491650

THE NEW GROVE
MOZART

THE NEW GROVE
DICTIONARY OF MUSIC AND MUSICIANS
Editor: Stanley Sadie

The Composer Biography Series

BACH FAMILY

HANDEL

HAYDN

MOZART

SCHUBERT

THE NEW GROVE

MOZART

Stanley Sadie

W. W. NORTON & COMPANY

NEW YORK   LONDON

Contents

List of illustrations

GENERAL ABBREVIATIONS

A	alto, contralto [voice]	orch	orchestra
acc.	accompaniment	orchd	orchestrated
add, addl	additional	org	organ
add, addn	addition	ov.	overture
ant	antiphon		
arr.	arrangement	perf.	performance
aut.	autumn	pic	piccolo
		pr.	printed
B	bass [voice]	pubd	published
b	bass [instrument]	pubn	publication
bc	basso continuo		
bn	bassoon	qnt	quintet
		qt	quartet
cl	clarinet		
conc.	concerto	R	photographic reprint
cont	continuo	r	recto
db	double bass	rec	recorder
		recit	recitative
edn.	edition	red.	reduction
		repr.	reprinted
f., ff.	folio(s)	rev.	revision
facs.	facsimile		
fl	flute	S	soprano [voice]
Fr.	French	str	string(s)
frag.	fragment	sum.	summer
		sym.	symphony
glock	glockenspiel		
gui	guitar	T	tenor [voice]
		timp	timpani
hn	horn	tpt	trumpet
hpd	harpsichord	tr	treble [instrument]
		trbn	trombone
inc.	incomplete	transcr.	transcription
inst	instrument		
		U.	University
Jb	Jahrbuch [yearbook]		
		v, vv	voice(s)
kbd	keyboard	v., vv.	verse(s)
		v	verso
lib	libretto	va	viola
		vc	cello
mand	mandolin	vn	violin
movt	movement		
ob	oboe		
obbl	obbligato		

BIBLIOGRAPHICAL ABBREVIATIONS

AcM	*Acta musicologica*
AMz	*Allgemeine Musik-Zeitung*
AnMc	*Analecta musicologica*
BMw	*Beiträge zur Musikwissenschaft*
CNRS	*Centre National de la Recherche Scientifique*
CMc	*Current Musicology*
IMSCR	*International Musicological Society Congress Report*
JAMS	*Journal of the American Musicological Society*
JbMP	*Jahrbuch der Musikbibliothek Peters*
KJb	*Kirchenmusikalisches Jahrbuch*
Mf	*Die Musikforschung*
MGG	*Die Musik in Geschichte und Gegenwart*
MJb	*Mozart-Jahrbuch des Zentralinstituts für Mozartforschung*
ML	*Music and Letters*
MQ	*The Musical Quarterly*
MR	*The Music Review*
MT	*The Musical Times*
NOHM	*The New Oxford History of Music*
ÖMz	*Österreichische Musikzeitschrift*
PRMA	*Proceedings of the Royal Musical Association*
RMI	*Rivista musicale italiana*
SM	*Studia musicologica Academiae scientiarum hungaricae*
SMw	*Studien zur Musikwissenschaft*
SMz	*Schweizerische Musikzeitung/Revue musicale suisse*
STMf	*Svensk tidskrift för musikforskning*
ZIMG	*Zeitschrift der Internationalen Musik-Gesellschaft*
ZMw	*Zeitschrift für Musikwissenschaft*

Preface

This volume is one of a series of short biographies derived from *The New Grove Dictionary of Music and Musicians* (London, 1980). In its original form, the text was written in the mid-1970s, and finalized at the end of that decade. For this reprint, the text has been re-read and modified by the original author and corrections and changes have been made. In particular, an effort has been made to bring the bibliography up to date and to incorporate the findings of recent research.✱

The fact that the texts of the books in this series originated as dictionary articles inevitably gives them a character somewhat different from that of books conceived as such. They are designed, first of all, to accommodate a very great deal of information in a manner that makes reference quick and easy. Their first concern is with fact rather than opinion, and this leads to a larger than usual proportion of the texts being devoted to biography than to critical discussion. The nature of a reference work gives it a particular obligation to convey received knowledge and to treat of composers' lives and works in an encyclopedic fashion, with proper acknowledgment of sources and due care to reflect different standpoints, rather than to embody imaginative or speculative writing about a composer's character or his music. It is hoped that the comprehensive work-lists and extended bibliographies, indicative of the origins of the books in a reference work, will be valuable to the reader who is eager for full and accurate reference information and who may not have ready access to *The New Grove Dictionary* or who may prefer to have it in this more compact form.

✶

I should particularly like to acknowledge – as was not possible when it was published in *The New Grove Dictionary* itself –

✸ *items dated 1981 & 1982 are included in the bibliography; also one for 1983.*

the generous help given to me in the preparation of this text by four Mozart scholars who read and criticized it: Peter Branscombe, Alec Hyatt King, Alan Tyson and Neal Zaslaw, and am specially grateful to Drs Tyson and Zaslaw for permitting me to use the results of their research, some of which was unpublished. I am also particularly grateful for the valuable help given to me by Anthony Hicks in drawing up the work-list.

S.S.

We are grateful to the following for permission to reproduce illustrative material: HM the Queen (fig.2); Internationale Stiftung Mozarteum, Salzburg (figs.3,6,7,17); Staatsbibliothek Preussischer Kulturbesitz, Musikabteilung, Berlin (fig.4); Civico Museo Bibliografico Musicale, Bologna (fig.5); Deutsche Staatsbibliothek, Berlin (figs.8, 12); Hunterian Art Gallery, University of Glasgow (fig.9); British Library, London (figs.10, 11, 15); Musikbibliothek der Stadt Leipzig (fig.13); Universitetsbiblioteket, Uppsala (fig.16); Gesellschaft der Musikfreunde, Vienna (cover).

Cover: Portrait (1816) by Barbara Krafft (Gesellschaft der Musikfreunde, Wien)

1. Ancestry and early childhood

The 'miracle which God let be born in Salzburg' – to quote the words of Mozart's father – entered the world on 27 January 1756. He was baptized in Salzburg Cathedral the next day, as Joannes Chrysostomus Wolfgangus Theophilus; the first two names note that 27 January was the feast day of St John Chrysostom, while Wolfgangus was the name of his maternal grandfather and Theophilus a name of his godfather (Joannes Theophilus Pergmayr; Mozart sometimes preferred the Latin form, Amadeus, more often Amadè, Amadé or the German form Gottlieb). He was the seventh and last child born to Leopold Mozart and his wife Maria Anna (née Pertl); only he and the fourth child, Maria Anna (Walburga Ignatia), or 'Nannerl', born in 1751, survived. The house in which he was born, in the Getreidegasse, is now a Mozart museum.

The paternal ancestry of the family has been traced back with some degree of certainty to Ändris Motzhart, who lived in the Augsburg area in 1486; the name is first recorded, for a Heinrich Motzhart in Fischach, in 1331, and appears in other villages south-west of Augsburg, notably Heimberg, from the 14th century. The surname was spelt in a variety of forms, including Mozarth, Mozhard and Mozer. Several early members of the family were master masons (i.e. architects), builders, craftsmen and sculptors; two, in the late 16th and early 17th centuries, were artists. Mozart's great-grandfather David (c1620–1685) was a master mason, his grandfather Johann Georg (1679–1736) a master bookbinder in Augsburg. Others of his paternal ancestors were from

Baden-Baden and Ober Puschthain. His mother's family
came mainly from the Salzburg region (her father held
important administrative and judicial posts at Hüllen-
stein, near St Gilgen, and Salzburg), but one branch may
be traced to Krems-Stein and Vienna. They mostly
followed middle-class occupations; some were gardeners.

Mozart's father, Johann Georg Leopold Mozart,
played a central role in his son's life. Born in Augsburg in
1719, he was educated in his native city and at the
Benedictine University in Salzburg, where he studied
philosophy and jurisprudence; he then turned to music
and took a post as violinist in the Kapelle of the prince-
archbishop of Salzburg, later becoming court and chamber composer and eventually (1763) deputy Kapellmeister. Until that time he was an active composer; but, deeply
aware of his responsibilities as the father of a remarkable
genius, he withdrew from composing in order to foster the
talent of his son. His reputation however rested less on his
composition than on his treatise *Versuch einer gründlichen
Violinschule* (Augsburg, 1756; many translations and
later editions), which although much indebted to Tartini
stands as one of the most important didactic and
theoretical works of its day.

Mozart showed his musical gifts at an extremely early
age. In his sister's music book, his father noted that he
had learnt some of the pieces when he was four. His
earliest known compositions, an Andante and Allegro
κ1*a* and *b*, were written, Leopold noted, early in 1761,
when he was five. They are very brief, and modelled on
the little pieces, many of them north German in origin,
that his sister had been given to play (and which he also
learnt; the 'Wolfgang Notenbuch' is a forgery). As they
survive only in his father's handwriting, it is impossible
to determine how far they are Mozart's own work.

Mozart's first known public appearance was at Salzburg University in September 1761, when he took part in a theatrical performance with music by Eberlin. Like other parents of his time, Leopold Mozart saw nothing improper in exhibiting, or in exploiting, his son's God-given genius for music. He took Wolfgang and Nannerl to Munich, for about three weeks from 12 January 1762, where they played the harpsichord before the Elector of Bavaria. No documentation survives for that journey. Later ones are better served – Leopold was a prolific correspondent and also kept travel diaries. The next started on 18 September 1762, when the entire family set off for Vienna; they paused at Passau and Linz for the children to perform before local noblemen or to give concerts. Except for a spell in December at Pressburg (Bratislava), at the invitation of a group of Hungarian patrons, they remained in Vienna until the end of the year, playing at the homes of various noblemen and appearing twice before Maria Theresia and her consort at Schönbrunn. The empress sent them a set of court clothes, which they wore for the well-known paintings later done in Salzburg, probably by P. A. Lorenzoni. Leopold's reports of the children's triumphs, in letters to his friend and landlord Lorenz Hagenauer, are corroborated by the diary entries of Count Zinzendorf (see Deutsch, 1962): Mozart 'plays marvellously, he is a child of spirit, lively, charming'.

The family returned to Salzburg on 5 January 1763. In February Mozart played the violin and harpsichord in a concert at the Salzburg court. A report in an Augsburg newspaper in May tells of the kinds of performance: he could play in an adult manner, improvise in various styles, accompany at sight, play with a cloth covering the keyboard, add a bass to a given theme, and name any note that was sounded. There are numerous anecdotes about his precocity, most of them coming from accounts of him prepared after his death by his sister and a family friend, J. A. Schachtner (a poet, Salzburg court trumpeter, violinist and cellist). One story tells of his remembering, correctly, that Schachtner's violin was tuned an eighth of a tone lower than his own; another, of his taking a second violin part at sight and playing it perfectly, although he had had no violin lessons. Those events were in 1763. He was only four or five when, according to Schachtner, he tried to compose a concerto, which looked 'a smudge of notes' but Leopold found 'correctly and properly' composed. Schachtner further wrote of his docile and tender disposition: he was afraid of the trumpet, demonstratively affectionate with friends, high-spirited, eager to learn anything but preoccupied with music. He was also proud and ambitious, and willing to play only before people who took music seriously.

2. Paris and London, 1763-6

Understandably, Leopold Mozart wanted to take his son to Paris and London, the largest, most prosperous musical centres. The family set out on this ambitious trip in their own carriage, with a servant, on 9 June 1763; their intention was to visit every significant musical centre on the route, particularly those with courts where the children might be heard and generous gifts bestowed. Mozart usually played the local church organ at towns where they made overnight stops. They also did a great deal of sightseeing.

Their first important stop was Munich, where Mozart played at court. Next they went to Augsburg, Leopold's birthplace; here there was no court and they gave three public concerts. They travelled on to Ludwigsburg, the Duke of Württemberg's summer residence (the duke was away, but they met Jommelli, his Kapellmeister, and the violinist Nardini); then to Schwetzingen, the summer palace near Mannheim of the Elector Palatine Carl Theodor, who heard the children on 18 July. They passed on to Mainz; the elector there was ill, so they gave a public concert instead of playing at court. In August they were in Frankfurt, performing four or five times. They played again in Mainz, then in Koblenz, and in Aachen before Princess Anna Amalia of Prussia (who piqued Leopold by compensating them only with kisses). They now passed into the Austrian Netherlands, to Brussels, where they spent six weeks, having waited five of them for permission to play before the governor, Prince Charles of Lorraine.

They reached Paris on 18 November, and remained there for five months except for two weeks at Versailles, where on 1 January 1764 they played before Louis XV. No doubt they gave other private performances; they also met several musicians active in Paris, notably the Germans Schobert and Eckard, as well as Baron Grimm, a leading figure in literary circles. There Mozart published two pairs of sonatas for keyboard and violin – his first music to appear in print – with dedications to a royal princess and to a lady-in-waiting. They gave two public concerts and then, in April, left for London.

The family spent 15 months in England. They appeared at court, where George III gave Mozart some difficult tests at the keyboard soon after their arrival and twice more in the succeeding months; the children were heard at four concerts, one of them in Ranelagh Pleasure Gardens, and Leopold invited music lovers to visit them in private and put Mozart's 'Talents to a more particular Proof'. Mozart was extensively tested by the philosopher Daines Barrington, who in 1769 furnished a report on him to the Royal Society; it mentions among other things his improvisations at the harpsichord, including songs of love and of rage in an operatic style. Among the composers the family met in London was J. C. Bach, who was particularly friendly; this was the beginning of a lifelong influence. They improvised together on the harpsichord, but there is no evidence that Bach, as is sometimes said, gave Mozart lessons. While the Mozarts were in London, Leopold was ill, and they moved to the suburban calm of Chelsea; it was probably there that Mozart composed his first symphonies, some of which were given at their next concerts. Here and elsewhere the advertisements lopped a

*1. Leopold Mozart and his children: watercolour
(probably 1763–4) by Louis Carrogis de Carmontelle*

year off his age.

After this profitable period in London, the family travelled to Dover (pausing at Canterbury to attend a race meeting and stay with Horace Mann; a planned concert there was evidently cancelled) and embarked for Calais on 1 August 1765. They were obliged to wait a month at Lille, as Mozart was ill, before going on through Ghent and Antwerp, where he played on the local organs, to The Hague, arriving on 10 September. There they gave two public concerts and played before the Princess of Nassau-Weilburg, to whom Mozart dedicated a set of six keyboard and violin sonatas published in The Hague. Some keyboard variations on Dutch songs and a *Gallimathias musicum* (a potpourri) also come from the months in the Netherlands. In The Hague first Nannerl and then Wolfgang succumbed to 'intestinal typhoid'. They moved on in January 1766, and gave concerts in Amsterdam, Utrecht and Antwerp before returning through Brussels to Paris, where they remained for two months. Baron Grimm again heard the children and commented on Mozart's 'prodigious progress' since the preceding visit. He mentioned his symphonies, which had been well received in Paris, and referred to his encounters with experienced musicians, in which the boy had undergone the most difficult tests that could be devised and had left his interlocutors baffled. Mozart (as Daines Barrington also said) sang weakly but with great expression, and was 'une des plus aimables créatures qu'on puisse voir, mettant à tout ce qu'il dit et ce qu'il fait de l'esprit et de l'âme avec la grâce et la gentillesse de son âge'. The final stage of the homeward journey took several more months. They paused to play in Dijon, Lyons, Lausanne and Zurich; then they went into Germany and spent 11 days at Donaueschingen, with four-hour musical sessions with the Prince of Fürstenberg on nine of the evenings. They passed on through Dillingen and Augsburg to Munich, where they appeared at court (Mozart had to improvise on a theme supplied by the elector) and where Mozart was again briefly ill. They arrived back in Salzburg on 29 or 30 November, bearing a large number of gold rings, watches and snuffboxes.

3. Vienna and Italy, 1766-71

Mozart remained at home for the next nine months: he wrote some fugues, but there is no evidence that he had formal musical tuition. Nor, probably, did he – at any time – undergo formal schooling. He learnt Latin when young, and soon had a command of Italian (later also some French and English); the report that he enjoyed arithmetic is borne out by various numerical games and jottings on his manuscripts. A remark by Schachtner implies, probably correctly, that all his tuition came from Leopold.

During these months he arranged some concertos, from sonatas mainly by composers he had met in Paris, and wrote three vocal works – a Latin comedy *Apollo et Hyacinthus* for the university, the first act of a joint work, the oratorio *Die Schuldigkeit des ersten Gebots* (Michael Haydn and Adlgasser wrote Acts 2 and 3), and a piece of Passion music. It was probably this last that, according to Daines Barrington, Mozart composed in isolation in a locked room so that the Archbishop of Salzburg could satisfy himself that the claimed compositions were in fact the child's own work; traditionally the piece concerned has been thought to be *Die Schuldigkeit,* but the state of the autograph, with Leopold's emendations, rules it out (see fig. 2).

In September 1767 the family set out for Vienna; their 15 months there are documented by Leopold's letters to Hagenauer. The visit was presumably timed to coincide with the festivities planned for the marriage of an archduchess, who however died during a smallpox

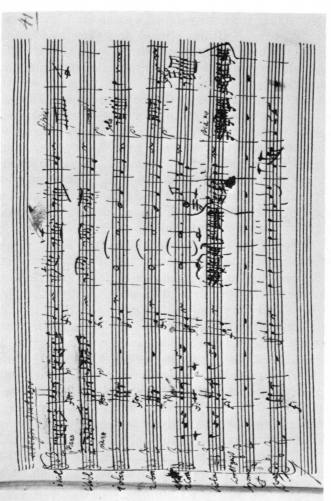

2. *A page from Mozart's 'Die Schuldigkeit des ersten Gebots' K35 (opening of no.4), composed early 1767*

epidemic before the wedding date. The combination of court mourning and the risk to their health induced Leopold to take his family out of Vienna after six weeks, on 26 October, to Brünn (Brno) and then to Olmütz (Olomouc). There Mozart and then Nannerl had mild attacks of smallpox. In December they returned to Brünn, giving a concert there, and arrived on 10 January 1768 in Vienna, where they were soon heard at court. By the beginning of February Leopold had conceived a plan for Mozart to compose an opera for production there; the emperor gave his consent and Gluck offered guarded encouragement. It was to be an *opera buffa*, called *La finta semplice*. The plan was unsuccessful. Leopold's letters, and his indignant petition in September to the emperor (sent with a catalogue of his son's works; see Zaslaw, 1982), tell a sordid story of intrigue. Mozart may have had some small compensation for the suppression of *La finta semplice* if, as is generally supposed, his one-act Singspiel *Bastien und Bastienne* was given privately, about October, at the home of Dr Franz Anton Mesmer, the inventor of 'magnetism therapy'. Moreover, on 7 December, he directed a performance before the imperial court of a substantial, festal mass setting (K139/47*a*), along with other works (notably a trumpet concerto, now lost), at the dedication ceremony of the Waisenhauskirche. About the end of the year they set out for Salzburg, probably pausing at the Lambach monastery, presenting to the library scores of symphonies by both Leopold and Wolfgang. This may have been in return for hospitality; they often stayed at monasteries rather than inns during their travels.

The Mozarts arrived back in Salzburg on 5 January 1769 and remained there nearly a year. During that time *La finta semplice* was performed at the theatre in the archbishop's palace, probably on or about 1 May, and Mozart wrote a new mass setting (K66) for performance, in October, at the first Mass celebrated by his friend Cajetan Hagenauer (Father Dominicus). To this period also belong some other, shorter sacred works, several sets of minuets for dancing, and three substantial orchestral serenades or cassations, of which two were probably 'Finalmusiken' for the ceremonies traditionally held by the faculties of Salzburg University at the end of the academic year. On 27 October Mozart was appointed, on an honorary basis, Konzertmeister to the Salzburg court.

Leopold had long planned to take his son to Italy, and was anxious to do so while Wolfgang was young enough for his talents to arouse wonder. He was doubtless also keen to visit the land that was the main source of stylistic novelty at the time, particularly in opera. They set out on 13 December, this time without Mozart's mother or sister. Their letters home are the principal source of information on their journey and activities.

The journey followed the now usual pattern: they paused at any town where a concert could be given, or where an influential nobleman might wish to hear Mozart play. They travelled to Innsbruck, giving a concert privately there, then to Rovereto, where Mozart played privately and on the organ at S Marco. In Verona he played at S Tommaso and at the Accademia Filarmonica, where he was given improvisation and sight-reading tests, and produced an impromptu written piece. He also had a portrait painted, probably by Saverio dalla Rosa (fig. 3); the piece of music shown on the harpsichord is taken to be a work by him, otherwise unknown (K72a). They next paused at Mantua,

3. Mozart: portrait (early 1770) probably by Saverio dalla Rosa, formerly attributed to Felice Cignaroli; the music he is playing is presumed to be by Mozart himself (this is its only source) and is entered in the Köchel catalogue (3/1937) as K72a

where the surviving programme of his concert, in the monthly series given by the Accademia Filarmonica, shows that he was put through tests of a particularly stringent kind. They passed on to Cremona, hearing there an opera by Hasse, and Milan, where they arrived on 23 January 1770. Here their chief patron was Count Firmian, the Austrian minister plenipotentiary, at whose house Mozart played several times as well as giving a public concert. Milan was an important cultural centre. They met G. B. Sammartini, the senior composer there, and Piccinni, and initiated arrangements for Mozart to write the first opera for the Carnival season in December; it seems that he was required to prove his ability to fulfil such a commission by submitting some arias (K88/73*c*, 77/73*e*).

They left Milan on 14 March; stopping the next night at an inn in Lodi, Mozart completed his first string quartet. They travelled through Parma, where they met the soprano Lucrezia Aguiari, reaching Bologna on 24 March; there they spent five days, giving a concert at Count Pallavicini's house, twice visiting the esteemed theorist and composer Padre Martini, with whom Mozart wrote some fugues, and meeting the famous castrato Farinelli. At Florence, where he played twice, privately, he met the castrato Manzuoli, an old acquaintance from London, and the English composer Thomas Linley, a boy of his own age, with whom he quickly made friends.

Mozart and his father then passed on to Rome, where they arrived on 10 April, in time for Holy Week, and stayed for a month. They gave several performances in private houses, and did much sightseeing. In the Sistine Chapel they heard the *Miserere* for double choir of Gregorio Allegri (1582–1652), traditionally, Leopold wrote, considered the exclusive preserve of the choir there; Mozart wrote it out from memory on a single hearing. He composed at least two symphonies in Rome. On 14 May they reached Naples, where they stayed until 25 June: they gave several concerts, did more sightseeing (including Pompeii and Vesuvius) and probably made two visits to the opera, one of them for Jommelli's *Armida*, which Mozart thought 'beautiful, but much too broken up and old-fashioned for the theatre'. Then they returned to Rome, where the papal Order of the Golden Spur was conferred on Mozart, and he had an audience with the pope; Gluck and Dittersdorf had also received the order, but Mozart's was in a higher rank, that of knight.

They left Rome on 10 July and travelled, through Loreto, Spoleto and Rimini, to Bologna. The summer was spent nearby at Count Pallavicini's house, where Mozart composed some sacred works and canons (and possibly symphonies) and received the libretto and cast list of his opera for Milan. Before they left Bologna he underwent and passed tests for admittance to member-ship of the ancient and esteemed Accademia Filarmonica; the surviving manuscripts of his test piece (an antiphon on a cantus firmus, K86/73v), with annota-tions by Martini, and his clean copy of a reworking, suggest that he had help. A similar honour from the Verona Accademia Filarmonica followed in 1771.

The Mozarts reached Milan on 18 October 1770. Work could now start in earnest on the composition of the opera, *Mitridate, rè di Ponto*. The libretto, by Vittorio Amadeo Cigna-Santi after Racine, had been set by Quirino Gasparini for Turin in 1767. Leopold discussed in his letters various intrigues among the singers, including the possibility of their substituting certain of Gasparini's settings for Mozart's; one of Gasparini's may in fact have been sung in the performance. He also reported the singers' enthusiastic approval of the music, but did not mention that – as the autograph material shows – Mozart rewrote several arias, presumably because the first versions failed to please. There were three recitative rehearsals, two preliminary orchestral rehearsals and two full ones in the theatre, and a dress rehearsal. The première, at the Regio Ducal Teatro, was on 26 December 1770; including the ballets (by other composers), it lasted six hours. Leopold had not been confident that the opera would be a success, but it was, and there were 22 performances of which Mozart, in the traditional way, directed the first three from the harpsichord.

The Mozarts left Milan on 14 January 1771 for Turin, then had four days back in Milan before going on to Venice, where they spent a happy month from 11 February with friends of the Hagenauers and gave a concert; they then moved on to Padua and Verona, pausing briefly to play in each, then back to Salzburg, where they arrived on 28 March. During these 15 months Mozart had increasingly added postscripts, usually addressed to his sister, to his father's letters home, supplementing Leopold's sharp, hard-headed, detailed reports with some high-spirited, boyish observation or an affectionate greeting, and occasionally some absurd obscenity. Later his notes often contained cryptic, amorous messages to girls in Salzburg.

4. Italian journeys, 1771-3

The Mozarts were not long at home. Before leaving Italy they had laid plans to return: a contract had been agreed for a further Milan opera at the end of 1772, and apparently an oratorio had been commissioned for Padua (though seemingly it was never performed); an opera for Venice was mooted, but Mozart would have had to be there when he was already committed to Milan, and the negotiations came to nothing.

The second Italian visit was in fact in 1771, not 1772. At Verona in March 1771 Leopold had received a letter commissioning a serenata or *festa teatrale* from Wolfgang for performance in Milan the following October on the marriage of the Archduke Ferdinand (his letter home expresses delight at news of the commission, but the idea must have been contemplated earlier: Burney, who saw the Mozarts in Bologna in the summer, referred in his diaries on 30 August 1770 to Mozart's projected opera for this wedding).

So Mozart had barely five months at home in 1771; during that time he wrote the Paduan oratorio, *La Betulia liberata*, some sacred works and probably some symphonies. He and his father arrived in Milan on 21 August. About a week later he was given the libretto, by Giuseppe Parini, for the serenata, *Ascanio in Alba*. Leopold remarked on the friendship and respect with which Mozart was treated by everyone, including Hasse (who was composing an opera for the festivities) and the singers. By 23 September the score was complete; there

were separate ballet and choral rehearsals, and four
general rehearsals, before the performance on 17
October. According to Leopold it was 'an extraordinary
success . . . I am sad to say that Wolfgang's serenata has
completely overshadowed Hasse's opera'. There were at
least two, possibly four, further performances. The
Mozarts remained until 5 December in Milan, where
Wolfgang wrote a divertimento and at least one symphony, and they gave a concert. It seems that Mozart
applied for employment in Archduke Ferdinand's service; a letter to the archduke from his mother, the
Empress Maria Theresia, advised him against burdening
himself with such useless people, and that the Mozarts'
habit of going 'about the world like beggars' would
degrade his service. Others, it seems, felt similarly. By
15 December the Mozarts were back in Salzburg.

The next ten months were spent at home. Just
after their return the prince-archbishop, Sigismund,
Count Schrattenbach, died: he had been a tolerant em-
ployer, ready to allow Leopold prolonged (if sometimes
unpaid) spells of leave. His successor, Hieronymus,
Count Colloredo, was enthroned on 14 March 1772.
For the celebrations Mozart composed a serenata, *Il
sogno di Scipione*, possibly performed in May. These
were prolific months: Mozart composed eight symphonies, four divertimentos and some substantial sacred
works. On 9 July he was formally taken into the employment of the court, with a salary as Konzertmeister
of 150 florins; he had held the post in an honorary
capacity for nearly three years.

The third and last Italian journey began on 24
October 1772. Probably Mozart had been sent the
libretto and cast list for the new Milan opera, *Lucio
Silla*, during the summer, and had already set the

recitatives; at any rate, it was the composition of a string quartet that occupied him on the journey. On his arrival in Milan he had to adjust the recitatives to accommodate changes made by the poet, Giovanni de Gamerra. He then wrote the choruses, and composed the arias for the singers in turn, having first heard each of them sing so that, in the accepted way, he could suit the music to their voices. There was a recitative rehearsal, then three rehearsals with orchestra and a dress rehearsal, interspersed with lengthy musical parties in the evenings given by Count Firmian. The première, on 26 December, which began three hours late and lasted six, was a mixed success, mainly because of a patchy cast, but the opera ran for 26 performances. In January Mozart wrote a solo motet, *Exsultate, jubilate*, for the primo uomo in the opera, Venanzio Rauzzini, who was himself a composer; some string quartets also belong to these months in Milan. The Mozarts remained there until the beginning of March: Leopold, anxious to find his son a post outside Salzburg, had applied to the Grand Duke of Tuscany and feigned illness to postpone the return journey while awaiting a reply. If one came, it was unfavourable.

They arrived back in Salzburg on 13 March. The next four months were spent at home, where Wolfgang composed four symphonies, a mass and probably some shorter sacred works and two divertimentos.

5. The early works

How much of the early music attributed to Mozart he himself actually composed can never be fully known. That
many of these pieces survive only in his father's hand, or
in composite autograph, often with heavily corrected
texts, does not necessarily argue conclusively against
Mozart's authorship; and stylistic arguments are even
more hazardous. Doubtless Leopold sometimes wrote
down Wolfgang's improvisations, made fair copies, partial or complete, of Wolfgang's unclear originals, and
inserted corrections of his own. Doubtless, too, he made
suggestions that found their way into Wolfgang's own
copies. Particular suspicion, however, is bound to attach
to those items where the surviving manuscripts are
largely in Leopold's hand, including the earliest keyboard pieces and parts of the Paris keyboard and violin
sonatas, K6–9, especially K8. (For a full and penetrating
discussion, see Plath, 1960–61.)

(i) Instrumental works

Mozart's earliest claimed compositions were short
keyboard pieces, probably dating from his sixth year.
Although most of them survive only in Leopold's hand,
these simple works are likely to be at least partly
Mozart's own; and Leopold left enough of naive charm
and harmonic solecism for plausibility. They imitate the
manner of the keyboard miniatures in the notebooks
Leopold drew up for his children's use. In the sonatas
for keyboard and violin published in Paris in 1764
– works in the most popular and commercially sal-

able form of the day – the models were the sonatas of Schobert and the other Germans in Paris. The music is somewhat mechanical in its textures (with much Alberti bass) and its melodic matter, with heavy reliance on sequential patterns; much here seems to represent an inventive boy's exploration of harmonic and textural possibilities.

The London sonatas, for keyboard and violin with optional cello (K10–15), show the same influences and preoccupations. But the London symphonies, or such of them as survive, represent a large step forward. Less so the very first (K16), which uses cliché with a mildly appealing simplicity and enthusiasm, than K19 in D, which shows in the first movement a remarkable grasp of the principles of J. C. Bach's symphonic style, for example the dramatic contrast of a *forte* motto opening with a *piano* continuation and the hint of a cantabile second subject, and possesses an Andante of Italianate melodic grace. Both symphonies have vigorous finales in 3/8 time, of a kind favoured by J. C. Bach and many Italian and English symphonists. As a parody of a well-formed style, this is an astonishing piece of work for a boy of nine, and its technical accomplishment is equally impressive. The same line of development is pursued in the B♭ Symphony K22 composed in The Hague, with its sharply outlined form and the maturer command of texture shown in the small-scale imitative writing. The accompanied sonatas written a few weeks later in The Hague (K26–31) sometimes show a neater handling of form than the earlier ones.

The next group of instrumental works comprises four keyboard 'concertos', prepared, presumably, for concert tours: they consist of sonata movements, mostly by German composers active in Paris (including Raupach,

Honauer and Schobert), to which Mozart added orchestral tuttis and accompaniments, making other minor
changes here and there. More important are the symphonies composed during or around the Vienna visit of
1767–8, where the influence of the Viennese symphonic
style is seen. It is notable in the full, energetic orchestral
style of K43, and in its inclusion of a minuet; slightly
less so in K45, a spirited D major work with strong
opera buffa overtones (it was in fact used as the overture
to *La finta semplice*); and strikingly evident in K48,
which has a first movement showing strong momentum,
busy textures, a substantial development section and a
well-defined recapitulation. This is Mozart's earliest
symphony first movement to include a clearly marked
restatement of the primary material; previous ones
follow the extended binary form preferred by J. C. Bach
and many Italians. The Andantes are mostly binary
movements of a simple melodic cast; that of K43 draws
on a duet from *Apollo et Hyacinthus*. There are typically
sturdy Viennese minuets, and finales which retain gigue-
like rhythm but are more fully worked out and formally
neater and better defined. Stylistic arguments indicate
that the 'New Lambach' symphony, rather than the 'Old
Lambach' K45a, may be Mozart's.

Three serenades probably date from the following
summer, K100/62a, 63, and 99/63a. Following the
Austrian serenade tradition, represented at Salzburg by
Michael Haydn, each has six or more movements and an
associated introductory (and perhaps valedictory)
march; there is a bustling, rather loosely textured opening allegro, two or even three cheerful minuets, and a
rollicking finale. The most refined invention is reserved
for the slow movements, of which one generally has a
concertante part (in K63 for violin, 100/62a for oboe

and horn) and the other is of a straightforward melodic character; K100/62*a*, in eight movements, also has concertante parts in a fast movement and the trio of one of its minuets, a pattern that later became standard.

The next orchestral works date from the first Italian journey. Probably Mozart wrote five symphonies in Italy. The four in D, K81/73*l*, 97/73*m*, 95/73*n* and 84/73*q* (the authenticity of K81 and 84 has been questioned, though not convincingly), may be the ones referred to in Mozart's letter of 4 August 1770: 'habe ich schon 4 itallienische Sinfonien componirt'. They are alike in their light textures, their lively, mechanical string figuration and their slender thematic material. Their first movements mostly have little or no development but a full recapitulation. Also from the Italian journey is K74 in G, similar in pattern to the D major works, whose linked first two movements suggest that it may originally have been intended as an opera overture, presumably to *Mitridate*. The manner of these symphonies shows Mozart influenced by the music he encountered in Italy, and keen to please Italian audiences, or both. There may also have been an element of emulation and competition, a pattern that was to continue.

Further symphonies followed between and during the two briefer Italian journeys. The more extreme aspects of Italian style have disappeared in K73, 75 and 110/75*b*, but the formal pattern remains. Of the three symphonies from late 1771, K96/111*b* is much concerned with orchestral brilliance and in particular the kind of imperious effect associated with the use of trumpets and drums in a C major work, and K112 is notable mainly for its first movement, a well-formed example of the *buffo* manner. K114 in A, composed back in Salzburg, embodies new elements. There is a chamber-music fineness of style, and a particular care over proportion and harmonic logic. While in most symphonies the outer movements require oboes and horns, and occasionally flutes instead of oboes in the slow movements, here there are flutes in all but the Andante; doubtless the choice of the higher instruments was dictated by textural considerations contingent on the use of high-pitched horns, needed in A major, but Mozart characteristically let the softer-toned wind section colour the actual invention.

Seven further symphonies belong to 1772. The first two (K124 and 128) show no special advance, except possibly in incorporating something close to development procedures in a predominantly *buffo* context, and in the growing textural interest of their slow movements; the next, K129, reverts surprisingly to the manner of J. C. Bach. All three throw greater weight on the finale than hitherto, and K130 goes further, with the most substantial finale Mozart had yet composed – in full sonata-allegro form, with a brief development but an extended second group. This symphony is exceptional, too, for the three-bar phrases in its Andantino and for its orchestration, with flutes preferred to oboes and (no doubt because extra players were briefly available) four horns. K132, Mozart's first symphony in E♭ since K16, and again requiring four horns, is more assured; its opening motto phrase, treated with the *forte–piano* polarity favoured by J. C. Bach, is one of a kind Mozart often used in this key (cf K364/320*d*, 375, 449, 482). The style here is mainly *buffo,* and the 'development' a neatly proportioned transition. For the slow movement, a 3/8 Andante, Mozart later provided a replacement, a 2/4 Andantino, shorter but texturally less plain. There is a minuet embodying a good deal of small-scale imitative treatment, a harmonically quizzical trio, and a *gavotte en rondeau* finale, more boisterously Viennese than French. The stylistic synthesis that this symphony represents is maintained in K133, whose D major brilliance places it firmly in the line of the Italianate symphonies. But it is texturally richer and better developed; and the implied 'Mannheim crescendo' of the opening is counterpoised by another Mannheim usage, the dramatic reappearance of the opening material, not previously recapitulated, in the coda. The influence of Haydn has been remarked (Wyzewa and St Foix, 1912–46), and of M. G. Monn (Fischer, Neue Mozart-Ausgabe preface). This group ends with another work in A (K134), like K114 using flutes and horns and in a more chamber-musical style. Its first movement is among Mozart's most closely argued, and its opening phrase is much heard in the exposition tuttis and in the development; the primary theme recurs at the end of the exposition, a usage associated with Haydn, lending logic to the absence of a full recapitulation. The expressive melodic tag that begins the Andante is one that Mozart specially favoured (cf 'Porgi amor', *Le nozze di Figaro*).

The symphonies of this group (which may be augmented by two: Mozart added finales, K120/111a and 161/141a, to make concert works out of two-movement overtures) were probably composed mainly for use in Salzburg, perhaps in connection with Mozart's post as Konzertmeister. Various other orchestral works were written for specific occasions. The three keyboard concertos K107 arranged, probably in 1772 (not 1765, as was long stated), from J. C. Bach sonatas may have been intended for performance on tour, when just two

4. Part of the autograph MS of Mozart's Piano Concerto in D K107 no.1 (3rd movement) after J. C. Bach; both Leopold's and Wolfgang's handwriting may be seen

violins and a bass instrument could be called upon; Leopold copied out the sonatas, Mozart added the ritornellos and accompaniments (see fig. 4). A 'Concerto ò sia Divertimento' K113 was written in Milan, his first use of clarinets; he revised it early in 1773, with oboes, english horns and bassoons, enabling the clarinets to be omitted.

The term 'divertimento' implies performance by a small ensemble, one to a part; 'serenade' implies orchestral performance. Four works of 1772 are known as 'divertimento', but for K131 the title is unauthentic and the work has characteristics in common with the cassations or serenades of 1769 and 1773–4. It has seven movements, and is scored for strings with only single oboe, flute and bassoon but (like the contemporary symphonies) four horns; there is some concertante flute writing and much ingenious, witty solo use of the horn ensemble, especially in the minuets and their trios. The work has the relaxed gait and loose structure typical of the Salzburg serenades, with an Adagio, clearly intended for solo strings, in the customary sensuous vein. The occasion for its composition is unknown, but the time of year means that its use on Colloredo's name day or for university Finalmusik cannot be excluded. For the three works for strings K136–8/125a–c, sometimes misleadingly known as 'Salzburg symphonies', the title 'divertimento' is again not Mozart's own, but that these compact and assured three-movement pieces are solo rather than orchestral music is made clear beyond doubt by the style; they are in effect lightweight string quartets. The similarity between the openings of the first and last movements of K136 has often been noted and is perhaps the most obvious among the numerous resemblances to be found between themes in different movements of a single work in Mozart's music of all periods, whether intentional, unconscious or fortuitous (for discussions of Mozart and cyclic form, see Engel, 1962–3, and Marx, 1971).

Apart from the single quartet (K80/73*f*) of 1770, to whose three movements he later added a rondeau in gavotte rhythm, Mozart's first true string quartets belong to the period of the third Italian journey. Each is in three movements, and the models are Italian, especially the quartets of G. B. Sammartini. The first, K155/134*a*, is in the manner of the 'divertimentos' K136–8; but in most of the remainder a genuine quartet style is apparent. The development section of K156/134*b*, with imitations against a dominant pedal figure, is both true quartet writing and true development, an unsurprising coincidence; and there are some carefully worked four-part textures in the slow movements, for example the E minor Adagio of the same quartet. Both this and K158 end with substantial minuets, in the favoured Italian style – on which Mozart had remarked in letters of 24 March and 29 September 1770. These six quartets follow, exceptionally, a cyclic key scheme, D–G–C–F–B♭–E♭, and four have minor-key middle movements, among them a fiery and extended G minor Allegro in K159.

(ii) Sacred works

The first vocal work recorded in the Köchel catalogue is the brief so-called 'madrigal' *God is our refuge* K20, presented at Leopold's wish to the British Museum as an example of his son's work; most of the handwriting is Leopold's. Sacred music occupied Mozart a good deal in the ensuing years. More than a dozen short liturgical or para-liturgical pieces were written up to

1773, as well as four masses and two litany settings. Stylistically, the models were clear; it is not surprising that, of the works by other composers that Mozart copied out, most of those formerly accepted as his own are sacred music. They include items by Eberlin, Michael Haydn, his own father, the younger Reutter, Padre Martini and Quirino Gasparini. Such were the composers he sought to emulate; the tradition was essentially Italian, imported to Austria, and its most famous representative was Hasse.

Mozart's first mass was the ceremonial K139/47a. Though nominally in C minor, it is mainly in the major; minor-key introductions lend solemnity to three movements. It has the usual mixture of solo items and choruses, which are mostly homophonic (the choir in block chordal writing against busy string textures) apart from the extended fugues that traditionally concluded the Gloria and Credo sections. Particularly original are the sombre textures of the 'Qui tollis', in F minor, the introduction (with trumpets and drums) to the 'Crucifixus' and the opening of the Agnus Dei on a trio of trombones. Probably from much the same time comes a *Missa brevis* (K49/47d), a brisk setting of the kind preferred for everyday liturgical use; it has only one, brief fugue, and its most interesting feature is the 'Et incarnatus' chorus with a light, ethereal texture and a chromatic treatment of 'passus et sepultus est'. Another *Missa brevis* (K65/61a) is equally perfunctory, apart from a chromatic duet setting of the Benedictus. A companion to K139, and more assured, especially in its 'rauschende Violinen' ('rushing violins') in the Austrian tradition, is the 'Dominicus' mass K66: the figuration of the G minor 'Qui tollis' is on the same pattern as that in the Agnus Dei of the Requiem (K626), and there are striking contrasts of texture and pace in the C minor 'Crucifixus'.

Mozart's first liturgical work, the offertory *Scande coeli limina* K34, consists of a graceful aria and a chorus of almost banal simplicity; but the pieces that followed, like the contemporaneous masses, show how quickly he grasped the techniques of choral writing, using plain block harmony, and applied the standard forms to church music. The *Regina coeli* K108/74d and *Litaniae lauretanae* K109/74e of 1771 include confident homophonic choral writing and ensembles or arias in the supplicatory style suggested by the texts; the longer *Litaniae de venerabili altaris sacramento* K125 of a year later shows more individuality of invention and a powerful command of writing for choir and orchestra, as well as considerable grasp of dramatic effect, with strong chordal writing against rushing violins, in such movements as the 'Verbum caro factum' and the 'Tremendum'. This work also contains tender arias, a lengthy choral fugue (of which Mozart made a shorter version) and, in the opening Kyrie, an elaborate ritornello structure with three levels – orchestra, chorus and soloists. His sacred music of 1770 includes some *a cappella* items, cantus firmus workings and canons, written in Italy and probably intended as contrapuntal studies for Padre Martini: these are his only technical exercises to survive, although possibly the *Te Deum* K141/66b, closely modelled on one by Michael Haydn, should be regarded in the same light. Mozart's best-known sacred piece of the early years is the Rauzzini motet *Exsultate, jubilate* K165/158a, a miniature vocal concerto in three movements, full of felicitous invention and culminating in a brilliant 'Alleluia'. Three of Mozart's 'church sonatas', for three-part strings

with organ continuo and intended for performance
between the Epistle and Gospel of the Mass, date from
the period up to 1773; these early examples are brief,
sonata-form miniatures, but Mozart later allowed the
form to be extended, in proportion to the mass settings
with which the pieces were associated, and in his last
church sonatas the orchestral forces are larger and the
organ part blossoms into first an obbligato accompaniment and ultimately a solo role.

(iii) Dramatic music

Barrington's story of his tests in 1764–5 makes it clear
that Mozart was already familiar with dramatic composition; he could improvise a plausible 'Song of Love'
and 'Song of Anger', and precede each with a proper
'five or six lines of a jargon recitative'. The Metastasio
setting *Va, dal furor portata* K21/19c, if elementary in
its invention, shows a knowledge of the standard mode
of treatment for such a text, as do the Metastasio settings of the following months, of which *Per pietà*
K78/73b, probably written in 1766, represents an attempt at the typical E♭ *aria di affetto* manner. Several of
these also show a grasp of the style of obbligato (or
accompanied) recitative.

His first more extended essay in dramatic music was
the act he contributed to *Die Schuldigkeit des ersten
Gebots* K35, a 'sacred Singspiel' in which a Christian
Spirit and a Worldly Spirit compete. That Mozart, at the
age of 11, could write music to reflect the sense of the
text is not surprising; the tradition was an established
one, and the emotion is generalized (with dance rhythms
and bravura for the Worldly Spirit and soberer music
for the other participants). Five of the arias are in full da
capo form, with middle sections usually in contrasting

tempo and metre; one, referring to the last trump ('Posaunenschall'), has an alto trombone obbligato and a rich accompaniment with divided violas. The invention is generally more elaborate here than in the school-drama *Apollo et Hyacinthus*, where the rhythms of the Latin verse often induced Mozart to compose in a somewhat facile triple metre. Here too there are several full da capo arias. Musically the duets are of particular interest, one being the graceful piece that found its way into the Symphony in F K43, the other a striking dialogue for the angry Melia and the innocent Apollo, where changes in texture and key already support the sense of the drama. Both these works belong in a tradition firmly established in Salzburg; Mozart must have been familiar with examples by such composers as Eberlin and Adlgasser.

For Mozart's next stage work, *La finta semplice* K51/46*a*, a new range of techniques needed to be acquired. This was a full-length *opera buffa* demanding from him first of all a command of the Italian language, then a grasp of the more rapid and fragmented mode of setting that a *buffo* context required, an ability to delineate an emotion quickly, a knowledge of the range of effective orchestral cliché that supplied much of the accompaniment, and a control of the extended, multi-section finale of the Goldoni–Galuppi tradition favoured in Vienna. The mastery of these techniques, in which he was admittedly helped by Coltellini's efficient but unsubtle libretto (after Goldoni), shows an amazing gift – even if partly one of deft imitation of his models – for a boy of 12 whose contacts with *opera buffa* must have been few. The actual invention is often on a fairly routine level, but there are several numbers of considerable interest, among them an echo aria (with an oboe providing the echo, and two english horns in the accompaniment), a drinking-song, an exquisitely scored aria in E for Rosina (the 'feigned simpleton' of the title) with divided violas and prominent bassoons, and a duel duet. The arias are generally shorter than those of the preceding works, and full da capo form appears only once; one aria comes from *Die Schuldigkeit*, now shortened, and another uses an idea from *Apollo*. *Bastien und Bastienne* K50/46*b*, composed just after *La finta semplice* though possibly begun earlier, is altogether simpler and more direct in style, both because of its topic, rural love, and because it belongs to the Singspiel tradition rather than the more sophisticated one of *opera buffa*.

With this selection of styles already mastered, Mozart ventured into the most important musical-theatrical form of his day, *opera seria*, with *Mitridate, rè di Ponto* K87/74*a*. The rejected drafts, totalling 11, suggest the extent to which he had to meet the singers' requirements. It has been remarked (by Tagliavini, 1968) that in several details of form and treatment Mozart modelled his setting on Quirino Gasparini's. The music of *Mitridate* is expansive, but there are no full da capo arias; eight are in shortened da capo form (often with middle sections in contrasting metre and tempo), four are in alternating slow and fast tempos, while six follow a sonata-like pattern and two a binary one. The most striking aria is a G minor Allegro agitato for the prima donna, with violin tremolandos, chromaticisms and a fragmented melodic line to represent the sense of the text.

La Betulia liberata, composed in summer 1771, is Mozart's first setting of an extended Metastasio text. The libretto is concerned more with the moral quality of the tale than with its drama: the story of Judith and

Holophernes is related wholly from within the besieged Bethulia. That ensures a setting somewhat formal and abstract in tone: even the dramatic central event of the work, Judith's killing of Holophernes, is related in a subdued obbligato recitative. The overture, in D minor (all Mozart's others of the period are in D major), is dark-toned and forceful, with thematic links between the outer movements, and perhaps with a Gluckian flavour; more markedly Gluckian is the C minor chorus for the Israelites at prayer, led by Ozias, which recalls the elegiac opening chorus of *Orfeo*. But *Betulia liberata* is no reform work, and stands firmly in the Metastasian tradition, with extended arias, often including bravura writing, and sometimes partial da capos.

Mozart's next two dramatic works were of the serenata or *festa teatrale* type, *Ascanio in Alba* K111 and *Il sogno di Scipione* K126. The style of the former, written to be performed alongside Hasse's *Ruggiero*, has been compared with Hasse's (Engel, 1960–61). It is a leisurely work, with pastoral choruses and ballets interspersed with the arias, among which those for Ascanius, sung by the alto castrato Manzuoli, are especially sympathetic. *Il sogno di Scipione*, composed for Salzburg rather than Italy, has a Metastasio text dating back to 1735. Like *Die Schuldigkeit*, it is a 'morality' – Scipio is wooed by Constancy and Fortune. The music is less tellingly characterized than that of the earlier work; the arias, mostly in shortened da capo form, are lengthy (averaging 185 bars, the highest figure for any Mozart work) and contain much bravura writing. It ends with an outburst in obbligato recitative from the rejected Fortune, followed by a *licenza* aria, of which two settings survive.

The final and most significant work of this group is an

opera seria, *Lucio Silla*, written at the end of 1772. It suffers from a verbose, sententious and ill-motivated libretto; but a more individual, less convention-bound expression of emotion may be found in this score than in any hitherto. This is true particularly of the music for the role of Junia, whose opening aria alternates between an intense Adagio and a fiery Allegro, and whose choral scene at her father's tomb again recalls Gluck. Her other music includes a conventional bravura aria and an aria of agitation. That role was written for Anna de Amicis; Rauzzini's primo uomo role is more conventionally brilliant although it includes an elaborate Adagio aria in Act 2 and a pathetic farewell minuet. The role of Celia, too, has a certain individuality, partly for its unusual light coloratura (doubtless designed for the singer's particular qualities). Sulla's, written for a novice, and reduced by Mozart's omission of two arias, is in the vein customary for an *opera seria* tyrant. The terzetto where, against the smooth lines and the sweet 3rds and 6ths of the lovers, Sulla expresses his anger is an early example of simultaneous differentiated characterization; and the obbligato recitatives are notably more powerful in expression than in any preceding work by Mozart.

6. 1773-4: The Vienna visit and its aftermath

Mozart and his father, having returned from Italy in March 1773, stayed in Salzburg until early summer. About this time the family moved from their apartment in the Getreidegasse to a large one in the Hannibalplatz (now Makartplatz). The move reflects the family's prosperity; although Leopold's salary had sometimes been withheld during his absences, the gifts they received had no doubt compensated. The family, it seems, were keenly conscious of their status in Salzburg society; their friends were professional people rather than fellow musicians, and they took care to be on good terms with the local nobility. They were not, however, content. Leopold's standing in the local musical establishment was less high than he wished, and he saw poor prospects there for his son.

It was probably to seek an opening for him at the imperial court that, after a busy four-month spell – which saw the composition of four symphonies, three serenades or divertimentos and a mass – Leopold took his son to Vienna. They arrived about 17 July and spent some ten weeks there; among the people they met were Dr Mesmer, the ballet-master J. G. Noverre, and the court Kapellmeister Giuseppe Bonno. Mozart played a violin concerto at a nearby monastery, and his Mass K66 was directed by Leopold at the Jesuit church. They had an audience with the Empress Maria Theresia, but if (as cryptic remarks in Leopold's letters imply) the intention was to secure a post, they were unsuccessful.

In other ways, however, the visit to Vienna was not unproductive, for it seems to have stimulated an intensification in Mozart's style. This has commonly been ascribed to his presumed contact with Joseph Haydn's latest music, in particular his string quartets (opp.9 and 17 and the recently published op.20); and doubtless Mozart also encountered other new Viennese music that interested him. While in Vienna he composed a set of six quartets K168–73, in a style markedly more Viennese than that of the Milanese set. Textures are more fully worked, with much imitative writing, not only in the development sections but integral to some of the thematic material on its first statement (even in one minuet, in K172, and in the Andante of K171). The carefree Italianate manner appears in some movements, like the first of K169 and 172 and some of the finales; but in others – like the variations (much in Haydn's manner) opening K170, or the Allegro of K171 with its recurring Adagio introduction and curiously varied pace, or above all the intense, chromatic Allegro of the D minor Quartet K173 – an altogether more intellectual approach to quartet composition is in evidence. So is it, still more, in the fugal finales of K168 and 173: not, like many quartet finales of the time, sonata movements with fugal sections but entire fugues, like those of Haydn's op.20 nos.2, 5 and 6. These were Mozart's first fugues outside church music, and are likely to have been provoked by Haydn's example. Their counterpoint is not Bachian, but in the traditional Austrian manner of Fux, and not without a certain selfconsciousness. Resemblances to works by several composers have been remarked, ranging from Handel (the F minor Andante theme in K168, no less indebted however to Haydn's op.20 no.5) to Gluck and to Gassmann. For the string quintet K174, Mozart's first, started early in 1773 and completed with some revisions at the end of the year, Michael Haydn provided the model with some quintets also from 1773. This is more polished and relaxed than the quartets, and the ensemble with two violas is treated in a variety of ways, notably in dialogues between first violin and first viola, with the richer sonorities used to good advantage. A comparison between the first version of the finale and the final one, where Mozart added a new theme at the beginning and turned his original opening idea into a subsidiary one, is instructive.

In Vienna Mozart completed a serenade (K185/167a) with a violin concerto section, probably for Salzburg University Finalmusik; it also has connections with the Andretter family, for whom he had written, most likely just before leaving for Vienna, a good-humoured divertimento (K205/167A). On his return he wrote several symphonies and his first original piano concerto. This last, K175, recalls in its manner the J. C. Bach parodies of two years before, but is larger in scale and surprisingly well developed in its finale, which starts with a contrapuntal gesture that recurs in various ways. Mozart later revived the work, equipping it in about 1782 with a new finale, the Rondo K382 (actually a theme and variations), which is out of style with the remainder of the concerto and on a level of charming triviality.

The symphonies, of which four were written shortly before the Viennese journey, a group immediately after, and a further group in 1774 – the dates are not entirely certain – are more important: it could be said that two of these, the earliest Mozart works to have an inalienable place in the concert repertory, mark his emergence from a preternaturally gifted youth into a great composer. The first four (K184/161*a*, 199/161*b*, 162, 181/162*b*) are reversions to the Italian type, with much brisk and mechanical figuration, simple textures, and three-movement form: in K184 and 181 the movements follow without a break, along the pattern of the Italian overture. K184 is the strongest of these, with a C minor Andante whose main theme is built on imitative writing; its dramatic style, marked in the driving unison passages and the sharp dynamic contrasts, was acknowledged by its adoption in the 1780s as overture to Gebler's *Thamos, König in Ägypten*, for which Mozart wrote incidental music.

K182/173*dA*, composed a few days after Mozart's return from Vienna, moves little beyond the preceding group. But K183/173*dB*, the 'little G minor', his first minor-key symphony besides the overture to *La Betulia liberata*, is music of a different temper. The urgent tone of the repeated syncopated notes at the start represents something new, and so do the dramatic falling diminished 7th and the repeated thrusting phrases that follow. The increased force of the musical thinking is seen in the strong sense of harmonic direction, the taking up of melodic figuration by the bass instruments, and the echo sections, which are no longer merely decorative but add intensity. Although the E♭ Andante is soft-textured music, with bassoons constantly echoing the violins, it is often chromatic, and the tone of the work is maintained, especially in the fiery finale. This tone is not unique among works of the period; there was a wave of minor-key symphonies, including G minor ones by Haydn (no.39), Vanhal and J. C. Bach (op.6 no.6) in the same manner as K183 (particularly J. C. Bach's, where there is even figuration close to Mozart's), which have been cited as musically analogous to the 'Sturm und Drang' movement in German literature.

Some biographers have suggested a personal 'romantic crisis' behind this symphony, but no known biographical circumstance supports that idea; such a work must, however, signify something in terms of spiritual development, even if, as is possible, it was written in emulation of similar works by other composers. No less of a landmark is the Symphony in A K201/186*a*, of April 1774 – also personal in tone, perhaps indeed more individual in its combination of an intimate, chamber music style with a still fiery and impulsive manner. The gentle appoggiatura phrase and dipping octave of the opening is dramatized and intensified by its *forte* repetition with the bass instruments in imitation. The Andante, calling for muted strings, is no different in its melodic style from several earlier ones, though it is more eloquent; here again elaborated repetition intensifies the music. The finale has an unusually long development section, urgent in tone, with much use of string tremolando and imitation between basses and first violins.

In May 1774 Mozart composed a further symphony, K202/186*b*, a D major work of a less developed and fairly light, serenade-like character. The Symphony in C K200/189*k* probably dates from November 1774 (or possibly 1773; the year is illegible on the autograph). It is far from the ceremonial manner associated with C major and the use of trumpets and drums in his earlier symphonies; the style is lighter, more *buffo*, the textures finer, the thematic ideas in the spirited outer movements neatly argued (and, like those of K202, seemingly related to one another).

Several other works of interest date from 1774.

There are two concertos, the Concertone K190/186*E* for two violins and orchestra, with solo parts for oboe and cello, and the Bassoon Concerto K191/186*e*. The Concertone ('large concerto') is a leisurely, amiable work in the sinfonia concertante style of J. C. Bach, with much dialogue and sequence: it has a minuet-rondo finale, a type J. C. Bach favoured. So has the Bassoon Concerto, whose particular interest lies in Mozart's brilliant assumption of a style to exploit the instrument's special qualities – its contrasts of register, its staccato, its latent eloquence. The occasions for which these works were composed, in spring 1774, remain unknown. In the summer Mozart wrote a serenade K203/189*b*, containing a violin concerto, probably for university Finalmusik or possibly for celebrations on Archbishop Colloredo's name day (it has been called the 'Colloredo Serenade').

The Colloredo connection is more firmly established with the sacred works of this period. Colloredo was a reformist churchman with, for his day, an austere view on music for worship. In a well-known letter of 1776 Mozart wrote to Padre Martini: 'a mass, with the whole Kyrie, the Gloria, the Credo, the Epistle sonata, the Offertory or Motet, the Sanctus and the Agnus, must last no more than three-quarters of an hour'. The masses of 1774, K192/186*f* and 194/186*h*, are of this type, unlike his only other since Colloredo's accession, the *Missa in honorem sanctissimae Trinitatis* K167, whose unusual setting with four trumpets (two high and two low) and chorus without soloists makes clear that it was meant for a special occasion. That work totals 863 bars; K192 and 194 have respectively 290 and 457. This style, more condensed than in the earlier *missae breves*, demanded a minimum of word repetition (some texts are even treated in continuous dialogue), simple choral de-clamation, and sparing musical treatment of verbal meaning, as well as unbroken Gloria and Credo settings without extended final fugues, though sometimes an imitative point is briefly worked out. As exercises in concision and ingenuity, they are impressive. The most interesting movement is the Credo of K192, held together by a motivic treatment of the word 'Credo' to the traditional tag, based on the 'Lucis creator' plain-chant, which Mozart used contrapuntally many times, most famously in the finale of his last symphony. Here it is sometimes treated contrapuntally, sometimes merely harmonized; the phrase gives rise to fugatos at 'Crucifixus' and 'Et vitam venturi', but its recurrences mostly serve as an affirmation of 'Credo'. The device is not, however, original; there existed a well-established Austrian tradition of 'Credo masses', to which com-posers like Donberger, Francesco Conti and Holzbauer had contributed, and with which Mozart must have been familiar (see Reichert, 1955). He had opportunity for sacred composition in a more expansive manner with the Lorettine litany setting K195/186*d*, whose scale suggests it may have been written for Salzburg Cathedral; it is a relatively elaborate, polished essay in the traditional Salzburg manner, like the previous set-ting (K109/74*e*), with choruses in a free homophonic style and much expressive melody and bravura writing for the soloists. Settings of the *Dixit* and *Magnificat* of the same period (K193/186*g*) contain some vigorous counterpoint.

7. 1775-7: Salzburg

In summer 1774 Mozart was invited to write an opera for the Munich Carnival season. He began work about September, and left Salzburg with his father on 6 December, probably with the score near-complete; his sister joined them later. The première of the opera, *La finta giardiniera*, was to have been on 29 December but was postponed to Friday 13 January (Mozart told his mother not to be worried by the unpropitious date). According to Mozart's report to his mother the opera was much applauded and there were two repeat performances. The work was later (1780) given by Johann Heinrich Böhm's travelling company, who performed it in German as a Singspiel, with spoken dialogue; as the autograph score of Act 1 is lost, and no original printed libretto is known, this version was preferred until the discovery of a source with the Italian original and its publication in the Neue Mozart-Ausgabe (1978).

La finta giardiniera, written just before Mozart's 19th birthday, was his first *opera buffa* for six and a half years. The libretto, generally thought to have been prepared by Coltellini after Calzabigi, had been set by Anfossi for Rome in 1774; Mozart may have known Anfossi's setting. It is a tale of disguises and mistaken identities. Although several of the arias are in the simple, direct manner called for by the straightforward humour of the plot, others, including two agitated ones in minor keys and several in amorous or pathetic mood, hint with their richer harmony and texture at Mozart's growing resources for the musical depiction of character and situation. There are two mad scenes, and two ensemble finales, that of Act 1 notable for its crisp and ingenious vaudeville-like treatment of the comic situation at the beginning, that of Act 2 for its poetic opening (where the characters are lost in a wood); but the structure of these extended scenes is not entirely sure, and in any case is hampered by the libretto.

While the Mozarts were in Munich they took part in local musical life; Leopold conducted liturgical music by Wolfgang in performances at court and they played at academies. They also went to masked balls. Mozart wrote an offertory *Misericordias Domini* K222/205a, in an elaborate, learned style, borrowing an Eberlin theme for the purpose; he later sent the work to Martini for approval. He was doubtless anxious to impress the court, for the idea of an appointment in Munich was never far from his mind or his father's. He took part in a keyboard contest with the virtuoso Ignaz van Beecke, also a former child prodigy: according to C. F. D. Schubart Mozart played weightily and sight-read perfectly but Beecke surpassed him in every other respect.

Mozart's earliest surviving piano sonatas date from about this time: K279–83/189d–h were seemingly written as a group, K284/205b a little later. They are not works of great individuality; their general style is most of all akin to that of J. C. Bach's sonatas, as in the graceful first movement of K283, although certain movements, like the second of K280, look to Haydn. The final sonata, written for Baron Thaddäus von Dürnitz (an amateur bassoonist for whom he probably wrote the duet sonata K292/186c), is longer and more brilliant; its pseudo-orchestral first movement anticipates the sonatas of 1777–8, and it is unusual in having a polonaise-rondeau central movement and a

5. *Mozart wearing the insignia of the Golden Spur:*
anonymous portrait (1777)

variation finale. The set may have been composed with a view to publication, but only the last sonata was printed in Mozart's lifetime. Approaches to publishers at this period met with no success.

Mozart returned to Salzburg on 7 March, and there began a period that apparently he found depressing. Opportunities in the Salzburg musical establishment were limited, and the archbishop was ungenerous over leave; feeling his talent stifled in provincial Salzburg, Mozart pined for the larger musical world where since childhood he had won so much applause. Leopold, ambitious for his son and almost pathologically suspicious and discontented – Hasse, in 1771, had commented sharply on this – no doubt fed his frustration. Convinced, probably correctly, that the archbishop looked on them unfavourably, the Mozarts felt insecure in his domain.

The period in Salzburg began, however, with a commission for a work to be performed on the visit of Archduke Maximilian Franz, on 23 April: a setting of Metastasio's *Il rè pastore*. Contemporary writers called it a 'Serenada' or 'Cantate', which implies that it was given in concert or semi-staged form. In the Metastasian tradition, the drama, and thus the musical clothing of it too, are highly stylized; the aria texts deal with the claims of love and of duty, and the deft libretto contrives opportunities for pathetic farewells and occasional passionate expression. That the musical setting is somewhat static is inevitable, but the arias show a grace and polish in keeping with the text and a nice appreciation of scale – prolonged arias like those in the earlier Italian works are rare. The incipient characterization of *La finta giardiniera*, however, was scarcely followed up in *Il rè pastore*; the text offered no real scope for it.

Mozart's other principal compositions of 1775 were instrumental: they comprise another serenade (K204/213*a*), almost certainly written as university Finalmusik, and five violin concertos. These represent – excluding the violin concertos built into serenades – his total output of concertos for the instrument, or at least of undoubtedly authentic ones. (Two more are ascribed to him, K268/C14.04 in E♭ and K271*a*/271*i* in D, which may include music of Mozart's in adulterated form: their sources are dubious and their style uncharacteristic. The 'Adelaïde Concerto', allegedly from 1766, is a forgery, probably written in the early 1930s.) The five fully genuine works span from April to December 1775 and show a steady gain in mastery of the form. In the first two, K207 and 211, the balance between virtuoso violin writing and thematic treatment is not quite assured; the solo passage-work does not relate entirely convincingly with the general musical fabric, particularly in K211, whose rather halting and formal first movement recalls late Baroque or early Rococo concertos like some of Tartini's and those of his successor Nardini, whom Mozart had met at Stuttgart and probably Florence. K216 in G, beginning with a theme from an aria ritornello in *Il rè pastore*, is altogether more confident in style and makes in its Adagio a new, telling use of expressive violin cantilena. So does K218; these two concertos also have in common finales in a variety of tempos and metres, at different levels of sophistication, including courtly dances alongside folk themes (among them, in K216, a musette-like melody whose origins account for Mozart's calling this the 'Strasbourger-Concert'; see Bartha, 1956). Suggestions that K218 was modelled on a Boccherini concerto are mistaken; the alleged source is another modern forgery. The diversity of material in the final work of the group, K219 in A, reflects Mozart's newly acquired control with its happy and graceful themes, its counter-subjects and its dialogues; the poetic Adagio episode introducing the soloist in the first movement and the 'Turkish' episode set into the minuet finale are specially notable. The occasions that called forth these concertos are unknown, but probably they were mostly composed for Mozart himself or for a friend called Kolb at Salzburg; later they were played by Antonio Brunetti, the Salzburg Konzertmeister from 1776, for whom Mozart supplied a new movement (K261) to replace the 'studied' Adagio of K219, and a Rondo K269/ 261a, probably to replace the one in K207.

In 1776 Mozart wrote a number of piano (or harpsichord) concertos, and his treatment of that form underwent an analogous development. The occasion for the composition of the first, K238 in B♭, is not known; the second, K246 in C, was written for the Countess Lützow, a member of a prominent Salzburg family. K238 is an amiable work, essentially in a *galant* manner, with fluent passage-work taking its place neatly in the structure; it marks no departure. In the K246 opening movement the soloist, for the first time, has a distinctive, lyrical secondary theme not heard in the preceding ritornello, a clear hint of the coming expansion of the form's scale and range although the actual invention is fairly conventional. The finale follows the minuet-rondo design favoured in several earlier concertos, as does that of the three-piano concerto K242, composed about the same time for the Lodrons, another leading Salzburg family – an ingeniously contrived work that also exists in a two-piano version. By the beginning of 1777, stimulated by the visit of a French keyboard virtuoso,

Mlle Jeunehomme, Mozart was ready to write a concerto on a far larger scale. K271 in E♭, quite apart from the inherent attractiveness, vitality and grace of its ideas, is one of Mozart's most subtle and highly organized works of any period in matters like its thematic relationships, its handling of phrase length and cadence to increase tension and strengthen its resolution, and, most strikingly, in its richly developed relationship between soloist and orchestra. It begins, arrestingly and unconventionally, with the piano answering in the second bar the orchestra's fanfare-like opening phrase; and though this dialogue has no effect on the movement's basic formal outlines it establishes an unusually flexible treatment of soloist and orchestra and gives rise to a large variety of possibilities, adventurously and wittily explored – not least the later exchange in dialogue roles, at the recapitulation, and the piano's unorthodox final intervention in the ritornello following the cadenza. There is a sombre C minor Andantino, notable for its exploitation of the violins' dark lowest register, its chromatic melody and affective harmony, and its elaborately embellished solo line. The finale is an extended rondo whose brilliant passage-work assumes a symphonic character, and whose thrust is tellingly relieved by an interpolated minuet, of which each strain is repeated with florid decoration. K271, written in the month of Mozart's 21st birthday, represents a new maturity, technical and emotional.

A stream of lighter instrumental works had flowed from Mozart's pen during the time between *Il rè pastore* and summer 1776. They include divertimentos for a wind band of pairs of oboes, bassoons and horns, cheerful outdoor music on a smallish scale, with brief sonata movements, variations and a polonaise and a contredanse as well as minuets; there are six in this group, though there may be doubts about the authenticity of the last, K289/271*g*. On a less unpretentious level are various occasional works, divertimentos and serenades, including two substantial, six-movement works (K247 and 287/271*H*) composed for the name days of Countess Lodron: each has two minuets and two slow movements (one an Adagio in the traditional amorous serenade style), with fast movements often including material of an almost rumbustiously popular character. At least two actual folk melodies appear in K287. These works are for two violins, viola, double bass (rather than cello) and two horns: they are solo, not orchestral, music. So is the septet divertimento K251, for the same combination plus oboe, traditionally supposed to have been composed for Nannerl Mozart, probably on her name day. There are two echo serenades, the charming K239 'Serenata notturna', consisting of a march-like first movement, a minuet and a rondo (with rustic episodes), where a group of two violins, viola and double bass is set against full strings and timpani; and the Notturno K286/269*a*, where the dialogue among four orchestras of strings and horns is ingenious and humorous, depending on echo effects. The single substantial orchestral work of the period is the noble Serenade K250/248*b*, composed for the marriage of Elisabeth Haffner, daughter of a prominent Salzburg citizen. This is a nine-movement work, with three minuets and an interpolated violin concerto, whose lithe, sparkling rondo is a tour de force both of composition and execution. The scale and character of the music, particularly its *maestoso* opening, make clear Mozart's view of the grandeur of the occasion; this is the weightiest and most symphonic of Mozart's occasional works to date, without prejudicing the D major trumpet-and-drum brilliance typical of the medium. A flute concerto by Mozart is said to have been performed in July 1777, but no such work is known; an oboe concerto may also belong to this period.

Mozart's other sphere of activity in these years was church music, required of him in connection with his court duties. He had composed one short mass, K220/196*b*, about the time of *La finta giardiniera* (it follows the tradition of cyclic use of material, the music for the Kyrie recurring at 'Dona nobis pacem'); four more, all in C major to accommodate the trumpets favoured in Salzburg, followed in 1776 and one in 1777. None requires violas, which evidently were not used, or were used merely to double the bass line, at Salzburg. The longest and most elaborate is the first, K262/246*a*, probably composed for Salzburg Cathedral at Easter 1776; it has, besides the customary concluding fugues to the Gloria and Credo, contrapuntal writing even at the Kyrie and the 'Et incarnatus', and extended orchestral ritornellos. The Benedictus, usually a solo movement followed by a separate Osanna or a repeat of the preceding one, is here set with solo phrases to the 'Benedictus' words and choral refrains to the 'Osanna', in a single movement. Points of interest in the next three, K257, 258 and 259, all of them of the *missa brevis* type, are in K257 the use of a repeated Credo motto, though not contrapuntally as in K192, and the appearance of the four-note 'Credo' phrase used in K192 in its Sanctus; in K258 the interesting solo–chorus treatment of the Benedictus and the curiously solemn florid writing of the last movement; and in K259 the use of the organ as a solo instrument in the Benedictus. This group of compact, direct pieces, firmly in the Austrian tradition of church music and indeed of the region's natural and gracefully decorative Rococo art as a whole, is rounded off by K275/272*b*, a work on a modest scale and of a simpler and more intimate character – in B♭, it lacks the usual trumpets. There are several epistle sonatas of this period, no doubt originally associated with particular masses: attractive pieces in an airily tuneful style, emphasizing the lack of any sharp distinction in Mozart's attitude to sacred and secular. Mozart's most important church work in this period, however, is the *Litaniae de venerabili altaris sacramento* K243. It embraces several styles unselfconsciously and without incongruity: simple homophonic choruses, dramatic ones, fugues, a plainchant setting, and expressive arias with florid embellishment.

8. 1777-80: Mannheim, Paris, Salzburg

The Mozart's discontent with their Salzburg situation came to a head during 1777. In August Mozart wrote a carefully worded petition – there is almost an undertone of insolence to it – asking the archbishop for his release from employment. In his faintly sarcastic note of reply the archbishop released both father and son; but Leopold could not afford to go and was evidently reinstated. So on this next journey Mozart was accompanied by his mother. The numerous and long letters exchanged between father and son during his 16 months' absence (this was the first time they had been away from one another) cast a sharp light on their relationship, particularly if read with some scepticism as to Mozart's frankness and indeed his truthfulness.

Mozart and his mother set out, in their own chaise, on 23 September. At Munich, where they spent 17 days, Mozart offered his services to the elector, and met with a polite refusal: 'there is no vacancy here'. At Augsburg they remained a fortnight: Mozart visited the piano maker J. A. Stein, amazed the monks at the Heilig-kreuz canonry with his fugal improvisations, attended an academy with the town patricians (where he was discomfited at being teased over the Order of the Golden Spur that he wore) and gave a concert including several of his recent works. He spent some time with his relatives and struck up a vivacious friendship with his cousin Maria Anna Thekla (his 'Bäsle', affectionate diminutive of *Base*, 'cousin'): in the ensuing months he wrote her several letters, full of the obscene childish humour, characteristic of Salzburg, that also runs through his letters home; there is no reason to imagine that their friendship was in any way sexual, as has been suggested. Mozart and his mother left Augsburg on 26 October and, after pausing at Hohenaltheim in the hope of playing to the Prince of Oettingen-Wallerstein, reached Mannheim on 30 October.

Mannheim was an important musical centre, with a fine orchestra and a court devoted to music under the lavish patronage of the Elector Carl Theodor. Mozart remained there until the middle of March. His letters give a graphic picture of musical life and the musical people there. He quickly became friendly with Cannabich, the Konzertmeister, and with others, including the Kapellmeister, Holzbauer (whose opera *Günther von Schwarzburg* and a mass impressed him), and particularly the flautist J. B. Wendling. He soon met the elector, talked to him about his children's musical tuition, and dropped hints about his interest in remaining at Mannheim; but it was another month before the elector made clear that there was no post for him. Mozart was acutely disappointed. It was now a bad time of year for travelling. So he found work, as well as diversion, in Mannheim: he did some teaching, wrote some flute music for De Jean, a surgeon with the Dutch East India Co., and stayed three more months taking part in much music-making. During that time he fell in love with Aloysia Weber, a soprano, aged 16, daughter of a copyist, and travelled with her and her father to Kirchheimboland to perform to the Princess of Nassau-Weilburg. He postponed moving on to Paris, and put to Leopold the notion of taking her to Italy to become a prima donna. This naive proposal infuriated

6. *Autograph letter from Mozart to his father (dated '30'
February 1778), written from Mannheim; it refers to the
aria 'Se al labbro'* K295 *that he composed for Anton Raaff*

Leopold: he had been pouring forth advice since Mozart
had left home – on routes, potential patrons, letters of
introduction, ways of ingratiating himself with
influential people, money matters and countless other
topics – and was now distracted by his son's ill-
conceived schemes, his dilatoriness, his irresponsibility
over money and his apparent family disloyalty. The
contrast between Mozart's gossipy, high-spirited, often
frivolous letters and his father's increasingly anxious and
irritable ones is revealing. Finally, on 11–12 February
1778, Leopold ordered his son onwards: '*Off with you to
Paris!* and that soon, find your place among great
people – aut Caesar aut nihil'. Further, Mozart's mother
was to accompany him to Paris; Mozart had hardly
shown himself fit to travel alone.

The Mozarts left Mannheim on 14 March and arrived
in Paris nine days later. Mozart followed up various
connections, through German acquaintances, Baron
Grimm and the Palatine ambassador, and found work.
He composed additional music, mainly choruses, for a
performance at the Concert Spirituel of a *Miserere* by
Holzbauer and, according to his letters home, a sinfonia
concertante κ Anh.9/297*B* for flute, oboe, bassoon and
horn, for his Mannheim friends; that, however, if it ever
was composed, was suppressed by the Concert Spirituel
director, Joseph Legros, and like the *Miserere*
movements is lost. (A work in E♭ for oboe, clarinet,
bassoon and horn, κ Anh.9/C14.01, discovered much
later in an early 19th-century copy, has been reckoned
to be a version of that work; but its credentials are
dubious, and any music by Mozart that it may contain
can be only in a corrupt form.) Mozart was not happy in
Paris; his letters make clear that he heartily despised
French music and French taste, that he was unwilling to

be duly deferential to possible patrons, and that like his father he always suspected malicious intrigue. He undertook a little teaching (his letter to Leopold of 14 May tells fascinatingly of his methods with an untalented composition pupil) and accepted some private commissions; he also hoped to write an opera. A post as organist at Versailles was offered to him, he told his father, but he intended to decline it. Two new works had hearings in June: a group of ballet pieces, for Noverre, given with a Piccinni opera, and a symphony composed for the Concert Spirituel, performed on 18 June and several times repeated. The symphony was warmly received, and after its success, Mozart wrote, 'I went off to the Palais Royal, where I had a large ice, and said the rosary as I had vowed to'.

By that date Mozart's mother was ill with a fever. They tried the usual family remedies, then called in Grimm's doctor; but nothing could be done, and on 3 July she died. Mozart's communication of the news to his father shows a new maturity and sensitivity. He wrote to say that she was critically ill, and by the same post wrote to the Abbé Bullinger, a close friend in Salzburg, telling him what had happened. Leopold was thus prepared when Bullinger broke the news to him. Mozart now went to stay with Grimm, who soon wrote frankly and pessimistically to Leopold about his son's prospects in Paris, pointing out that his visit had unfortunately coincided with the Gluck–Piccinni controversy, and that he would have done better in Paris with half the talent and double the shrewdness. Meanwhile Mozart had another symphony given at the Concert Spirituel, on 8 September (he claimed in a letter that it was a new work, but that seems to be untrue), renewed his old acquaintance with J. C. Bach, over from

London to hear the Paris singers before composing an opera, and wrote a scena (now lost) for Bach's friend the castrato Tenducci. His friendship with Grimm (an ardent Piccinniste; Mozart was anxious to keep clear of the controversy) deteriorated. Mozart owed him money, and reacted in a manner typical of one who feels an irksome obligation.

On 27 August Leopold wrote to Mozart, enjoining on him the need to work towards earning a living in Paris. Four days later he wrote again: Mozart must come back to Salzburg, where a better post was open to him; he would still be a Konzertmeister, but now court organist, with accompanying duties, rather than violinist. The archbishop had offered a salary increase and generous leave. So Mozart, who had hoped to escape from the provincial atmosphere of Salzburg and to secure a full Kapellmeistership – although, as Leopold pointed out, he was too young for that – set out for home. He left on 26 September; Grimm arranged the journey and put him on a slow coach through Nancy to Strasbourg, where he gave three unprofitable concerts. Then he went to Mannheim, where he remained a month, although, as Carl Theodor had become Elector of Bavaria and moved to Munich, the orchestra was largely disbanded. There he heard a melodrama (a theatrical work consisting of declamation with music) by Georg Benda, and resolved to write one himself; the work, *Semiramis*, was listed in the Gotha *Theater-Kalender* from 1779 but, even if written, was never performed and is now lost. He also started writing a concerto for piano and violin. Leopold, incensed at his son's having gone to Mannheim, where there were no opportunities, summoned him home. Mozart reached Munich on 25 December. There he remained – again to the irritation of Leopold, who was afraid that his dawdling might jeopardize the Salzburg appointment – until 11 January: he presented dedication copies of a set of sonatas, newly arrived from the engraver in Paris, to the Electress Elisabeth Auguste, and stayed with the Webers. His reception from Aloysia, now singing in the court opera, was apparently cool; 'I really cannot write – my heart is too full of tears', he wrote to Leopold. And it seems that his inquiries about a post or an opera commission there proved fruitless. He arrived home, anxious about the welcome he would receive, in mid-January.

Mozart had been away 16 months. He had received no worthwhile offer of a post or even a major commission; he had fallen deeply in love and been disappointed; his mother had died; his actions had worsened the family finances and strained the family affections – though there is no doubt that the eagerness to see one another again, repeatedly expressed in the father–son correspondence, was genuine and indeed heartfelt. His letters of these months hint at several important aspects of his personality. He had always been told by Leopold to be natural and friendly with noblemen but aloof, 'like an Englishman', with other musicians; deeply implanted in him was a mistrust of his own professional colleagues (perhaps exaggerated in his letters, to satisfy his father), and that consorted uneasily with his natural youthful openness and liveliness. His comments on musical matters often show a certain arrogance; he knew the extent of his own skills, could see the weaknesses of other men's, and (as his music repeatedly bears out) was keen to outshine any potential rival. He had a strong and sincere, quite conventional, religious feeling, with a hint of selfconscious moral rectitude, in no way contradicted by his smutty humour.

Immediately on his return Mozart formally petitioned the archbishop for his new appointment as court organist, which was granted with a salary of 450 gulden (the same as his predecessor Adlgasser's). His duties included playing in the cathedral, at court and in the chapel, composing as required, and instructing the choirboys. The years 1779–80 were uneventful for him. He wrote several sacred works, and symphonies, presumably for use in court ceremonial; also from this period came some concertos and, each summer, a divertimento or serenade. His interest in dramatic music remained strong, and when Johann Heinrich Böhm's troupe visited Salzburg in mid-1779 and winter 1779–80 Mozart's music to Gebler's *Thamos, König in Ägypten*, may have been used. He began work on a Singspiel, now known as *Zaide*, intended either for this troupe or for Emanuel Schikaneder's, in Salzburg for winter 1780–81, or with thoughts of production in the new German opera house in Vienna.

9. Music of 1777-80

Like his youthful journeys, the Mannheim-Paris one of 1778 had its influence on his music. The first echo of the Mannheim style came in the Piano Sonata K309/284*b*, written for Cannabich's young daughter Rosa (its Andante was designed, Mozart said, to portray her): Mozart's sister wrote that 'anyone could see it was composed in Mannheim', and Leopold that 'it has something of the mannered Mannheim style about it, but so little that your own good style is not spoilt'. They were doubtless referring to such characteristics as the sharp dynamic contrasts in the first two movements and the aura of 'sensibility', even expressive affectation, that pervades the Andante. A similar atmosphere is evident in the Andante of the next sonata, K311/284*c*, though the lines are less elaborate, and the work as a whole is of a more brilliant and expansive cast. These two were published in Paris by Mozart's friend Mme Heina (her husband had been Mozart's only companion at his mother's funeral), along with his first minor-key sonata, K310/300*d* in A minor, probably also composed there. He may have written the A minor work for his performances in the Parisian salons; it follows up the tradition of fiery keyboard writing that Schobert and others had pursued in Paris, though Mozart's textures are less orchestral than theirs, the sense of agitation more consistent and deeper.

The six sonatas for piano and violin printed in Paris and dedicated to the electress were begun in Mannheim early in 1778, and they bear the impress of the local style. That however is not the sole influence; when passing through Munich Mozart had commented favourably on a set of sonatas by Joseph Schuster, then popular there, and had thought of writing a similar set. Schuster's (ed. in NM, nos.229, 232–3) are texturally slender but ingenious, and their use of the 'accompanying' violin is enterprising for the date. Mozart employed several of his devices, and in particular derived from Schuster the structure of the first movement of K303/293c where, in effect, the Adagio introduction represents the first subject and recurs at the recapitulation. The emotional world of these sonatas is however closer to that of Mannheim than that of Schuster's light, crisp pieces, and each sonata touches on a different aspect of Mannheim expressiveness. At one extreme is K304/300c, Mozart's only work in E minor, with its spare textures and hesitant, wistful manner representing a world of delicate sensibility – its concluding minuet in particular, a rondo on an elegant, pathetic melody of a French cast with a gentle second episode in E major providing harmonic balm. At the other is K306/300*l* in D, the only three-movement sonata of the published set, a showy and energetic piece with a hint of orchestral style in some of the keyboard writing and a finale in two contrasting tempos and metres. Those two were probably the last to be written. The individuality of expression in these sonatas, and the inventiveness yet essential simplicity of the piano–violin textures, is also evident in such movements as the graceful finale of K302/293d in E♭. One further sonata was written in Mannheim, a three-movement work in C (K296) in a light, almost playful style, composed for Mozart's pupil Therese Serrarius, daughter of his landlord there.

Other products of the Mannheim months are

Mozart's flute works, written slowly and unwillingly for De Jean; the commission was never finished, the fee never fully paid. The second of the two concertos (K313–4/285c–d) is probably an arrangement of an oboe concerto, possibly the one referred to in a letter as having been written for the Salzburg oboist Ferlendis, and thus rather earlier. Both are essentially in the manner of the violin concertos of 1775, with no perceptible Mannheim influence; an additional Andante (K315/285e) may have been intended as a simpler slow movement for K313 rather than as part of a third concerto. Mozart wrote that he had composed three flute quartets for De Jean , but only two (K285 and 285a) can be assigned to this period. Of his other two, K298 is much later (1786–7), and K Anh.171/285b, if fully authentic, probably belongs to the early Viennese years. Mozart told his father that he disliked the flute; but the writing is too professional and idiomatic to betray anything of the kind. He wrote again for flute in Paris, a double concerto with harp (his only work for that instrument) for the Count (not Duke) of Guines and his daughter, composed with care and evident affection as well as a sharp sense of a style apt for aristocratic French patrons: the Andantino, with divided violas, has a sensuous warmth, and the finale is a courtly gavotte.

The most significant Paris work is the symphony written for the Concert Spirituel and, following Leopold's counsel, carefully tailored to local taste. It begins with the obligatory *premier coup d'archet*, made the more sharply effective by the *piano* phrase that follows; marked dynamic contrasts, vivacious rhythms, powerful unison and octave passages, brilliant tuttis, and exposed writing (equally for the string and wind sections) characterize the first movement, a specially inven-

7. The Mozart family; portrait (c1780) by Johann Nepomuk della Croce; Mozart's mother (d 1778) is depicted in her portrait of c1775 (probably by Lorenzoni or Franz Joseph Degle)

tive piece, obviously designed to dazzle the Parisians'
ears and exploit their large orchestra. That such was
Mozart's purpose is left in no doubt by his letter of 3
July 1778, in which he referred to the unusual *piano*
opening of the finale and the effect it had. The familiar
6/8 Andante, the weight of evidence suggests, was
composed later as a replacement for the original,
simpler 3/4 movement. The other surviving Paris
work is the ballet *Les petits riens*, which contains some
sharply characterized dances of an aptly elegant kind,
though it is not easy to be certain which of the smaller
pieces are Mozart's new movements and which the
'wretched old French airs' that he said were included.

The Mannheim and Paris experiences left their mark
on the music composed on his return home; he was
doubtless pleased to display his command of inter-
national styles in provincial Salzburg. That command is
especially clear in the orchestral music. Soon after his
return he wrote two symphonies, of which the first,
no.32 (in the traditional numbering) in G K318 is in
Italian overture form – possibly it was intended for a
theatrical performance, but there is no firm evidence. It
consists of an Allegro into which, at the end of the
development section, an Andante is inserted; then the
Allegro resumes, with its second subject, and finally the
first subject returns. This 'reversed recapitulation',
favoured by certain Mannheim composers, ought not be
regarded as progressive or innovatory; rather it
represents an older, binary pattern, in which the first
subject was not recapitulated at all, now supplemented
by the rhetorical device of having the opening music
crown the movement by serving as coda. Mozart did
this in the first movements of two sonatas (K306 and
311) and in the Andante of his next symphony, K319 in

B♭. While K318 bears, in its brilliant and prolonged tuttis and its dramatic style, signs of Mozart's recent experiences, K319 is a much more chamber-musical work, in the Salzburg tradition. Interestingly, the 'development' sections in its original three movements – the minuet was added later – each begin with fresh material (with thematic links between them, incidentally): this too, often reckoned as bold or forward-looking, is again a reversion to an earlier procedure.

These works were followed by Mozart's last Salzburg serenade, K320 (see fig. 8), probably composed as university Finalmusik. Its concertante insertion is a pair of movements with solo woodwind instruments, mainly flute and oboe, but sometimes a six-part ensemble; the whole work has an opulence of orchestration beyond that of the preceding serenade, K250. Its first movement in particular, though in Mozart's typically extrovert D major manner, has tuttis of exceptional variety and ingenuity, using (as does Symphony no.32) Mannheim-style crescendos, and the finale incorporates hints of contrapuntal development, while the D minor Andantino touches on emotions of a sombre kind not normal to serenades. The use of a posthorn in the second trio of the second minuet gives the work its nickname. This group of works ends with the vigorous and spacious Symphony no.34 in C K338, composed a year later, in August 1780, by when the stylistic novelties were more fully assimilated: the tone is assured and individual. Here the first-movement 'development' makes no reference to exposition material, and there is both a normal recapitulation and a last-minute reappearance of the first subject. There are three movements; the minuet K409/383*f* may have been intended for it but scarcely accords with it in style.

Mozart composed a further four substantial instrumental works in this period: a piano and violin sonata (K378/317*d*); his last Salzburg divertimento, K334/320*b*, for strings and horns, possibly intended for the Mozarts' friends the aristocratic Robinig family, and notable for its exquisitely graceful first minuet; and two double concertos. That for two pianos K365/316*a* is a work of vivacity and charm, with much ingenious dialogue; it is not known to have been commissioned and was probably intended for Mozart and his sister. That for violin and viola, the Sinfonia concertante K364/320*d*, is a major work, comparable in its significance to the Piano Concerto K271, also in E♭. The sinfonia concertante was a favoured form in Mannheim and Paris, with their orchestras of virtuosos; Carl Stamitz composed several for violin and viola. Mozart possibly wrote one for wind, and began one for piano and violin, of which he wrote 120 bars, and one for string trio, of which he wrote 134. He may have stopped work because there was no likelihood of a commission or performance; but the possibility should not be overlooked that the intractable formal problems posed by the instrumental layout gave him pause. In K364 they are less acute, for it is a double concerto rather than an ensemble one, and the instruments can interchange material freely; they mostly play separately, in dialogue – the viola often taking over phrases heard on the violin, presenting them in a different light and turning them in different directions – and come together only at the ends of sections. The orchestral writing is markedly Mannheim-influenced, and enhanced by the rich texture of divided violas, needed to reflect the violin–viola symmetry. An impassioned, elegiac tone, characteristic of Mozart's C minor slow movements,

8. First Page of the autograph MS of Mozart's 'Posthorn'
Serenade κ320, composed 1779

marks the Andante, its dialogues full of unexpected melodic twists leading to highly chromatic harmonies.

The vocal works of this period are comparatively few. Mozart wrote four arias on the Mannheim and Paris journey. For Aloysia Weber he set first a Metastasio text, *Non sò d'onde viene*, K294: 'because I know [J. C.] Bach's setting so well, and like it so much . . . I wished to see whether I could not write an aria totally unlike his'. It is indeed like J. C. Bach in style, but not like his setting; it is an eloquent *aria d'affetto*, written lovingly for Aloysia's voice. An ornamented version, prepared for her instruction, is extant. *Io non chiedo* K316/300*b*, presented to her in Munich, tests her coloratura. He also composed an aria for Dorothea Wendling, and one for the elderly tenor Raaff, a good friend to him at Mannheim, beautifully suited to his old-fashioned portamento style and allowing him generous opportunities for breath. Back in Salzburg, Mozart wrote four substantial sacred works. First among them is the Coronation Mass K317, traditionally believed to have been composed for the ceremonial crowning of an image of the virgin in a church near Salzburg. Written in March 1779, it has claims to be counted Mozart's finest Salzburg mass. It is in *missa brevis* style, but less condensed than his earlier examples and considerably tauter in structure, with more use of recurring material (in particular, the 'Dona' matching the Kyrie). The symphonic drive of the Credo is broken off for an Adagio 'Et incarnatus', touching on distant keys and with delicate violin arabesques; and the Agnus is a soprano solo whose resemblance to 'Dove sono' in *Le nozze di Figaro* has often been remarked.

In the next (and last) of the Salzburg masses, K337, the Agnus, with solo oboe, bassoon and organ, resembles the Countess's other aria in *Figaro*; this, also a short mass, is otherwise of limited interest, apart only from the exceptional treatment of the Benedictus as a severe *a cappella* fugue. Mozart's only two complete settings of the vesper psalms were composed in 1779–80, probably for use in Salzburg Cathedral. Each is a sequence of six movements, not (like a mass or litany setting) a unity; only the keys of the outer movements correspond. Most movements have a basis of homophonic choral writing with solo episodes, but in each work the pattern is changed for the 'Laudate pueri', at first strictly fugal or canonic, and generally contrapuntal throughout, and also for the succeeding 'Laudate Dominum', a soprano aria – in K321 with organ obbligato, and in K339 a simple long, floating melody whose beguiling beauty attracted many 19th-century arrangers.

The technique of writing vivid dramatic music to support declaimed speech – picked up from Benda, and to have been applied in *Semiramis* – was used in *Zaide*, as the unfinished, untitled Singspiel to a text arranged by J. A. Schachtner is known. Its opening scene in particular is striking, with chromatic harmonies and highly expressive figuration supporting the enslaved hero's words of despair; and it culminates in a minuet aria of exquisite grace in the manner of J. C. Bach. *Zaide* was left incomplete presumably because performance prospects had faded; but it has several strong and elaborately worked items, notably a fiery G minor aria for the heroine Zaide and two ensembles, the second of them a quartet in which the characters' differentiated expressions of love, anxiety and vengeance are treated in the same way as in the later *Idomeneo* quartet. But the opera's topic and characterization generally make it more readily seen as a step towards *Die Entführung*. The other dramatic music of this time consists of three choruses, two of them probably reworkings of ones composed in 1773, three entr'actes and a melodrama for Gebler's play *Thamos, König in Ägypten*, his only incidental theatre music (Mozart was a keen follower of theatre, non-musical as well as musical). The serious, intense tone of the instrumental pieces – most likely composed in 1776–7, though the whole achieved its final form probably in 1779 – and the exalted nature of the ritual music in the new final chorus testify to Mozart's involvement in the drama, which like *Die Zauberflöte* deals with the triumph of good over evil. When *Thamos* fell out of the repertory Mozart's music was used in K. M. Plümicke's play *Lanassa*.

10. 1780-81: Munich

During the summer of 1780, Mozart at length received the commission he had hoped for to compose a serious opera for Munich; probably Raaff had helped him secure it. The Salzburg cleric Gianbattista Varesco was engaged to prepare a libretto based on Danchet's *Idomenée*, set by Campra (Paris, 1712). The plot concerns King Idomeneus of Crete, who promises Neptune that if spared from a shipwreck he will sacrifice the first person he sees, and is met on landing by his son Idamantes. Mozart began to set the text in Salzburg: he already knew several of the singers, from Mannheim, and could draft some of the arias in advance. On 5 November he left for Munich to complete the task, working with the singers, the intendant (Count Seeau), the designer (Lorenzo Quaglio) and the ballet-master (Le Grand, in effect the producer too). His letters to Leopold, who was in close touch with Varesco, provide a fascinating picture of the genesis of the work and in particular of the ways in which it was modified during rehearsal. The matters that chiefly occupied Mozart's mind – apart from assuring his father about the singers' enthusiasm – were, first, the need for cuts, because the text was overlong; second, the need to make the action more natural; and third, the need to accommodate the requirements (and the weaknesses) of the singers. As rehearsals, act by act, continued during December, more cuts were made. Even after the libretto was sent to the printer at the beginning of January Mozart continued to trim the score and eventually it was decided to have a second libretto printed to show the final text (although in the event still more adjustments were made, as the performing score makes clear). Because of the opera's excessive length at the rehearsals, Mozart omitted at this late stage not only much recitative of both kinds but also sections of the ceremonial choral scenes and three arias in the last act. The planning, and composition, of the opera had in fact been seriously miscalculated: the libretto was far too long, particularly for the elaborate, expansive setting Mozart envisaged and the ruthless cutting necessitated by the realization of this at so late a stage was bound to affect the work's proportions. The opera was performed, after post-ponements, on 29 January 1781. Leopold was now in Munich, so Mozart sent no report; but clearly it was a considerable success.

In *Idomeneo* Mozart depicted serious, heroic emotion with a richness unparalleled elsewhere in his works. He certainly set great store by the opera himself. Although nominally an *opera seria*, it departs substantially from tradition: with its French source, it has a more natural attitude to emotion, a more complex structure, and a greater emphasis on the participation of the chorus, while its scoring – for the virtuoso Mannheim orchestra, now at Munich – is exceptionally full and elaborate. Gluck's influence, notable in Mozart's setting of the oracle scene with trombones (cf *Alceste* – though the idea, in any case obvious in view of the association of trombones with ritual, was put forward by Leopold), is often remarked. The influence of Piccinni's French operas – Mozart had heard *Roland* in Paris – is also strong; so perhaps is that of Holzbauer's *Günther von Schwarzburg*. Mozart had no interest in eliminating either bravura singing, which he used to a dramatic rather than an exhibitionist end (as above all in Idomeneus's 'Fuor del mar'), or, unlike Gluck in his 'reform operas', in eliminating simple recitative – though he often elided recitative of either kind with the lyrical music so as to make the texture more continuous.

A remarkable feature is the opera's abundance of orchestral recitative, much of it vigorous and dramatic, and often extremely colourful and expressive in its harmony, sharply reflecting the sense of the words. Some of it involves the use of motif: it is clear that Mozart employed certain patterns of phrase throughout the opera with consistent reference to individual characters and their predominant emotions, like Ilia's grief and Electra's jealousy (see Heartz, 1974; also *MJb 1973–4*, 82ff). There are also fairly well defined relationships between particular keys and the dramatic contexts in which they appear, affecting the recitative as well as the arias; similar patterns may be found in the later operas. An unorthodox key treatment – a false recapitulation in C minor in a D minor aria – is clearly intended to suggest that Electra is disorientated or even unhinged. The traditional device of analogy between natural events and represented emotion is used with particular force in the same aria, Electra's in Act 1, where the storm at sea is paralleled by her turbulence; and Idomeneus's 'Fuor del mar', a traditional simile aria, gains special force because it is the raging sea itself that is responsible for the raging emotion within him. If the music for Idamantes is less inspiring, that may be because Mozart found the singer, an inexperienced castrato, inadequate; but the richness and warmth of the music for Ilia, notably her E♮ *aria d'affetto* with prominent wind parts, speak unmistakably of Dorothea Wendling's capacities as well as Mozart's sympathy for the character. In the opera's orchestration many new and brilliant details are to be found, like the evocative flute, oboe and violin passages in 'Fuor del mar' (as in bars 9–10) or the solemn effect of the big choral scenes: sustained wind against inexorable string triplets and muted trumpet fanfares in 'O voto tremendo', or pizzicato violin arpeggios against wailing flute and oboe phrases in Idomeneus's prayer. Of the individual numbers, however, the most powerful is the Act 3 quartet in which Idamantes resolves to seek death, a tour de force in which intensely chromatic music embraces truthfully four characters' diverse emotions.

Idomeneo had three performances in Munich. Later in 1781 Mozart considered revising it 'more in the French manner', with a bass Idomeneus (as he had initially expected to have for the première) and a tenor Idamantes, but his hopes came to nothing. He did however give a performance, probably a concert one, at the Auersperg palace in Vienna in 1786, for which he arranged the castrato part of Idamantes for a tenor, writing an extended new aria with violin obbligato and a new duet, and making other modifications and cuts.

While he was in Munich Mozart composed a number of short vocal works, his Oboe Quartet, and possibly the Serenade K361/370*a* (or part of it) and three piano sonatas. These, K330/300*h*, 331/300*i* and 332/300*k*, long ascribed to his months in Paris but now known to belong to this period in Munich or Mozart's early years in Vienna, are among his most popular keyboard works, especially K332 in F (which in its 1784 published form has a richly embellished slow movement recapitulation, presumably Mozart's own second thoughts) and K331 in A, famous for its first movement, a 6/8 pastoral theme with variations, and its 'Rondo alla turca' finale, a brilliant response to the current fashion for janissary music.

Mozart, his father and his sister remained in Munich until early March. They then spent a few days in Augsburg, no doubt visiting their relatives. On 12 March Mozart, back in Munich, was summoned to Vienna, where the Archbishop of Salzburg and his retinue were resident during celebrations of the accession of Emperor Joseph II.

11. Early Viennese years, 1781-4

Mozart reached Vienna on 16 March and lodged with the archbishop's entourage. At table he was placed below the valets but above the cooks; fresh from his triumphs in Munich, where noblemen had talked with him on equal terms, he was insulted and resentful. He equally resented the archbishop's refusal to let him earn money by playing at concerts. His letters home over the next three months reflect not only his increasing irritation – many sections are written in the cipher Mozart and his father used for material they did not want the Salzburg censors to understand – but also a growing enthusiasm for the possibility of earning his own living in Vienna. On the evening of an entertainment given by the archbishop, for which he supplied a rondo for the violinist Brunetti, a song for the castrato Ceccarelli and a sonata for himself (K373, 374 and 379/373a), he could, had the archbishop released him, have played before the emperor and earned the equivalent of half his annual Salzburg salary. On 9 May matters came to a head, and at a stormy interview with the archbishop, who according to Mozart poured out abuse unworthy of his station and his calling, Mozart asked for his discharge. At first he was refused, but at an interview with the chief steward Count Arco on 9 June he was finally and decisively released from Salzburg service, 'with a kick on my arse ... by order of our worthy Prince Archbishop', he wrote. Leopold's letters of these months do not survive, but their content is easily inferred from Mozart's replies. Clearly he was apprehensive for his own situation and anxious about his son's future. Mozart replied with strong – almost too strong – protestations about his honour, about how ill he had been used, and about the rosy prospects of a career in Vienna; he also answered various reproaches about supposed improper behaviour and failures in his religious observations, and his answers ring true.

By this time Mozart had moved from the quarters occupied by Colloredo's retinue to the house of his former Mannheim friends the Webers. In 1780 Aloysia had married a court actor, Joseph Lange, and now Mozart's name came to be linked with that of the third of the four daughters, Constanze. In a letter to Leopold, Mozart dismissed such rumours as 'entirely groundless': he had never thought less of getting married, which would be a misfortune to him, and anyway he did not love the girl. But to scotch the gossip he moved elsewhere in September. He was making a modest living by teaching, one of his three or four pupils (see Hamann, 1962–3) being Josepha von Auernhammer, for whom he wrote his two-piano sonata and to whom he dedicated a set of accompanied sonatas, published by Artaria in November; she was very ugly – Mozart was repelled by her amorous feelings towards him – but musically talented and a true friend. Probably she later saw some of his publications through the press. At the end of July Mozart had been given a libretto for a Singspiel, *Die Verführung* (later *Entführung*) *aus dem Serail*, on which he unhurriedly worked; it was soon clear that there was no prospect of an early production. Other compositions included a wind serenade for a group of 'poor beggars who . . . play quite well together' to perform to a lady on her name day; he wrote it 'quite carefully' as an influential court official was to hear it. The 'poor beggars' surprised Mozart by playing it to him on his own name day two weeks later. During these months he took part in concerts in various noblemen's houses. In December he played at court in a private, informal competition with Clementi; they improvised, separately and together, and played sonatas. In a letter to his father Mozart called Clementi a 'mere technician'; Clementi later spoke of him more generously. Although Mozart was evidently regarded as the winner, his hopes for a court appointment were no nearer to fulfilment.

During the autumn and winter of 1781–2 the relationship between Mozart and Constanze Weber grew deeper. Mozart did not refer to her in his numerous letters home between his urgent denials of 25 July and his firm statement on 15 December of his love for her. On that date he wrote to Leopold of his virtuous life as regards relationships with women, his need for a domestic existence (which he said would represent an economy) and his conviction that Constanze was a para-gon despite the unpleasantness of her family. Events gave Mozart little choice: doubtless through his future mother-in-law's scheming, he was placed in a position where, because of his alleged intimacy with Constanze, he was required to agree to marry her or to compensate her. The letters containing Leopold's reactions were later destroyed by Constanze.

Mozart's main energies during the early part of 1782 were concentrated on the completion of *Die Entführung aus dem Serail*. He may have given his first Viennese concert (or 'academy') in March; he certainly took part in one in the Augarten in May. During this time he played regularly in Sunday concerts at the home of Baron Gottfried van Swieten. Act 1 of *Die Entführung* had been finished the previous August, when Mozart

9. Constanze Mozart, née Weber: portrait (probably 1782)
by Joseph Lange

had hoped for a production in the autumn; the remainder was written by May, and rehearsals began at the beginning of June. The première, on 16 July, was evidently a success – Mozart's letter home describing it does not survive, but he referred to the 'good reception' after the second performance three days later. According to Niemetschek's biography of Mozart (1798), the emperor remarked that the opera had 'very many notes', to which Mozart replied 'Exactly the necessary number, your majesty'. Gluck, the doyen of composers in Vienna, with whom Mozart had lately become friendly, requested an extra performance. The opera remained in the repertory for several years and was soon given in various German cities. Other works of these months include, besides the accompanied sonatas for publication, the Haffner Symphony (written as a serenade for the ennoblement of Sigismund Haffner in Salzburg), a further wind serenade, a group of piano concertos intended for publication, and the first of a set of string quartets.

A few days after the première of *Die Entführung* the difficult situation in the Weber family came to a head and Mozart decided to go forward with marriage arrangements. He wrote to his father on 31 July 1782 asking his consent (also expressing pain at Leopold's cool reaction to the opera's success); on 2 August the couple took communion together, on 3 August the contract was signed, on 4 August they were married at St Stephen's Cathedral. On 5 August Leopold's grudging consent arrived. Constanze was 20, Mozart 26. Their marriage seems to have been very happy. Constanze was loyal and affectionate, if sometimes a shade thoughtless. Mozart occasionally reproached her, for not writing to him, or for frivolous behaviour; she may not have shared his long-practised disdainful attitudes. According to Mozart's description of her to Leopold, she had no wit, but plenty of common sense and the kindest heart in the world. None of Constanze's letters to Mozart survives; her few to his relatives testify to her poor literacy and her almost embarrassing eagerness to please. His to her testify to a relationship of warmth and intimacy, and often sound a note of almost paternal solicitude for her health and well-being. There is little reason to imagine that she was solely, or even primarily, to blame for their chronic money troubles, which began only weeks after their marriage when they had to borrow from the friend, Baroness Waldstätten, who had provided their bridal supper. It has often been suggested that Constanze was extravagant, and indeed Mozart felt bound to deny it, to Leopold, even before their marriage. The truth probably lies somewhere near Nannerl's statement, in 1792, that Mozart was incapable of managing his own financial affairs and that Constanze was unable to help him. In this context it is interesting to note that Leopold, in a letter to Baroness Waldstätten shortly after the wedding, set down his own thoughts on his son: the familiar complaint that Wolfgang was apt to procrastinate is enlarged upon, and his tendency to be easygoing or indolent on the one hand is contrasted with his impatience and impetuousness on the other.

Mozart was anxious to take his wife to Salzburg, to meet his father and sister. To Leopold's irritation, the visit was several times postponed: because of the weather, because of Mozart's pupils, because of his concert commitments (including an important academy of his own before the emperor on 23 March), and because Constanze was pregnant. Their first child, Raimund Leopold, was born on 17 June 1783, while

Mozart was working on his D minor String Quartet.
Then again he delayed, ostensibly because he was afraid
that in Salzburg he could be arrested by the archbishop.
He and Constanze set out in July (leaving behind their
child, who died on 19 August) and spent about three
months in Salzburg. Clearly Mozart had had anxieties
about the success of the visit, and particularly about his
father's reactions to Constanze; and one may infer from
the later correspondence that these months were not
wholly happy. Mozart's two violin–viola duets probably
date from this period, allegedly written for Michael
Haydn, behindhand with a commission; and the Kyrie
and Gloria of the mass he had resolved to write in
thanks for his marriage had their first hearing, possibly
with Constanze singing, at St Peter's Abbey on 26
October (the work, K427/417*a*, was never completed).
He also conferred with Varesco about a libretto for a
new comic opera. On the return journey he paused at
Linz, where he composed a symphony – no.36 in C
K425 – 'at breakneck speed' for a concert, as he did not
have one with him. Probably the Piano Sonata K333/315*c*
dates from this time.

Back in Vienna, Mozart resumed his teaching, which
provided his basic income, and entered on what were the
busiest, the most successful and probably the happiest
months of his life (despite an illness, possibly a kidney
infection, in August). In a letter home he listed his
engagements over five weeks, covering the Lenten concert season, including 19 concerts during the month of
March, mostly at the houses of Count Johann Esterházy
and the Russian ambassador, Prince Golitsïn, but
including concerts of his own, both private and at the
theatre. In February he had started keeping a list of his
new works, *Verzeichnüss aller meiner Werke* (see fig.

10. The first page of Mozart's 'Verzeichnüss aller meiner
Werke', begun in February 1784

10), recording the incipit and the date of each; many of
the entries however were made well after the actual time
of composition, and several dates must be wrong. The
first works noted are the great piano concertos from
K449 onwards, most of them composed for the concerts
in which he was engaged; other early entries are for the
Quintet for piano and wind, which Mozart counted 'the
best work I have composed', and the Sonata for piano
and violin K454, written for the violinist Regina
Strinasacchi – this is the work he is said to have
performed from a blank or fragmentary copy, and it is
clear from the autograph that the violin part was written
first and the piano one added later. This sonata, with
two others for solo piano (K284, 333), was published by
Torricella, and three (K330–32) were issued by
Artaria; other publishers made available in manuscript
the group of piano concertos written in 1782–3, K413–
5/387a, 385p, 387b, which Artaria printed in 1785,
and a wind-band arrangement (not by Mozart) of *Die
Entführung*. A wind serenade of Mozart's was given at a
concert by Anton Stadler, the clarinettist; this may have
been the Serenade for 13 instruments K361/370a,
probably begun in Munich in 1781 and completed in
Mozart's early months in Vienna. In the first days of
1785 Mozart completed the last two of the six quartets
published by Artaria later in the year with a dedication to
Haydn. His second child, Carl Thomas Mozart, was born
in September 1784.

12. 1782-4: Vocal works

Mozart's 1780 correspondence with Leopold about *Idomeneo* gives a picture of the mechanics of planning an opera for the stage. That about *Die Entführung aus dem Serail* is revealing in other ways. Mozart's letter of 26 September 1781 refers not only to some restructuring of the libretto (to expand Osmin's part, and to move an ensemble to a more effective position) but also to specific expressive devices: the key relationships, which he said needed some degree of remoteness to express Osmin's immoderate rage, and the orchestration, where the violins in octaves expressed Belmonte's throbbing heart, and muted violins with flute the 'whispering and sighing'. He further referred to the 'sacrifice' of one of the arias for Constanze (that his fiancée and his heroine shared a name was coincidental), 'Ach ich liebte', to the singer's 'flexible throat', and mentioned that he had included the lively janissary chorus and the drinking-duet to please the Viennese taste. In another letter, evidently responding to Leopold's criticism of the literary quality of J. G. Stephanie's libretto, he pointed out that it 'could hardly be better written for music', adding: 'in an opera the poetry must be altogether the obedient daughter of the music ... when music reigns supreme and one listens to it, all else is forgotten'.

Music indeed reigns supreme in *Die Entführung*; in fact the force and the scale of the music, and certain aspects of its structure (like the integration of the overture and the opening aria), carry the work beyond the accepted limits of the Viennese Singspiel tradition to which it belongs. The colourful 'Turkish' music (exotically scored, with piccolo and an enlarged percussion section) and the comic scenes with the Pasha's grotesque steward, Osmin, belong squarely in that tradition, as do the vaudeville finale and the songs for the servant Pedrillo – one is a 'Moorish' ballad with pizzicato accompaniment, the other the parody 'Frisch zum Kampfe', where the grandiose, military D major setting with trumpets and drums is contradicted by music to represent his quaking with fear. On a different plane are, above all, the deeply felt arias for Constanze in Act 2: first a chromatic lament, using material from *Zaide*, given a particularly pessimistic slant by its ending in the home key, G minor, with material earlier heard in B♭ major; and the expansive 'Martern aller Arten', 293 bars long with an undramatically lengthy opening ritornello of 60 bars, with four obbligato instruments, where although there may seem to be further concessions to Cavalieri's throat the bravura is not without dramatic function. Other noteworthy features are Belmonte's ardent arias and the quartet finale to the second act, resembling the chain finales of *opera buffa* but, unlike them, not propelling the action. It is characteristic of the Singspiel that the crucial elopement scene is not set to music but conducted in spoken dialogue.

The German opera company for which *Die Entführung* was composed lasted only briefly. Mozart, though an enthusiast for opera in German, now sought Italian librettos. He started work on two comic operas during 1783, one, *L'oca del Cairo*, with Varesco, and the other, *Lo sposo deluso*, with Lorenzo da Ponte; but he soon abandoned them, doubtless because he came to realize how feeble were the librettos. He composed a number of separate arias during this period, including a group for insertion in Anfossi's *Il curioso indiscreto* for singers (among them Aloysia Lange) unsuited by the existing ones. Also for his sister-in-law was *Mia speranza adorata* K416, in the increasingly popular rondò form, with a slow section followed by a fast one (sometimes twice over, *ABAB*), which Mozart later often employed in his operas. From 1783 or rather later come a group of vocal chamber pieces, notturnos for two sopranos and bass with clarinets or basset-horns, lighthearted yet with an operatic vein of expression, apt to their Metastasio texts: these were written for a circle of friends connected with Gottfried von Jacquin, whom Mozart apparently permitted to pass the pieces off as his own.

Mozart had little call to compose sacred music during this period. A beautiful and richly scored Kyrie K341/368a, in D minor – in contradistinction to the C major of most of the Salzburg church music – is usually dated from just after *Idomeneo* (though a much later date has been suggested); the next sacred work is the C minor Mass K427/417a, partly written by January 1783, and left incomplete. Written not to commission but in fulfilment of a vow, it was to have been a large-scale 'cantata mass', unlike any other of Mozart's, and is reckoned to have been designed for Constanze to sing. The special stylistic features of the C minor Mass require that it be viewed in the wider context of Mozart's activities and compositions of the period. In 1782 he had come into contact with Baron Gottfried van Swieten, at whose house he regularly played. Van Swieten, while ambassador in Berlin, had developed a taste for late Baroque music, then little heard in Vienna except in antiquarian musical circles. Mozart's interest was caught, and he asked his father to send fugues by the Bachs (C. P. E., W. F. and J. S.) and Handel. Various of his works of these months reflect his response to the challenge of a new technique. He copied several Bach fugues and attached new preludes to some of them, in a solemn but personal vein, showing no awareness of stylistic incongruity; about the same time he wrote a suite, sometimes unauthentically called 'in the style of Handel', and several fugues for keyboard. Almost all these pieces were left unfinished. Some were composed for Constanze, who (he told Leopold) liked fugues. His persistent failure to complete them suggests not only that Mozart lost interest once he had met the form's basic challenges but also that he regarded fugue as essentially irrelevant to his real manner of musical expression. Some scholars (notably Einstein, 1945) have ascribed a deep significance to Mozart's encounter with Bach and with fugue in particular; but although some absorption of contrapuntal techniques cannot be excluded, their influence on Mozart's central musical development is easily overrated.

The contrapuntal treatment in certain instrumental works of this period, for example the String Quartet in G K387, can be traced to other influences; and the fugues in the C minor Mass do not significantly depart from the traditional Austrian ecclesiastical model. The work is however marked by a certain archaic flavour, new in Mozart's music, that seems likely to derive from his experiences at van Swieten's. It is noticeable not only in the statuesque, grave choruses (some in eight parts, or five, as well as the customary four), among which the massive and relentless 'Qui tollis' on an ostinato bass of the Baroque descending tetrachord pattern is the most powerful, but also in several of the solo items, like the

'Domine Deus' duet or the 'Quoniam' trio, which have some almost Handelian counterpoint, figuration and bare continuo texture. Others of the solos are in the usual Austrian church style, with expressive melody and florid decoration, like the 'Laudamus te' and particularly the 'Et incarnatus', with wind obbligatos. The work has often been criticized for inconsistency of style. The Kyrie and Gloria were completed, and for the Sanctus and Benedictus Mozart's intentions for completion are easily deduced; but only part of the Credo was written, and none of the Agnus Dei. Einstein called the work a noble torso. In 1785 Mozart re-used the complete numbers, to a libretto specially provided (perhaps by Da Ponte), along with two new arias, to form a cantata *Davidde penitente* K469 for performance at the Vienna Tonkünstler-Sozietät.

13. 1781-4: Chamber and instrumental music

Mozart's first Viennese publication was a set of six piano and violin sonatas. It included K296, composed at Mannheim but not published in the earlier set; K378/317d, written either in Salzburg or early in 1781 before his arrival in Vienna; and K379/373a, composed just after his arrival for Colloredo's entertainments. These sonatas are broader in conception than the earlier ones. The first-movement development sections normally begin with fresh material; an exception is the particularly brilliant K377/374e in F where the first subject is thoroughly worked out and the development section elided with the recapitulation. That sonata ends with an extended minuet-rondo, in the *amoroso* style of J. C. Bach, following a variation movement. K379 in G ends with variations, and begins with a short but intense Adagio leading directly into a G minor Allegro of exceptional vigour; perhaps the unorthodox form and the temper of the music reflect Mozart's way of asserting himself at the archbishop's soirée. K376/374d, again in F, almost reverts to the playful mood of the Serrarius sonata K296, apart from its Andante, characterized by veiled accompanying textures as well as its unusual form. The final sonata, K380/374f in E♭, is the grandest in manner with its rhetorical contrasts between full chords and rapid passage-work and its strong sense of harmonic direction. A reviewer of the publication in Cramer's *Magazin der Musik* (4 April 1783) commented not only on the richness of the ideas and the signs of Mozart's genius but particularly on the ingenuity with which the violin accompaniment is combined with the keyboard so that the instruments 'are always kept in equal prominence'. They remain piano sonatas with accompaniment, and contain entire pages where the violin 'part could be omitted without damaging the music's continuity; but increasingly the violin part, instead of merely filling in harmonically, supporting, or adding interest to the texture, carries essential material, melodic or even contrapuntal, or engages in dialogue. Mozart's sonatas, both the 1778 set and these, have conspicuously more textural variety and fullness than most others of the time.

Mozart began work on a small further group of accompanied sonatas for Constanze, probably late in 1782; but they suffered the fate of most of the music intended for her and were left unfinished. They are miniature in scale and slender in content; one was evidently to have included a fugue. There exist completions by Maximilian Stadler. The K454 sonata for Strinasacchi is however in the mainstream of Mozart's development. The violin part, understandably, has even greater prominence, and the work is virtually a duo with the instruments on equal terms. It is interesting to note that again the first movement development begins with new material (more precisely, a figure from the exposition's cadence chords); the succeeding sonata, K481, of 1785, notable particularly for the far-reaching enharmonic modulations of its Adagio, has parallel treatment at the corresponding point. K454 is however of unprecedented richness in the variety of its melodic material, its phrase structure and its harmonic pace as well as its texture.

But the central chamber works of this period are the six string quartets dedicated to Haydn. Mozart's personal acquaintance with Haydn probably dated from 1781. Where or how they met, and the degree of intimacy of their friendship, is uncertain, but it is known that they were at quartet parties together more than once. The English composer Stephen Storace gave such a party in 1784, reported in Michael Kelly's *Reminiscences* (1826), where the players were Haydn, Dittersdorf, Mozart and Vanhal. Another took place on Leopold's visit to his son in 1785, when Haydn said to him: 'Before God, and as an honest man, I tell you that your son is the greatest composer known to me in person or by name. He has taste, and, what is more, the greatest knowledge of composition'. Mozart chose to dedicate his first mature quartets not to a noble patron for the favour of gifts in return, but to the acknowledged master of the string quartet. In his warm, florid Italian dedication, he referred to Haydn as his 'most dear friend' and to the elder composer's expressed satisfaction with the works (see fig. 11).

Mozart also referred to his quartets as 'the fruits of long and laborious endeavour', a claim that is borne out by the state of the autographs and the existence of numerous rejected sketches. That he sought to emulate Haydn's op.33, published in 1781, can scarcely be doubted. Like Haydn's, these works are characterized by textures conceived not merely in four-part harmony but as four-part discourse, with the actual musical ideas ineluctably linked to a freshly integrated treatment of the medium. The debt to Haydn lies rather in this general approach to quartet style than in the specific resemblances that have been pointed out (like the kinship of the minuets of the E♭ quartets, op.33 no.2

11. Title-page of the six string quartets, κ387, 421/417b, 428/421b, 458, 464 and 465 (Vienna: Artaria, 1785)

and K428/421*b*), though such resemblances are sufficiently marked to leave no doubt about Mozart's knowledge of the Haydn works or his interest, conscious or no, in vying with them.

The Mozart works form a collection more heterogeneous than any set of Haydn's. They do however have several features in common, some of them new to Mozart's music. One is the use of counterpoint for intensification: in for example the first movements of the D minor, K421/417*b*, the most sombre and dramatic work in the set, and of K464 in A, where each of the principal themes is soon subjected to imitative treatment. The Andante of K428 follows a similar procedure, supported by an increasing level of chromaticism; the upward-resolving appoggiaturas have prompted comparisons with *Tristan und Isolde*. This quartet as a whole is remarkable for its chromatic writing; also notable is the multiplicity of motif in its first movement. The most famous use of dissonance is, of course, in the C major K465 whose slow introduction (Mozart's only one in a string quartet) became an analytical *cause célèbre* (see Vertrees, 1974). K458 (the 'Hunt', after its 6/8 opening), the most relaxed of the six, inaugurates the second half of the set, which Leopold understandably regarded as lighter in style than the first, and is the only one with a development section quoting no exposition material; but its coda, with contrapuntal discussion of the opening theme, draws the movement together. Its Adagio, also lacking development, has some textural detail of exceptional richness. The minuet (placed before rather than after the slow movement), notable for the unorthodox phrase structure of its eight-bar opening strain, is much briefer than the others, several of which are in effect miniature sonata-form designs; their trios are often in the minor mode, with invention of a more sophisticated cast. Two quartets have variation movements, K421 (finale, on a theme akin to that of the variation finale of Haydn's op.33 no.5 but also to a variation in the K377 sonata) and K464 (slow movement). Each follows to some degree the 'quatuor concertant' scheme whereby the instruments take turns at carrying the main interest, but this potentially banal notion is transfigured by Mozart's textural inventiveness into a pattern of increasing complexity and, again, intensification. Two of the finales are of particular interest. That of K464 is virtually a monothematic movement, built from the pair of tags heard in the first four bars. That of K387 begins with a fugal exposition, and incorporates another (on a theme contrapuntally compatible with the first) in its second subject; it is not however a fugal movement like those in Haydn's op.20 or Mozart's K173, but a sonata-type form (a rounded binary, for it lacks a first-group recapitulation) with fugal material. To cite this as a sign of Bachian influence is to disregard the fact that a steady stream of sonata-type movements with fugal sections had been composed during Mozart's time, including many by composers whose work he knew, like Michael Haydn, F. X. Richter and Wagenseil.

Other chamber works of this period include two duets for violin and viola, written with an ingenuity that goes some way towards concealing the textural thinness of the medium, and various arrangements of Bach fugues, with and without preludes (the exact number is in doubt); there is also the ingeniously composed horn quintet, set with two violas so that the solo instrument is not too readily covered, and the happy oboe quartet written in Munich at the time of *Idomeneo*. More impor-

tant than these is the Quintet for piano and wind K452, a
difficult medium because of the limited capacities of the
wind instruments (oboe, clarinet, bassoon, horn) to
blend or to sustain a prolonged line, and the risk of their
sound beginning to cloy. Mozart designed his melodic
material accordingly, casting it in short phrases which
create and resolve tensions at a rapid rate. The result is a
work of exceptional mastery and inventiveness,
melodically, rhythmically and in its use of instrumental
sonority.

Wind music proper falls into a separate category,
being designed rather for open-air band performance
than as chamber music. Mozart's three substantial wind
serenades date from around this time; they are his last
works for wind ensemble, apart from some small
masonic pieces and the lightweight divertimentos
K Anh.229/439b, which are contemporary with the
similarly scored Jacquin notturnos (and which survive
in some state of disorder; see Flothuis, 1973–4). The
earliest of them is probably K375, originally for pairs of
clarinets, bassoons and horns but more familiar in its
later form, with additional oboes making up the standard 'Harmonie' ensemble. It opens with the martial
rhythm Mozart often used in works in E♭, and is on the
expansive, leisurely scale apt to serenade music; there
are five movements, with two minuets. Its companion
piece K388/384a, Mozart's first true C minor work, is
presumably the 'Nacht musique' that, according to a
letter, he was required to write in great haste. The fact
that Mozart later arranged it for string quintet
(K406/516b) is in itself a commentary on its character.
A work of driving energy and consistent intensity, with
its chromatic writing, its strikingly unorthodox phrase
structure, its pulsating inner parts and its vigorous sfor-

zandos, it lifts the wind serenade medium to a level perhaps out of accord with its social purpose; the learned canons of the minuet and especially its trio (4 in 2, *al rovescio*), indebted more to Haydn (cf Symphonies 44, 47) than to the Baroque, demand a more attentive listener than do the serenades of Mozart's youth, as indeed do the instrumental ingenuities of the concluding variations. For enterprise in the handling of instrumental colour, however, the Serenade for 13 instruments, or 'Gran Partita', K361/370a, stands supreme: this is a seven-movement work, for the eight-part Harmonie ensemble supplemented by two basset-horns, two horns and double bass. By using thematic material of a dialogue character, or involving contrasts between the tutti and smaller groups, Mozart allowed the maximum scope for varied instrumental combinations; and the inclusion of a variation movement, and of two trios to each of the minuets, provided yet more opportunities for kaleidoscopic writing. The expressive variety and instrumental range of these works stand without parallel in wind music.

Despite Mozart's activities as pianist and piano teacher, this period produced little solo piano music. Except in so far as they provide a commentary on his preoccupations at the time, the abortive fugues, the prelude and fugue K394/383a and the pseudo-Baroque dance suite K399/385i are unimportant. The fantasias of the same period (these works are all, plausibly, supposed to belong to 1782), which include the one in D minor K397/385g, argue that his interest in the Bach family extended to Carl Philipp Emanuel, whom he is reputed to have admired but whose influence on him is otherwise small; Mozart's sympathy for the north German style must have been limited. The fantasias were all left unfinished. To some extent they may represent written-out versions of his concert improvisations. So too do the variations, of which one important set (K455) and one whose entire authenticity has been much argued (K460/454a) belong to this period. K455 typifies, as much as any single work can, Mozart's variation technique: it comprises a series of variations of progressive brilliance interspersed with others of textural ingenuity, including one in the tonic minor, has an Adagio as the penultimate variation and finally an extended one in a changed metre. The only sonata of these years is K457 in C minor, which was published in 1785 along with the Fantasia K475; the pairing implies that continuous performance was intended, with the formal orderliness of the sonata resolving the tensions of the impassioned and irregular fantasy, notable for its remote modulations and its unpredictable structure and textures. The sonata is itself the most forceful – it has been called Beethovenian, and certainly it influenced Beethoven – that Mozart composed, taut in form and characterized by the driving, triadic themes of its fast movements, which enfold an Adagio notable for the increasingly elaborate embellishments of the main theme.

Finally mention should be made of Mozart's two strongly contrasted two-piano works, the brilliant, good-humoured Sonata in D K448/375a and the Fugue in C minor K426. The latter, based on a theme of Baroque ancestry, is elaborately worked, using inversions and many varieties of stretto, and derives a certain harshness from the prevalence of chromatic appoggiaturas. Neither the counterpoint nor the treatment, with a homophonic final climax, could be called Bachian. In 1788 Mozart arranged the fugue for strings, prefixing it with an Adagio (K546). These are Mozart's only two-piano works, apart from some fragments and the incomplete Larghetto and Allegro in E♭ (K*deest*; see Croll, 1964).

14. 1781-4: Orchestral music

Mozart's Viennese piano concertos may well be reckoned his greatest achievement in instrumental music. They represent a corpus of music of exceptional quality and originality, far beyond the concertos of his predecessors or his contemporaries in their scale, their thematic richness and their subtle, highly developed relationship between soloist and orchestra.

The origins of the structural patterns of Mozart's piano concerto opening movements lie in the ritornello form of the aria or concerto first movement of the late Baroque, expanded in the light of the sonata principle. Closely analogous structures may be found in the arias of his early operas. This was a form that varied considerably according to the character of the material, except in its basic scheme of tonalities, which essentially conformed to the sonata pattern used in virtually all Mozart's and his contemporaries' music. The commonest schemes in his concerto first movements of this period usually follow some such lines as these: an opening ritornello in the tonic, comprising a primary theme and (after a tutti) a secondary one, with a cadential group; then, in effect, a sonata-form exposition for soloist and orchestra, beginning with the former primary theme (sometimes with prefatory solo material), including the former secondary theme and often a new solo one, both in the dominant, and cadential material; a central ritornello; a widely modulating development or 'free fantasia', with sequential writing and solo bravura and little thematic working; a recapitulation, including material from both the opening ritornello and the exposition, now in the tonic; and a cadenza and closing ritornello. Mozart's thematic fertility and his particular method of devising flexible links, between themes, bravura passages and ritornello material, ensured a high level of interest within each concerto as well as great variety within the series as a whole.

Mozart wrote three piano concertos in 1782–3 and six in 1784; a further eight were to follow. He described the 1782–3 set to his father (28 December 1782):

These concertos are a happy medium between what is too easy and too difficult; they are very brilliant, pleasing to the ear, and natural, without being vapid. There are passages here and there from which connoisseurs alone can derive satisfaction; but these passages are written in such a way that the less learned cannot fail to be pleased, though without knowing why.

K413/387*a* is the slightest and most conservative of these three: its finale reverts to the minuet-rondo type favoured by J. C. Bach and used by Mozart as far back as 1774. K415/387*b* is in the pompous, formal manner of many of Mozart's C major symphonies, with brisk, military rhythms and brilliant passage-work; Mozart's sketches show that he planned a C minor Adagio, then settled for a graceful Andante in F (he used the C minor material for a pair of slow episodes in the 6/8 finale). The most distinctive of these three works is K414/385*p*, with its exceptionally delicate orchestral layout, its easy succession of melodies, and its unassuming bravura writing. The main theme of the Andante quotes, not necessarily intentionally, an overture by J. C. Bach (to *La calamità dei cuori*, 1763, published 1770); the music's elegiac character has led to its being interpreted as an act of homage to J. C. Bach, who had lately died. Mozart wrote two finales, the Rondo K386 being presumably a rejected first attempt; that both are 2/4 Allegrettos, light and gentle in character, suggests that he had a clear view of the kind of movement he wanted to write before finding the right material.

These concertos, Mozart said, were written for performance with an orchestra including oboes and horns – in fact K413 additionally calls for bassoons, 415 for bassoons, trumpets and drums – or even 'a quattro', presumably meaning just four string instruments, which made them apt for domestic use. The next, K449 in E♭, composed for Mozart's pupil Barbara Ployer, can also be played with strings alone. Although it thus lacks the variety of colour that marks the greatest of the series, it may be counted as the first of the mature concertos. Its opening movement, like that of K414, abounds in melodic ideas, but here they are more diverse in character, and the form is enlarged so as to comprehend a wider range of material. There is an unusually taut development section, built on a phrase from the cadential group. This movement has something close to the textbook 'double exposition', otherwise unknown in the mature works, by virtue of its modulation to the dominant in the opening ritornello. The finale is Mozart's most brilliant, elaborate and ingenious to date. Outwardly a sonata-rondo, of a specially complex kind, it incorporates procedures closely akin to those of monothematic movements, sonata or ritornello, and at the same time its opening theme is subjected to constant melodic variation – to the extent that a coda turning to 6/8 metre, a procedure normal in variation movements, seems a natural outcome. Its contrapuntal inclinations have also been much remarked.

Mozart composed the next two works, K450 in B♭ and 451 in D, to play at concerts. 'They are both concertos to make you sweat', he wrote to Leopold (26 May 1784). K450 represents a distinct advance in its newly elaborate writing for wind instruments and in its re-conciliation of a more selfconscious virtuoso style with, again, a wide range of thematic material; in K451, in the tradition of brilliant D major music (the orchestra in-cludes trumpets and drums), the style is again virtuoso, and there is a new, spacious symphonic character, but the music is more homogeneous and lacks the thematic variety and interest of the other concertos of this period. The next two were composed for Barbara Ployer (K453 in G) and the blind virtuoso pianist Maria Theresia von Paradis (K456 in B♭), though Mozart undoubtedly played them himself; both, particularly K453, are techni-cally less demanding than the two preceding. The use of wind instruments is even more elaborate; much of the principal thematic material is entrusted to them, and this strikingly affects the nature and phrase structure of that material, especially in the dialogue themes of the first movement of K456. The two opening movements follow virtually identical groundplans, and share too a new method of weaving piano bravura writing into interest-ing, often motivically constructed orchestral textures, so that it becomes less of an end in itself, more of a con-tinuation of the musical development. The Andante of K453 is characterized by its distant, often dramatic modulations and its rich woodwind writing; the finale is a set of variations (mainly double ones), on a theme close to one Mozart noted in his commonplace book as sung by his pet starling. The K456 slow movement, in G minor, is (like that of K450) a set of variations, whose expressive force is barely lessened by their being some-what schematic for a work otherwise so fluid; possibly they also seem foursquare, but the strains are in fact of eight and 13 bars. The finale (again like that of K450) is of the 'hunting' type. With K459 in F, the last of the 1784 concertos, the finale (560 bars long) bears more weight; it is in a variety of sonata-rondo form, enriched by fugato episodes and much semi-contrapuntal use of orchestral material against piano bravura. This follows a pastoral Andantino and a martial first movement, thematically less varied than its predecessors but no less tautly developed, exploiting the march-like rhythm that Mozart had also used to begin K451, 453 and 456.

Mozart's only other concerto of the early 1780s is K417, for horn. Of the next for horn, K447, the Romance probably dates from 1784 but the outer movements are seemingly later (1786–7). These works, and K495 of 1786, are altogether smaller in scale than the piano concertos, and do not have a comparable subtlety, though basically they follow the same formal outlines. Composed for Joseph Leutgeb, an old Salzburg friend who was now a Viennese cheesemonger, they exhibit, not least in their multi-coloured autograph annotations, Mozart's humour. They also, characteristically, show Mozart turning the natural horn's limitations to profitable ends, even to the point where the different timbre of stopped notes may be musically advantageous. Each concerto possesses, predictably, a spirited 'hunting' finale. K417 and 495 have much in common; K447 is the most adventurous, with unusual scoring – clarinets and bassoons replace the oboes and horns – and a slow movement in A♭ rather than B♭, meaning that the available natural notes fall differently in the scale and so give rise to a new range of melodic possibilities. K412/386*b*, long dated 1782, has been established (by Tyson) as from 1791; it comprises a compact, neatly turned first movement and a 'hunting' rondo, incomplete in the autograph (the sole true source: the score sometimes dated 1787 is probably a 1792 completion).

Mozart had no regular call to compose symphonies in these years as he did concertos. Between 1781 and 1788 his few symphonies were written as occasional pieces; no.35 was originally a serenade, composed for the Haffner family in Salzburg at the time of the *Entführung* première, and written in the brilliant and effective serenade key, D major, which Leopold (according to Mozart's letter of 27 July 1782) favoured. It originally had five movements, with two minuets. The autograph makes clear that the flutes and clarinets in the outer movements were added later. The music is essentially in the serenade manner, with dashing outer movements, a warm-toned Andante and a formal, foursquare minuet; but the substance of the first is strengthened by the way its main motif is woven into the texture, and the finale is a brilliant *moto perpetuo*, recalling that of the Paris Symphony. That a serenade could take its place as a symphony is in itself a commentary on the course Mozart's music was taking. Symphony no.36, hastily composed at Linz, does not pursue that course much further: in spite of its slow introduction, a new feature for a Mozart symphony, it is primarily an extrovert work, clear and spacious in its form, with sturdy, emphatic tuttis. Viennese influence, specifically Haydn's, has been noted in the use of an introduction, the siciliana-style slow movement (though the F minor episode in its development was surely suggested by one in the Michael Haydn symphony to which Mozart at the same time composed an introduction) and the ländler-type trio; the wit in the finale, with its successive instrumental sallies, seems wholly personal.

15. Vienna and Prague, 1785-8

On 11 December 1784 Mozart had become a freemason at the lodge 'Zur Wohlthätigkeit'. The master there was Baron von Gemmingen, whom he had met in 1778 and whose *Semiramis* he had planned to set; the master at another lodge Mozart attended, 'Zur wahren Eintracht', of which Haydn was briefly a member in 1785, was the well-known scientist Ignaz von Born. Mozart's lodge was later amalgamated into 'Zur gekrönten Hoffnung'. He wrote some music for masonic ceremonial and for other use at lodge meetings. The society was essentially one of liberal intellectuals, concerned less with political ideals than with the philosophical ones of the Enlightenment, including Nature, Reason and the brotherhood of Man. Although there was tension between Austrian freemasonry and the Catholic church, the organization was in no sense anti-religious; membership was perfectly compatible with Mozart's faith, and there is no reason to think that he abandoned his religion even if his formal observances became less regular.

Mozart's surviving correspondence for 1785, and indeed the ensuing years, is sparse. A few letters from Leopold, visiting his son in Vienna for ten weeks early in the year, to Nannerl (now Frau Berchtold zu Sonnenburg) give a graphic account of Mozart's activities: they comment on his lavish apartment, the bustle of his daily life and the character of his latest music. Leopold attended several of his concerts; during the Lenten season Mozart gave six at the Mehlgrube and one at the

Burgtheater, and took part in various others. He also gave three later in the year, during Advent. This period represents the peak of his reputation as composer and pianist. *Die Entführung* was carrying his name to many German cities. His teaching activities continued: one of his pupils was the English composer Thomas Attwood, whose surviving exercises illuminate Mozart's careful, systematic teaching methods, and perhaps carry hints as to how Mozart himself had been taught (see Heartz, 1973–4). A good deal of his music was published, in print or in manuscript copies. At the end of the year the *Wiener Zeitung*, in a concert review, referred to Mozart's 'merited fame' and said that he was 'universally valued'. In spite of all this he was in financial straits; a plea for a loan, probably not the first, went to his friend the composer and publisher F. A. Hoffmeister in November. Compositions of 1785 include three piano concertos, a replacement Andante for a violin concerto, a piano quartet, several songs and various masonic works – a cantata, a funeral piece, songs and choruses, and (for brother masons but probably not for ritual use) some movements for clarinets and basset-horns. There were also arias for use in other composers' operas.

Opera remained central to Mozart's ambitions. His short Singspiel *Der Schauspieldirektor* K486 was completed early in 1786 for performance in the Orangery in Schönbrunn Palace, along with a work by the court composer Salieri; both were commissioned for a visit by the Governor-General of the Austrian Netherlands. In March a private performance of the revised version of *Idomeneo* (see chapter 10) was given. But his main project was the collaboration with Da Ponte on *Le nozze di Figaro*. The topic was no doubt carefully chosen. Beaumarchais' play had been given in Paris in

April 1784, and a German version had been printed in Vienna when, at the beginning of 1785, performances by Schikaneder's theatre company had been banned; further, the play was a sequel to *Le barbier de Séville*, of which Paisiello's operatic version had been a great success. Although both Da Ponte and Michael Kelly, the Irish tenor who first sang the roles of Basilio and Curzio, left garrulous memoirs, neither was specially informative about the opera's genesis. Letters from Leopold to Nannerl make it clear that composition had started by October or November 1785, and that there was a good deal of intrigue (allegedly by Salieri and Righini) against the opera. It finally came to the stage at the Burgtheater on 1 May 1786, and was well received; many items were applauded and encored at the first three performances, inducing the emperor to restrict encores at later ones to the arias. In Vienna the opera was given nine times in 1786, then revived for 26 performances in 1789–90; it was quickly taken up by travelling companies and widely performed in other German cities, usually in German.

The months in which *Figaro* had been composed were otherwise uneventful. The only important works besides the opera had been three piano concertos, one written in December 1785 and two in March 1786, the customary time of year for them because of the traditional Lenten concert season. That this year he gave only a single concert in Lent (there may have been others in Advent) must be a commentary on the fickle taste of the Viennese public. The fee of 450 gulden for *Figaro* – Da Ponte received 200 – did not lessen his financial anxieties. During the summer he was able to sell various recent works to the Prince of Fürstenberg, but his hopes of a retainer fee were not realized. In the

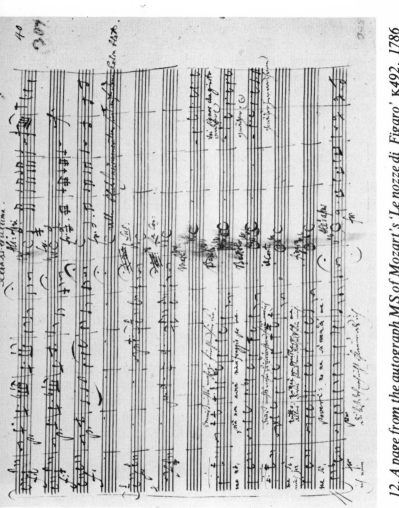

12. A page from the autograph MS of Mozart's 'Le nozze di Figaro' K492, 1786
(Act 2 finale, beginning of the last scene)

autumn he conceived a plan for going to England, accompanying or following his friends Stephen and Nancy Storace, Kelly and Attwood, but that foundered when Leopold advised against it and declined to look after Mozart's children. A third child, Johann Thomas Leopold, was born on 18 October and died on 15 November.

Towards the end of the year, however, Mozart accepted an invitation to Prague, where *Figaro* had been a great success. He spent some four weeks there, from 11 January 1787; it is clear from a letter he wrote to Jacquin that he relished his popularity in the city. He saw one performance of *Figaro* and directed another, and gave a concert including a new symphony (K504) written for the occasion. He also went to a Paisiello opera but chatted through it. The Prague impresario Bondini commissioned him to write an opera for production the following autumn; on his return to Vienna he asked for another libretto from Da Ponte, who though engaged on texts for Salieri and Martín y Soler started work on *Don Giovanni*.

In April 1787 Mozart heard that his father was seriously ill, and wrote a letter of consolation, including a famous passage expressing his view, based on masonic teachings, of death: 'As death . . . is the true goal of our existence, I have formed during the last few years such close relations with this best and truest friend of mankind that his image is no longer terrifying to me but rather very soothing and consoling'. Leopold died at the end of May. Mozart renounced his share of the estate to Nannerl for 1000 gulden; he asked for his manuscripts to be sent to him, but some were given to the Heiligkreuz monastery at Augsburg and others evidently went astray.

Mozart is not known to have made any public appearance in Vienna during some eight months of 1787. In April he moved from his apartment behind the cathedral to what was presumably a more modest one; about that time he was briefly ill. Teaching activities continued: in the spring, he may have given lessons to Beethoven, then on his first, very brief visit to Vienna; he also taught Hummel who, not yet ten, probably lived with the Mozart family.

His compositions since the time of *Figaro* seem to have been planned primarily with a view to publication, which represented a source of ready cash. There were several chamber works, including a piano quartet, three piano trios and a string quartet in 1786 and two string quintets and a piano and violin sonata in 1787; most of them soon went into print, as did several songs. The reason for the composition of the K503 piano concerto is uncertain: it may have been intended for a projected series of Advent concerts, or possibly for performance in Prague. Nor is it known what occasions called forth the *Musikalischer Spass* or the *Kleine Nachtmusik*.

Those two works immediately preceded *Don Giovanni*. Mozart left for Prague on 1 October 1787, with much of the score written. The première had been planned for 14 October, but because of inadequate preparation *Figaro* was given instead and *Don Giovanni* was postponed until 29 October. According to Constanze's later recollection the overture, the last part of the opera to be written, was finished two days before (other sources support the one-day legend). The Prague public received the work warmly; a report stated that Mozart was greeted with threefold cheers. He directed three or four performances before returning to Vienna in mid-November. He spent much time in Prague with

the Dušek (Duschek) family in their villa outside the
city; the difficult aria *Bella mia fiamma* K528 was
composed for Josefa, an old Salzburg friend.

Mozart arrived back in Vienna in mid-November and
was soon offered the post of court *Kammermusicus*, at a
salary of 800 gulden (Gluck, who had just died, had
been paid 2000). He was apparently required to do little
more than write dance music for court balls. Though not
a court Kapellmeister, and not a Kapellmeister at all
except in a very loose sense, he could at least sign
himself as a court musician in the imperial and royal
service. Clearly he welcomed this appointment, both for
the dependable income associated with it and for its
advancement of his standing in Viennese musical life.
He had been hoping for something of the kind for five
years; there is no reason to suppose that he specially
valued independence from patrons. The extra income
scarcely seems to have eased his situation. He moved to
a new apartment, where a daughter (Theresia) was born
on 27 December; she died on 29 June 1788, just after
another move, to a smaller apartment in a suburb. By
then the pitiful sequence of letters to Michael Puchberg,
a merchant, freemason and musician, had begun. Four
were written in June and July, pleading urgently for
loans: one refers to Mozart's hopes of quick repayment
when he received money for a planned concert series
(which probably never took place); another to the poor
response to his solicitation for subscriptions to the
publication of his new string quintets, and to
embarrassing debts to a former landlord; and a third to
dealings with a pawnbroker. In one, requesting a large
long-term loan, he wrote of 'black thoughts' that he could
banish only 'with great effort', mentioning however that
since the recent move he had been able to work more
productively.

The works on which he was engaged were the three last symphonies, completed, according to his catalogue, on 26 June, 25 July and 10 August. The earlier part of 1788 had indeed been relatively unfruitful: there were various dances, a little piano music, songs and arias, a piano concerto (written in February, though no concert in Lent is documented) and three new items for the Viennese première of *Don Giovanni* on 7 May. The opera cannot have been unsuccessful, for it had 14 further performances, but there is evidence that the story of its having a mixed reception, with some of the audience regarding the work as prolonged, contrived and over-elaborate, is not unfounded. Similar criticisms were levelled at *Figaro* and *Die Entführung*. Later in 1788 Mozart composed more dance music, a piano trio, a string trio which he gave to Puchberg, and vocal canons; he also arranged *Acis and Galatea*, the first of several Handel works (to include *Messiah* in March 1789) for concerts under Baron van Swieten's auspices.

16. 1785-8: Chamber and instrumental music

(*i*) *Works without piano*. After the disciplined style of the six 'Haydn' quartets of 1782–5, Mozart's string chamber music of the following years is more relaxed and more expansive, and often more concerned with sensuous beauty of harmony or texture. The only quartet of these years is K499, known as the 'Hoffmeister' after its original publisher. Its first movement, Allegretto rather than the usual Allegro, is characterized by the all-pervading falling phrase of its opening theme, by its varied though less conscientiously egalitarian quartet writing, with the viola in particular colouring the texture, and by its chromaticisms and its remote modulations. The minuet again is coloured by a high viola part, the Adagio by smooth, euphonious writing, with many parallel 3rds and 6ths – these intervals are prominent melodically throughout the quartet. The finale's rapid triplets, chromatically inflected, show high spirits tempered by hints of wryness in a way that was to become increasingly characteristic.

Mozart's two string quintets of spring 1787 represent a peak in his chamber music. He seems to have found the five-part texture easier to handle than four-part. The new possibilities of symmetry clearly attracted him: violin set against cello, with three-part harmony in the middle (K515, opening; K516, introduction to finale); a pair of violins against a pair of violas, above the cello (K515, first movement, bars 94ff); violin against viola with string trio accompaniment (K515, second movement; K516, third movement, bars 30f); and a high trio against a low one (K516, opening). Many other, more elaborate, quickly shifting patterns also appear; and there is a general harmonic and textural richness, without any thickness or heaviness, since the total tessitura is enlarged compared with the quartets. The C major K515 (perceptively discussed by Rosen, 1971, pp.264ff) is Mozart's longest four-movement chamber work, generously proportioned in every particular, with spacious, harmonically slow-moving themes and broad structural spans. The first movement is remarkable for its remote modulations and its complex rhythmic structure, in which the opening five-bar phrases, later tautened by overlapping into orthodox fours, represent one of many subtleties; it is balanced by a finale of 539 bars, more conventional in phrase structure but with a huge sonata-rondo framework embracing a great deal of contrapuntal development. Again it is touched by that ambivalent emotional quality of many of Mozart's overtly high-spirited finales of this period. The Andante is largely an elaborate dialogue for violin and viola, the minuet a highly individual movement using ten-bar phrases and intense chromaticisms (diminished 7ths with clashing appoggiaturas).

The complementary quality implied by the composition alongside a minor-key work of a major-key one in the same genre – Mozart's usual procedure in his maturity – is seen in other aspects of the C major and G minor quintets. The first movement of K516 is faster-moving harmonically and sharper in its melodic contours, with a more directly emotive thematic content in its aspiring phrases and falling chromaticisms, and a more closely imitative style. This emotive manner is maintained in the accented off-beat chords of the minuet, and in the softening of the trio's turn to the major, the more so because it takes the cadential phrase of the minuet as its starting-point. After an Adagio with all the instruments muted, enriched by much real five-part harmony, distant modulation and textures of a rare feathery beauty, a dark slow introduction precedes the finale proper, a G major Allegro in 6/8 which has been criticized as an abnegation of the consistent emotional world of the remainder of the work; again, however, there is a hint of ambiguity. The existence of a discarded G minor opening leaves no doubt that Mozart weighed different possibilities.

Only two other string works belong to this period. One is the C minor Adagio K546, a stern piece influenced by French-overture rhythms, which Mozart prefixed to a string arrangement of the two-piano fugue in C minor K426. The other is the 'divertimento' for string trio, K563 – so titled, no doubt, mainly because of its six-movement plan, with two minuets and a set of variations. Folklike melodies have been noted in the fourth and sixth movements. Though in no sense in the manner of the earlier divertimentos, it has by virtue of its light textures and concertante writing a generally less concentrated style than the quartets or quintets. Mozart's only string trio, it shows great resource in its handling of the limited medium in a lengthy work. The nocturne or *Kleine Nachtmusik*, for string quartet and double bass, shows in its direct, appealing invention the aristocratic ease and mastery that Mozart could now bring to entertainment music; its antithesis is the *Musikalischer Spass*, whose harmonic and rhythmic gaffes serve to parody the work of incompetent composers. Another kind of musical joke, a *quatuor d'airs dialogués*, is the flute quartet K298, with ideas from a song by F. A. Hoffmeister, a French traditional melody, and an aria from Paisiello's *Le gare generose* – this last fixing its date as not before autumn 1786. A dozen miniature duos for horns, a genre usually intended for open-air music-making, date from this period; they make the most of a medium severely circumscribed by the natural horn's limitations.

(ii) Works with piano. The first products of Mozart's new interest in the popular forms of keyboard chamber music from 1785 were two piano quartets, K478 in G minor and K493 in E♭, another of the characteristic major–minor pairs. While the piano trios are still to some extent accompanied sonatas, in the quartets the string ensemble is balanced against and contrasted with the piano, which has a role of a virtuosity akin to that in Mozart's concertos of the time. There is a major-key finale to K478, but its first movement has much of the intense, sombre character associated with G minor. The E♭ quartet is more lyrical and expansive, with extended second-group themes; written during the opening run of *Figaro*, it is a particularly happy work.

If the material of the trios is often more conventional, that is understandable in this extended piano-sonata form. The first and last of the group, K496 and K564, each in G, and each possessing a variation movement, particularly bear the imprint of the accompanied sonata style, though K496 has an Andante with elaborate yet economical four-part counterpoint, not unlike string quartet textures. K502 in B♭, though not stylistically very different, is more original and more concentrated in invention, with the second-group theme derived from the first, and continuously developed in a manner

Mozart may have learnt from Haydn; that a new theme provides an interlude at the beginning of the development is however entirely characteristic, particularly in a movement with a thematically economical exposition. From mid-1788, the period of the last three symphonies, come three piano trios, one in G already referred to, and works in E (K542) and C (K548). This last, like K564, is polished but somewhat routine in its material and its procedures. K542, Mozart's only work in E, is richly poetic in its first movement, where the pellucid textures and graceful, chromatically inflected lines introduce hints of melancholy. Understandably, the trio with the truest three-instrument style is K498, for clarinet, viola and piano, probably composed for music-making with the Jacquin family; its veiled colour, its spare textures and its concentrated use of material place it among the most unified in feeling of Mozart's works. Lastly among these keyboard chamber works, the K526 piano and violin sonata should be mentioned, Mozart's last full-scale work in the medium and the most integrated in its piano and violin writing: the first movement has a new level of elaboration in virtuoso interchange between the violin and the piano right hand, and the very brilliant finale shows an array of textures in which the priority between piano passage-work and lyrical accompaniment (often flowering into melody) varies fascinatingly.

To this period belong a number of important keyboard works, including two substantial duet sonatas, K497 and 521, which carry the form beyond its usual domestic context. K497 proclaims its seriousness with an Adagio introduction and maintains it in its extended scale and the unusual frequency of contrapuntal writing as opposed to the customary dialogues and homophonic accompaniments. Mozart's most persistently contrapuntal piano writing appears in K533, the sonata he put together by adding two movements to the Rondo K494 – which he expanded, supplementing it with a cadenza to give it weight more nearly to balance the new movements. The first is exceptionally spare in texture and economical in material, and contrapuntal thinking pervades all its sections; it also derives a strong sense of direction from its purposeful sequences and its free use of discord. The Andante looks to C. P. E. Bach in its affective appoggiaturas, but the intense chromaticism, remote modulations and release in florid melody are characteristically Mozartian. This remarkable movement also affords an outstanding example of the 'principle of increasing animation' in Mozart's music (Lowinsky, 1956), by which phrase lengths increase at the end of a period, stresses are shifted (often with overlapping phrases) and rhythms quickened; it was by such methods, and his use or subtle avoidance of symmetrical phraseology, that Mozart so successfully controlled the structure not merely of periods but also of sections and entire movements, perhaps even whole works. This control over pace, harmonic and rhythmic, is an important factor in Mozart's 'perfection of form'.

Some smaller piano works of these years typify particular tendencies. The Rondo K485 – a rondo only in title – is based on a melodic tag which Mozart used many times at different periods, and which also appears in J. C. Bach's music (op.11 no.6) in just the form used here; if this piece leans towards the urbane grace and brilliance of J. C. Bach, the A minor Rondo K511 is more akin to C. P. E. with its appoggiatura-laden, introspective tone. Other piano works of the period include a still more chromatic Adagio K540, a remarkably emotional work, characterized by suspensions and diminished 7ths, in a key (B minor) Mozart otherwise scarcely used. This highly personal piece was composed in the difficult spring of 1788. A little later, at the time of the last symphonies, came the popular sonata 'for beginners' K545. Its first movement includes Mozart's only true example – there is a remote parallel in the finale of the K387 quartet – of a recapitulation beginning in the subdominant; it is not, however, merely a transposed version of the exposition, for in order to fix the home key more firmly the transition moves on to the dominant before settling in the tonic. Even in conventionally planned sonata movements Mozart was inclined to adjust the recapitulation transition in order to consolidate the tonic.

17. 1785-8: Orchestral music

(*i*) *Piano concertos.* The piano concertos of 1785, the pair in D minor K466 and C major K467, abandon certain aspects of the plan that had served for those of 1784. Each concerto of that group opened with a well-defined theme that the soloist could take up on (or immediately after) his initial entry. These two begin with material that does not lend itself to solo performance, and a new kind of integration between soloist and orchestra is implicit. So is a different kind of solo entry. K466 has a significant new theme for the soloist, which is apt only for a piano entry after a tutti and is used and developed in just that context in the development section. The movement's basic outline remains unaffected; during the statement of the opening primary material in the exposition proper its restless syncopations are glossed by urgent semiquaver figuration. In K467 the entry has a mild flourish of virtuosity before a trill which serves to accompany the orchestral motto theme, a theme whose symphonic character and contrapuntal potentialities find a clear analogy in the forceful and strongly directed piano bravura. Although its development section barely alludes to material stated earlier, this is Mozart's most densely argued concerto movement and among his broadest in structure. The novelty and increasingly symphonic nature of these first movements is paralleled by the departures in the other movements, less in the K466 Romance (in simple rondo form, with the traditional stormy second episode) than in the

extraordinary Andante of K467, with its reliance on a
new richness of cantilena, harmony and texture, or the
K466 finale, constructed on a scale and with a density of
argument comparable with the first movement's – it is in
a variety of sonata-rondo form, with material exclusive
to the soloist, and a substantial development section.
The 'daemonic' character of K466 made it Mozart's most
popular concerto in the 19th century. Beethoven wrote a
characteristic pair of cadenzas for it.

The concertos written at the time of *Le nozze di
Figaro* do not consistently pursue the new symphonic
approach. All require clarinets, not previously used in
piano concertos; the wind colouring, a feature of the
concertos since K450, almost dominates K482 in Eb
through its influence on the shape of the thematic
material. This is a leisurely, expansive work, allowing
the ear to relish the sensuous piano and wind sonorities,
with an Andante in variation form (the wind dominate
two of the variations) and a traditional 'hunting' finale
that incorporates as an episode, like K271 in the same
key, a slow minuet with a variation. The emphasis in
K482 on bravura writing may be contrasted with the
much more gentle nature of the passage-work in K488 in
A; lacking its predecessor's trumpets and drums, this
concerto draws on another, softer range of tone colours,
of a piece with its graceful themes. Its first entry reverts
to the usual pattern, but a departure is represented by
the presentation of the new second-subject matter after,
rather than before, the central ritornello, thus placing it
analogously with the fresh development themes that
Mozart often introduced; the analogy is pursued in that
the entire development is based on this theme – which
however is later recapitulated in the orthodox position.
The Adagio, Mozart's only F♯ minor movement, is

famous for its poetry and its pathos, derived from its gently falling phrases, siciliana rhythm, 'Neapolitan' harmony and expressive woodwind writing.

Those two concertos and the C minor K491, all composed during the writing of *Figaro*, make up a mutually complementary group, like the pairs already discussed; but the C minor is more profitably considered alongside the other 1786 concerto, the C major K503, for in these two the symphonic approach of K466 and 467 is pursued alongside the treatment of colour and character of K482 and 488. They are not however alike. K491, where the orchestra, uniquely, requires both oboes and clarinets, has many thematic ideas (though no true second-subject one in the first tutti): this material, some of it motivic, lends itself to development to an extent new in the concertos, and in the recapitulation it is drawn together, with the ideas re-ordered, elaborated and orchestrally enriched. In K503 the first-movement material is almost neutral in character, comprising broken-chord patterns, figures of three repeated notes (masonic significance has been ascribed to them) and scales; and its themes are relatively formal – bland, foursquare and minimally expressive. This concerto is thus in the line of descent from K415 and 451, but now the proportions are grander and the organization more taut, particularly through the capacity of the material to serve for contrapuntal working and rigorous, continuous development. The other movements show parallel features. In the C minor the second, like a Romance, is a rondo with faster-moving episodes where material stated by the wind band is elaborated by piano and strings. The finale is a set of variations, mainly double ones, the repeat of each strain in effect a new variation (as in

K450, 453 and 456), allowing for greater elaboration and variety of orchestral colour without increasing the time-scale; two major-key sections (Ab, bar 97; C, bar 165) have the relaxing effect of episodes although they are thinly disguised variations.

There were no concertos in 1787. The solitary one of 1788, K537 in D, is to some extent in the manner of K503, with similar neutral material, but less amenable to strongly organized development and more inclined towards decorative passage-work; it is hard, especially in the Romance-type second movement, not to sense some falling off in inventive vigour. The solo part left hand is not complete in the autograph; Mozart, expecting to play the concerto himself, had no reason to fill in detail. Similar considerations naturally apply to ornamentation: many concertos have conspicuous lacunae in this respect, for example K488 and 491 (second movements) and K482 (finale, including the repeats of the interpolated minuet).

(*ii*) *Symphonies*. In his mature years Mozart wrote no symphonies for use in Vienna at least until his last three of 1788; he did however perform there some earlier ones, including sections of serenades and the revised version of the Haffner K385 (1782). That work and the symphony for Linz were the only ones he composed after he had settled in Vienna until late 1786, when he wrote the Prague Symphony K504, presumably for use in that city. It is in three movements, with no minuet – more probably because he had reason to think that the Prague audiences were accustomed to three-movement symphonies than for any aesthetic reason. While preserving much of the traditional D major brilliance, in style it is close to the K503 concerto: it depends more on the arrangement and development of motifs than on thematic material. The first movement, after a slow introduction, has a structure of great originality and integrity, borrowing perhaps from Haydn's so-called monothematic type: its initial second-group idea starts as a chromatically inflected variant of the first, with a contrapuntal and sequential continuation, but a distinct lyrical theme ensues. Further, the tutti material of the groups is similarly related. The development includes contrapuntal workings of various of these motifs, and elides with the recapitulation, which in turn fuses – using the ambiguity of the inflected variant – the two groups in an extraordinarily subtle way. It has been pointed out (Larsen, 1956) that this unconventional form is best understood in relation to ritornello structure, which in view of Mozart's recent preoccupation with the piano concerto is not entirely surprising. The Andante, though lyrical in temper, remains motivic in style: all its ideas are based on the changing and developing repetition of essentially brief figures. So in a more relaxed way is the finale.

The great triptych that stands at the end of Mozart's symphonic output is obscure in its origins. It is not clear why he should have written symphonies just then: if for a series of concerts (a letter to Puchberg suggests he had one in mind), concertos might have been more understandable. These works are mutually complementary, a pair that grew into three: the pairing of G minor with E♭ and C had recent precedents, in the piano quartets and the string quintets respectively. The E♭ symphony is scored with clarinets rather than the usual oboes. The G minor is without trumpets or drums; Mozart later rearranged the wind layout, incorporating parts for clarinets and modifying those for the oboes.

The treatment of form is plainer and more conventional in all three first movements than in that of the Prague Symphony. No.39 is especially clearcut: after a sombre slow introduction based on dotted rhythms, the material is consistently lyrical and the development so traditional as to start with a subdominant statement of a second-group theme. The basic material in no.40 is less homogeneous. Its impassioned opening, with its original and beautiful throbbing accompaniment on divided violas, is set against a secondary theme in dialogue, but the falling-note figure from the opening (cf K478) persists at various levels and lends an undercurrent of agitation. Here the development section, quickly contradicting the conventional tonal expectation, begins with the first-group material in F♯ minor and includes contrapuntal argument around it; there is more during the recapitulation. The passion and urgency generally ascribed to this symphony have not been universally acknowledged; Schumann spoke of grace and charm, and others have detected only *opera buffa* character (see Westrup, 1955). No.41 is more formal and consciously grand, with *forte–piano* contrasts at the opening, tuttis with military rhythms, new superimposed counterpoints and expansive second-group material. For all that, *opera buffa* is not far distant: the gestures of the first bars could be those of the Count's knocking at the door answered by the Countess's pleas (in *Figaro*), and a cadential theme (bar 101) is identical with one in an aria, 'Un bacio di mano' K541, composed for an Anfossi opera.

The slow movements are marked by a new tone in Mozart's music: their tutti sections, often in minor keys, with high violin writing, chromatic wind and low-lying harmony for the middle string instruments, have an

13. Mozart: silverpoint drawing (1789) by Doris Stock

almost anguished emotional force (no.39, bars 30ff; no.41, bars 23ff). The Andante of no.39 makes much use of its two opening phrases; in sonata form without a development section, it has a recapitulation that is effectively a developmental elaboration of the exposition. The Andante of no.40 is more conventional in pattern, with a short development touching at its end heights of chromatic pathos (bars 69ff). Its basic two-note figure may be seen as linked with that of the first movement. Much the most complex in melodic structure, orchestration and chromatic harmony is the Andante of no.41, and here too, although there is a development section, new elaborations are introduced in the recapitulation; as in no.39, a *piano* statement of the opening material begins the coda.

The tendency to assign more weight to the finale of a multi-movement work can be seen in Mozart's symphonies since K130, and to some extent in his piano concertos (e.g. K466); Haydn was moving in the same direction. That of no.39 is relatively straightforward, a monothematic sonata-form movement, its secondary theme a varied version of the primary enhanced by a poetic, distantly modulating passage, with a vigorous development involving imitative writing. No.40 has a famously fiery finale, thematically rather foursquare (as indeed is the first movement); its remarkable development section begins with a tonally disorientating flourish, then embarks on a four-part contrapuntal working-out of the material, ending in the remote key of C♯ minor, where the music pauses before being wrenched back to the tonic for a regular recapitulation. The finale of no.41 is even more famed, for its 'fugue'. It does not possess a fugue, as such; rather, this is a sonata-form movement including fugal material. In this it is in the same tradition as the к387 quartet (see chapter 13) and, more particularly, as symphonies by various Austrian composers, including Michael Haydn, which Mozart may be assumed to have known – though in scope and execution it far surpasses any models. To discover J. S. Bach's influence is to sentimentalize and to ascribe to Mozart 20th-century historical attitudes; if any more distantly past influence should be noted it might rather be that of Fux and his school, the more so as the four-note tag that serves as fugue subject has its ancestry in a plainchant, 'Lucis creator', extensively set by those composers. The movement sets out conventionally, then at the transition includes a fugal exposition on the opening subject; and its main second-group theme is workable in various degrees of close imitation. Much of the tutti and accompanying material, mostly scale figures, also proves to be amenable to contrapuntal treatment. Some of the possibilities are further explored in the development section, but it is not until the coda (at bars 371ff) that the whole is drawn together in an apotheosis of invertible five-part counterpoint without parallel in the symphonic literature.

18. Key associations

Mozart's last four symphonies are in keys with specially strong associations in his music. Much has been written about his comparative consistency in the use of keys for particular types of work. This should be seen in a wider context of key traditions and associations, and instrumental characteristics. C. F. D. Schubart (*Ideen zu einer Ästhetik der Tonkunst*, 1806; written in the 1780s) distinguished between the 'tinted' and neutral keys, referring to the keys with sharps in their signatures as 'wild and strong', those with flats as 'sweet and melancholy', and the neutral ones as 'innocent and simple'.

D major was orchestrally the most brilliant key, specially effective for string instruments, and preferred by Mozart for almost all his Salzburg serenades as well as his Italian symphonies and overtures and such concertos of a calculated brilliance as K451 and K537. D and C were the keys in which trumpets and drums were habitually used, and the extra depth of C seems to have led to Mozart's preferring it for works of a more ceremonious character, including several early symphonies, three mature piano concertos (K415, 467, 503) and Symphonies nos.34 and 41. E♭ was the traditional key of the operatic *aria d'affetto* and the warm emotion associated with it, reflected in such works as the Sinfonia concertante K364/320*d* and Symphony no.39; the use of the clarinet, regarded as a specially expressive instrument, was common in this key. F and G were considered more neutral, and Mozart used them relatively infrequently in his mature music; F has certain pastoral associations, and the light quality of G, partly a result of high-pitched horns – still more marked in A and sometimes in B♭ – gave it associations with rural jollification, as in the choruses of *Le nozze di Figaro* and *Don Giovanni*. For his operatic love duets Mozart habitually used A major, with its associations of soft, warm texture; and in his operas D minor is almost invariably linked with ideas of vengeance. Minor keys however are relatively rare in any music of this period, and are never without special emotional significance of a dark or passionate kind; in his Viennese years Mozart wrote only two substantial instrumental works in D minor (K421/417*b* and 466) and three each in G minor (K478, 516 and 550) and C minor (K388/384*a*, 457 with 475, and 491). In his maturity he composed only single works in E major (K542), A minor (K310/300*d*) and E minor (K304/300*c*), a few movements in A♭ and no more than isolated ones in B minor (K540) or F♯ minor (K488); his only F minor works (K594 and 608) are for mechanical organ. Equal temperaments were not fully in use even for keyboard instruments in Mozart's time – this was a factor in the 'tinting' of the keys – and the unacceptability of certain intervals to his sensitive ear may have affected his choice.

Though his internal tonal contrasts, in development sections, range wide, Mozart was unadventurous compared with Haydn in his choice of keys for slow movements: in major-key works, he generally used the subdominant, less often the dominant and rarely the relative minor; in minor-key ones, commonly the relative major or the submediant. Mozart essentially used tonality to secure a broad unity, not for rhetorical effect; the very broadest of his tonally unifying schemes are found in his operas.

19. Last years, 1789-91

Early in 1789 Mozart accepted an invitation from Prince Karl Lichnowsky to accompany him to Berlin. They left on 8 April, pausing at Prague (where Mozart visited friends and discussed with the impresario Guardasoni possibilities of a new opera commission) and then at Dresden. During six days there he played chamber music privately (including the K563 trio) and was unexpectedly asked to perform at court, where he played the K537 concerto; he heard a mass by J. G. Naumann, which he dismissed as 'very mediocre', and listened to the playing of J. W. Hässler, who had 'merely memorized old Sebastian Bach's harmony and modulations and could not play a fugue properly'. They moved next to Leipzig, where Mozart is said to have improvised at the Thomaskirche organ in the presence of J. F. Doles, the Kantor and a former Bach pupil. They reached Potsdam about 25 April, but Mozart returned to Leipzig (8–17 May) to give a concert (including the K456 piano concerto) which was well received though financially unrewarding. Little is known about his time in Potsdam and Berlin; probably he heard *Die Entführung* at the opera house, and he went to a concert at which Hummel played. He also appeared at court, on 26 May, and may have been invited to compose quartets for King Friedrich Wilhelm II, who was a cellist, and sonatas for the princess – he later told Puchberg that he was composing quartets and sonatas for the Prussian court, but made no reference to a commission (his letter, moreover, was partly motivated by a concern to reassure Puchberg about repayment of a proposed loan). He almost certainly started work on the quartets on the return journey; for K575 and part of K589 he used manuscript paper originating from a mill between Dresden and Prague (see Tyson, 1975, and fig. 15). He arrived home on 4 June 1789; in his eight weeks away he had sent some 11 letters to his wife, full of news about his activities, eagerly affectionate and indeed sometimes very intimate in content, and showing concern not only about her health but also about the propriety of her conduct in his absence.

The letters to Puchberg this summer read pitifully. Both Mozart and his wife had spells of illness: he was unable, he said, to work, and he could secure only one subscriber, van Swieten, for a proposed concert series at his home (he had moved back to central Vienna at the beginning of the year); and Constanze had to go to Baden, a spa about 25 km from Vienna, for a cure. She was again pregnant; a daughter, Anna, was born in November and died the same day. While Constanze was in Baden, Mozart wrote two replacement arias for a new production of *Figaro* on 29 August; Adriana Ferraresi del Bene, who sang Susanna, was evidently not suited by the existing music. Cavalieri sang the Countess. The most important compositions of the summer were a piano sonata, and the clarinet quintet for Anton Stadler, first heard at a Tonkünstler-Sozietät concert in December. At the end of the year Mozart's main energies were expended on *Così fan tutte*, the third of his operas with Da Ponte. The others had been successes; they were travelling through the German lands and beyond and were generally well received, although many listeners found *Don Giovanni* bold, extravagant and complex. *Così fan tutte* had rehearsals on 31 December at Mozart's home and 21 January 1790 at the theatre; Puchberg and Haydn probably attended both. The première was on 26 January; there were four further performances, then a break because of the death of Joseph II in February, and five more in the summer.

Yet again, the fee for the opera seems to have had little effect on Mozart's financial situation. There were eight letters to Puchberg in the first half of 1790, requesting still larger loans and offering still less convincing promises of repayment. His poverty was not, however, desperate in the sense that he and his family starved or went unshod; basic necessities, like food, clothing, a carriage and servants, were cheap enough to be available to anyone in his social class. Constanze was able to take a cure at Baden, where Mozart spent some time in June. He still had his court salary and two pupils (he was anxious for more) as well as some income from publications; concert plans are often referred to in his correspondence, but whether they materialized is uncertain. He completed the third of the 'Prussian' quartets in June, and according to a letter to Puchberg had to sell the set for 'a trifle' to obtain cash quickly; they were not published until just after his death, and they bore no dedication to Friedrich Wilhelm II. In July he made two more Handel arrangements for van Swieten.

With the accession of the new emperor, Leopold II, Mozart hoped for preferment at court. None was forthcoming; but to take advantage of the coronation festivities, in which he had no official role, he went in September to Frankfurt, taking Franz de Paula Hofer, husband of his sister-in-law, and a servant. They arrived on 28 September. His concert, on 15 October (see fig. 14), was apparently a success musically, although the orchestra was small (only five or six violins, according

Mit gnädigſter Erlaubniß
Wird Heute Freytags den 15ten October 1790.
im groſen Stadt-Schauspielhauſe
Herr Kapellmeiſter Mozart
ein groſes
muſikaliſches Konzert
zu ſeinem Vortheil geben.

Erſter Theil.

Eine neue groſe Simphonie von Herrn Mozart.

Eine Arie, geſungen von Madame Schick.

Ein Concert auf dem Forte piano, geſpielt von Herrn Kapellmeiſter Mozart von ſeiner eigenen Kompoſition.

Eine Arie, geſungen von Herrn Cecarelli.

Zweyter Theil.

Ein Concert von Herrn Kapellmeiſter Mozart von ſeiner eigenen Kompoſition.

Ein Duett, geſungen von Madame Schick und Herrn Cecarelli.

Eine Phantaſie aus dem Stegreife von Herrn Mozart.

Eine Symphonie.

Die Perſon zahlt in den Logen und Parquet o fl. 45 kr.

Auf der Gallerie 24 kr.

Billets ſind bey Herrn Mozart, wohnhaft in der Kahlbchergaſſe Nro. 167. vom Donnerſtag Nachmittags und Freytags Frühe bey Herrn Caſſirer Scheidweiler und an der Caſſe zu haben.

Der Anfang iſt um Eilf Uhr Vormittags.

14. *Handbill for the concert Mozart gave in Frankfurt (15 October 1790) during the festivities on the coronation of Leopold II; the programme included the piano concertos* K537 *and* 459

to an eye-witness, insufficient for works like the K459 and K537 piano concertos and the new 'grosse Symphonie' he gave); but it was poorly attended and financially a failure. Mozart's letters to Constanze are full of affectionate assurances about his anxiety to be home and optimistic suggestions about how they would overcome their money worries. On his return journey he gave a concert at Mainz, heard *Figaro* at Mannheim, and played before the King of Naples at Munich. He reached home about 10 November, joining Constanze at the new apartment in central Vienna to which she had just moved.

In December 1790 Mozart saw Haydn leave for London; he himself had just declined an invitation from an opera promoter there but had been promised another, like Haydn's, from J. P. Salomon. His compositions during the winter months include a string quintet (another followed in April), a piano concerto, two pieces for mechanical organ and numerous dances for court balls. He played a concerto at a concert organized by the clarinettist Josef Bähr in March; and an aria and a symphony, perhaps one of the last three, were given at the Tonkünstler-Sozietät concerts in April. During that month Mozart petitioned the city council for the reversion to the important and remunerative post of Kapellmeister at St Stephen's Cathedral, where the incumbent Leopold Hofmann was aged and ill; he was appointed assistant and deputy, without pay. Hofmann lived until 1793.

During the early summer Constanze, once more pregnant, was away at Baden; Mozart often visited her there, and became friendly with the choirmaster, Anton Stoll, for whom he composed the motet *Ave verum corpus*. Their sixth child, Franz Xaver Wolfgang

Mozart, was born in July. Mozart's frequent letters to Constanze suggest a happier frame of mind, with their affectionate concern and cheerful banter, the latter directed at F. X. Süssmayr, his pupil and a close friend in these months. It seems that financial matters were less pressing, and perhaps his spirits reflected the happy collaboration on which he was engaged with his old acquaintance the actor-manager Emanuel Schikaneder, whose company gave plays and Singspiels in a suburban theatre. This collaboration was on *Die Zauberflöte*, which occupied him during part of the summer. Early biographers suggested that in his wife's absence Mozart indulged in various kinds of excess during 1791, in company with Schikaneder, but there is no evidence of that, nor of any kind of loose living on Mozart's part at any time. Nothing more licentious than a fondness for billiards is reliably documented.

While he was at work on *Die Zauberflöte* he received another commission, when a stranger asked him to compose a requiem under conditions of secrecy. This commission came from Count Walsegg-Stuppach, who wanted to pass off as his own composition a requiem for his wife. Then, probably about the middle of July, Mozart was asked by the Prague impresario Guardasoni to write the opera for the festivities in September at Leopold II's coronation as King of Bohemia. This was to be *La clemenza di Tito*, a setting of Metastasio's 1734 text; the Dresden court poet Caterino Mazzolà was then in Vienna and it would seem probable that Guardasoni and Mozart arranged for him to cut and reshape the libretto to meet modern requirements. (Other possibilities have been put forward about the opera's origins, linking it with plans mooted by Guardasoni and Mozart in 1789, and attempting to explain how an aria apparently from the opera might have been performed in Prague as early as April 1791: see Volek, 1959; Lühning, 1974; and Tyson, 1975.)

Mozart set out for Prague on about 25 August, with his wife and Süssmayr. His earliest biographer, Niemetschek, said that he started work on the opera in the coach, and composed it in 18 days, but there are good reasons for believing that he had already written most of the ensembles and two of the arias for Titus (he knew the singer, the Ottavio in *Don Giovanni*), and had drafted more (see Tyson, 1975). The simple recitatives were supplied, it seems, by Süssmayr (see Giegling, 1967). Mozart had a spell of illness in Prague, but went to a performance of *Don Giovanni* on 2 September, finished work on *Tito* on 5 September, and conducted the première the next night. It apparently had only a mixed reception (the empress called it 'una porcheria tedesca'), but like most of Mozart's operas it soon rose in public esteem, and the final performance on 30 September was much applauded.

On that same night *Die Zauberflöte* had its first performance at the Theater auf der Wieden (or Freihaustheater) in Vienna, with Schikaneder as Papageno, the composer Benedikt Schack as Tamino and Mozart's sister-in-law Josepha Hofer as the Queen of Night. Again, initial reactions were cautious, but by 7 October Mozart could write to Constanze, at Baden, that several numbers had been encored and that the opera was steadily becoming more esteemed. Mozart took his mother-in-law to one performance, and to another his son Carl as well as Salieri and the soprano Cavalieri – Salieri greeted every item with 'bravo' or 'bello', Mozart noted. At another performance Mozart delighted the audience by playing the glockenspiel in the wings, deliberately mistiming it in relation to Schikaneder's actions. About this time he completed a clarinet concerto for Stadler; and in November he composed a masonic cantata, directing a performance on 18 November at his lodge.

That cantata was his last completed work. The illness he had suffered in Prague, which may have been linked with his spells of poor health the previous year, apparently never quite left him. Later accounts of his last weeks tell of his working feverishly, on his return from Prague, at the Requiem, with premonitions of his own end; these seem hard to reconcile with the high spirits evident in his letters from much of October. At the end of November he was confined to bed, and attended by two leading Viennese doctors, Closset and Sallaba. He was nursed by Constanze and her youngest sister, Sophie. His condition seemed to improve on 3 December, and the next day a few friends (Schack, Hofer and the bass Gerl) gathered to sing over with him parts of the unfinished Requiem. That evening, according to the moving account of his death written by Sophie Haibel in 1825, his condition worsened; Closset, summoned from the theatre, applied cold compresses; and just before 1 a.m., on 5 December, Mozart died. The cause of his death was registered as 'hitziges Friesel Fieber' (severe miliary fever) and later diagnosed as 'rheumatische Entzündungsfieber' (rheumatic inflammatory fever) by a medical authority on evidence from Closset and Sallaba. That seems perfectly consistent with the symptoms and Mozart's medical history, more so than the various rival diagnoses, such as uraemia; there is no evidence to support the anyway improbable notion that he was poisoned, by Salieri or anyone else (for a full discussion see Bär, 1966, 2/1972). He was quietly buried in a mass grave, in accordance with contemporary Viennese custom, at St Marx churchyard outside the city, on 7 (not 6) December. If, as later reports say, no mourners attended, that is consistent with Viennese burial customs at the time; but Jahn (1856) wrote that Salieri, Süssmayr, van Swieten and two other musicians were present. The tale of a storm and snow is false: the day was calm and mild.

The obituary notices were unanimous in acknowledging Mozart's greatness. Various concerts and requiems were given in his memory, including some for Constanze's benefit. The estate was considerable, though its financial valuation was small (for details, including the books and music in Mozart's library, see Deutsch, *Mozart: die Dokumente seines Lebens*, 1961, Anh.II). Constanze applied for and was granted a court pension, which amounted to one third of Mozart's salary; Puchberg did not press for the money due to him, about 1000 gulden, but later asked for it and was repaid. In the ensuing years Constanze sold many of Mozart's manuscripts, a large proportion in 1799–1800 to the publisher J. A. André.

20. The Da Ponte operas

Mozart is sometimes presented as primarily a composer of *opera buffa*. But it is clear from references in his correspondence that serious opera and German opera were at least as important, perhaps even more so. He was a professional; and when the Viennese court theatre wanted *opera buffa*, he was ready to write it, once he could find a librettist to supply him with adequate texts. Da Ponte, as his memoirs indicate, took care to suit his librettos to the composers for whom they were intended. His three for Mozart, *Le nozze di Figaro* (1786), *Don Giovanni* (1787) and *Così fan tutte* (1790), exhibit an exceptional complexity of character and motivation; their plots contain many traditional and conventional elements, but treated in such a way as to allow a new seriousness.

The most straightforwardly comic is probably *Le nozze di Figaro*. Many political elements in Beaumarchais' original, including most of the direct expressions of social resentment, were pruned by Da Ponte; but the social tensions remain, to be expressed in, for example, Figaro's 'Se vuol ballare' in Act 1, the Act 2 finale, and the Count's music early in Act 3. The nature of the individual arias also reflects the social standing of the various characters: this may be exemplified by a comparison between the two D major vengeance arias, the blustery, parodistic 'La vendetta' for Bartolo and the Count's 'Vedrò, mentr'io sospiro', with its overtones of power and menace, or between the breadth and smoothness of the Countess's phraseology as opposed to

Susanna's. Arias showing extensions of the emotional
range of *opera buffa* include the two in which the
Countess mourns the loss of her husband's love,
Cherubino's two evocations of adolescent passion (particularly 'Non so più') and Figaro's cynical tirade against
woman's infidelity.

Some of the ensembles carry more complex kinds of
expression, like the ironic humour of 'Via resti servita';
and one, the Letter Duet, is a musical-dramatic tour de
force, the music representing the dictation of a letter,
with phrases realistically repeated and a condensed recapitulation serving for the reading-back of the text.
In general however the ensembles, following *opera buffa*
tradition, carry the action forward. This applies particularly to the finales. The first of the four acts in fact
ends with an aria rather than an ensemble, the brilliant
'Non più andrai', a favourite ever since Mozart's time;
and the third ends with a dance scene, which uses, as the
only concession to Spanish local colour, a traditional
fandango melody, close to that in Gluck's ballet *Don
Juan*. (The opera clearly prefigures the new two-act
structure used in *Don Giovanni* and *Così fan tutte*; the
traditional three-act plan is altogether abandoned.) The
other two finales are long, multi-section ensembles, with
changes in tempo, metre, tonality and orchestration resolving existing tensions and creating new ones, always
closely keyed to the action. Several such sections, especially in Act 2, are in effect substantial, symphonically
developed movements (for example the B♭ Allegro, bar
167). In the Act 4 finale, particularly, passing modulation is used strikingly to mark out incident, and the
mock pleas of love from Figaro to the 'Countess' –
Susanna in disguise – are paralleled by the parodying
character of the music. Each extended finale is streng-

thened by its unity of key, so that the pull of tonality draws them together: that of Act 2 begins and ends in E♭, that of Act 4 in D, the basic key of the opera (an increasingly common procedure in contemporary *opera buffa*). It is the symphonic force of the music, and its high degree of orchestral elaboration, that lends life to the characters, depth to the situations and seriousness to their resolution, and places the opera apart from the generality of Italian *opere buffe* of the period, however closely it may resemble those of such composers as Sarti, Anfossi, Paisiello, Cimarosa or Martín y Soler in its manner and its material.

Recent research on *Figaro* has thrown important new light on Mozart's method of composition. Analysis of papers and inks in the available part of the autograph implies that he did not compose the opera from beginning to end within six weeks as Da Ponte sent him the libretto (Da Ponte's tale – anyway belied by biographical evidence), but according to the character of the items: first the playful-undramatic ones, then the comic-dramatic, third the action scenes and last the lyrical arias (Köhler, 1967). The arrangement of numbers in the autograph of Act 3, available only since 1980, seems to preclude the revised order suggested in 1965 (Moberly and Raeburn) and since then widely accepted.

While *Don Giovanni*, like *Figaro*, is based on the tensions of class and sex, its plot, which dates back at least to the time of Tirso de Molina (1571–1641), is less obvious material for an *opera buffa* (strictly, it is a *dramma giocoso* in the tradition deriving from Goldoni): partly because of the serious and supernatural issues involved, and partly because the story was simply too short. Da Ponte drew on what was in effect a one-act libretto by Bertati, set by Gazzaniga for Venice early in

1787, and filled it out with extra episodes; it accordingly lacks the integrity of the *Figaro* plot, with its close network of functional relationships. But the force and the 'daemonic' character of the music have exercised a special fascination for audiences and for connoisseurs, giving rise to a vast literature, critical, interpretative and purely fanciful, by among others E. T. A. Hoffmann, Kierkegaard, Mörike, Baudelaire, Gounod and Jouve.

A difference in approach between *Don Giovanni* and *Figaro* is evident in the long and tonally unified scene that opens the opera: the overture, in D minor and major; a comic aria in F major for Leporello; an ensemble in B♭ as Anna pursues Giovanni from her chamber; a modulating scene as Giovanni fights and kills the Commendatore; a brief simple recitative, then an orchestral one for Anna and Ottavio, leading to their duet, back in D minor. Much of the opera's basic material is thus exposed in what is virtually an unbroken musical span. The more conventionally *buffo* material that ensues takes the normal form of alternating simple recitative and lyrical numbers – among the latter are Leporello's Catalogue Aria (in an unusual fast–slow pattern) and two movements establishing Elvira's grotesque, tragi-comic situation (the first with over-dramatic leaps and pauses, the second in an old-fashioned, pseudo-Handelian style) – before the quartet 'Non ti fidar', in which the serious and comic sides converge, and which leads with only a very brief, non-modulating recitative to Anna's recognition of Giovanni and her call for vengeance: again the serious side of the opera is sustained by virtually continuous music.

The material that follows – including two scenes for Zerlina and Masetto, the Act 1 finale, the mock seduction of Elvira, Leporello's escape, and various arias – is, essentially, interposed, with some of its ideas borrowed from Bertati's text; its links with the outer parts of the opera are fragile. It also contains Giovanni's own three arias, all to some extent conventional in type (the serenade with mandolin may be compared with 'In Mohrenland' from *Die Entführung*), as well as music providing social characterization comparable with that of *Figaro*, in Zerlina's simple tuneful songs and, more particularly, in the extraordinary ball scene of the Act 1 finale: here different groups dance simultaneously to the aristocratic minuet, the middle-class contredanse and the peasant German dance, played by three stage orchestras. This finale is another long, composite movement in a closed tonal scheme, though the resolution of one section by the next is less striking than in the parallel (Act 2) finale in *Figaro*, reflecting the more episodic nature of the plot.

The plot's main thread resumes in the cemetery scene and (after Anna's final aria, in the two-tempo rondò form normally reserved for the prima donna) the supper scene, an extended finale. Its first part includes passages, played by a stage band, from popular operas by Martín y Soler, Sarti and Mozart himself (*Figaro*), as table-music; in its central part, as the statue of the Commendatore consigns Giovanni to hell, the original tonic of D minor is at last established, with the music heard at the beginning of the overture. The climax is heightened by the use of trombones to suggest solemnity and the supernatural, the hieratic dotted rhythms, the extreme chromaticism, and the changing harmonic movement, growing increasingly irregular until it lurches wildly as Giovanni is overcome by the flames. But this is an *opera buffa*, and throughout the scene, cowering under the supper table, is Leporello, proffering advice and the common man's wry or facetious observations, just as he had while Giovanni killed the Commendatore and during the mock seduction (to genuinely tender music) of Elvira: comedy subsists alongside serious drama, and both are reflected in the music. And at the end of the opera, the remaining characters draw the moral and plan their future in a cheerful sextet, in G and finally D major.

For the Vienna performances of 1788 Mozart made various revisions: there was a replacement aria for Ottavio, a dramatically feeble duet scene for Zerlina and Leporello, and a scena for Elvira; it has been suggested, though probably mistakenly, that the final sextet was omitted. Both Ottavio's arias, and the new scene for Elvira, are commonly given in present-day performances although their inclusion scarcely strengthens the dramatic structure or the characterization.

Così fan tutte, composed just over two years after *Don Giovanni*, and also having sources in Tirso de Molina, is widely reckoned to be the most carefully and symmetrically constructed, and the most consistent in style, of the three Da Ponte operas. It has also been the one most severely criticized for moral shortcomings. The subject of the comedy, feminine fickleness, was found shocking even quite shortly after the opera's composition, and is made the more so by the convention (standing equally in *Figaro* and *Don Giovanni*) that the action should span no more than 24 hours. The opera is however susceptible of more positive interpretations, for example as a commentary on the strength and uncontrollability of amorous feelings and on the value of a mature recognition of them.

The plan of the opera and the make-up of the cast lend themselves to symmetrical treatment, with three

men (a pair of officers and their friend) and three women
(two sisters and their servant), each having an aria in
each act, and with a treatment of the ensemble
movements calculated so that the four principals are
kept in their pairs (officers, sisters) and given relatively
little personal identity until well on in Act 2 – by which
point the sisters are emotionally affected by the
'Albanians', their disguised lovers. Thus their arias in
Act 1, Dorabella's 'Smanie implacabili' and Fiordiligi's
'Come scoglio', while basically serious music, embody
an element of parody: the emotions voiced, and the
musical style in which they are couched, are as
disproportionate to the situation as are the self-
dramatizing protestations of a romantic girl. The music,
in fact, truthfully represents the situation's different
levels. There is a similar duality to the two quintets in
Act 1, the over-emotional 'Sento, o Dio' and 'Di
scrivermi ogni giorno', a touching farewell against
Alfonso's chuckles. Further, the music often parodies
particular styles and works.

While in Act 1 the emotions expressed are those
conventionally considered proper to the situations, in
Act 2 they become more personal in tone. The arias'
messages are no longer simply the predictable ones;
and the two sisters and the two officers are differentiated from one another in a way that lends logic to the
original couplings. In particular the dilemma of the
sterner sister, Fiordiligi, is strongly conveyed in the
heroic music of her rondò aria 'Per pietà'; the pain of
her capitulation, represented by a piercingly chromatic
oboe phrase in her duet with Ferrando, is contrasted
with the ease with which Dorabella, whose Act 2 aria is
playful, joins in a sensuous duet with Guglielmo. And
the quicksilver emotions of Ferrando, represented in the

phraseology and particularly the key scheme of his aria
'Tradito, schernito' (C minor–E♭–C minor–C major:
an uncommon pattern for Mozart), are set against the
cynicism of Guglielmo, expressed partly in his aria but
more so in the canonic quartet in the wedding scene,
where Mozart characteristically made a virtue of neces-
sity by assigning different music, and words to match, to
the baritone, who could not join in the canon at a pitch
apt to sopranos and a tenor. This solemn canon, for the
wedding toast, is one section of the second-act finale,
which later introduces allusively quotations from music
heard earlier in the opera – the march at the officers'
departure, two numbers familiar from the scenes where
the officers were disguised, and one mystifying passage
(bar 496) which can only be a quotation of material
Mozart decided to omit.

The canonic music, like that in the final sextet of *Don
Giovanni*, draws on a tradition now familiar chiefly
through Rossini's finales (*Il barbiere di Siviglia*, Act 1)
and Beethoven ('Mir ist so wunderbar', *Fidelio*); Mozart
must have known the examples in Martín y Soler's *Una
cosa rara* and Storace's *Gli equivoci*. Precedents may be
found for several other features of Mozart's Da Ponte
operas, including in several cases clear reminiscences, in
music by Sarti, Gazzaniga, Piccinni, Paisiello and
others (some are cited by Dent, 1913; Abert, 1919;
Einstein, 1945; etc). Sometimes, as in the 6/8 G major
peasants' music in *Don Giovanni*, this was partly a
matter of common coin. But the subtlety of characterization, the richness of orchestral development, the tonal
and symphonic control of long expanses of music, the
vitality of the recitative (simple as well as obbligato) and
the range of serious emotion combine to place these
three works on a different plane from other *opere buffe*
of their time.

21. Late instrumental works

Così fan tutte has characteristics – irony, restraint, serene detachment, symmetry – distinct from the other Da Ponte operas; these have been seen as elements of a specific Mozartian 'Spätstil'. Some commentators have dated this style back to the time of the last three symphonies (summer 1788), others to that of *Don Giovanni* (autumn 1787) or a few months before – to the period of the two great string quintets and, significantly, the letter to Leopold about death. How this late style may relate to the circumstances of Mozart's life, like his lack of professional progress, his financial troubles, his marriage, his father's death, and in particular his embracing of freemasonry, is of course open to speculation. It may seem that these changes represented a slow process, starting after (or even during) the period of his most lyrical music – early 1784 to summer 1786 – and continuing, with several important landmarks, including the K503 concerto and the Prague Symphony as well as the works just cited, so that by 1789 he had arrived at a style noticeably more austere and refined, more motivic and contrapuntal, more economical in the use of material, and harmonically and texturally less rich. His late music is melodically less abundant and less expansive; there are fewer new themes in development sections or in exposition codas, and second-group themes are more often derived from primary ones by some form of extension or contrapuntal treatment. Contact with Haydn's mature music may have stimulated this last development, but in general Mozart was now past the stage when he would omnivorously draw to himself all that he found worthwhile in other men's music. By the middle 1780s the process of synthesis that governed his earlier development had effectually finished, and the changes of this late period were of a more internal kind, with few parallels in other composers' music; arguably they may be regarded as analogous to the neo-classicism that was affecting the arts generally.

It has been suggested that at this time Mozart was finding composition increasingly difficult, and the multiplicity of extant sketches from his last years, mostly discarded beginnings, has been cited in support. Whether the existence of such sketches is evidential may be questioned since later material could anyway be expected to survive in larger quantities. Their existence also reflects the greater complexity of his later music. A certain amount of sketch material, mostly drafts of beginnings, from a few bars to entire expositions, but also detailed workings-out of brief passages, survives from most periods of Mozart's adult life; it testifies that composition was not as effortless to him as some romantic biographers thought, and that his works were not always visualized entire in his mind before being consigned to paper.

He seems to have found the string quartet a specially difficult medium. For the three 'Prussian' quartets, K575, 589 and 590, there were several false starts, as in the quartets dedicated to Haydn, and work on them was strung out over many months (Mozart did not, however, as was long imagined, call on earlier material; see Tyson, 1975). He must have realized that the new, elaborately wrought four-part style he had previously used would not serve for the kind of concertante quartets he wanted to offer the cellist king of Prussia. To

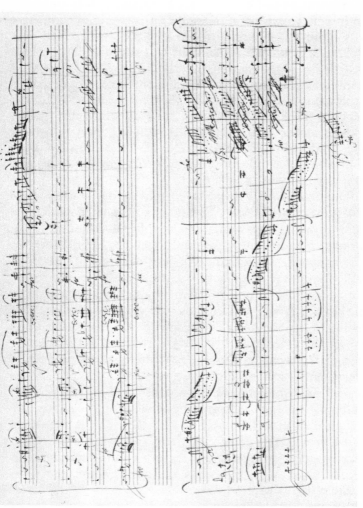

15. *Autograph MS from Mozart's String Quartet in D*
K575, *1789, end of the first movement*

write quartets in which the cello was consistently prominent would have violated Mozart's ideas of stylistic integrity; except in the slow movements, where there was more scope, and the trio of K575, he arrived at a style in which each instrument was for symmetry's sake assigned melodic matter. For the last two movements of K589 and the last three of K590 the idea of the cello's prominence seems virtually to have been abandoned; perhaps the Prussian hopes had faded. Here the quartet style is closer to that of the Haydn set, particularly in the finale of K590; the finale of K575 is also more contrapuntal, and more closely organized, than any other movement in that work.

These quartets are polished music; but if they were the only examples of Mozart's 'late style' it would be hard to avoid regarding it as involving something of a falling off in inventiveness and ingenuity. While the two late quintets, K593 and 614, bear a similar relation to K515–16 as the 'Prussian' quartets to the Haydn ones, they make a more positive impression. Each first-movement Allegro (K593 has a Larghetto introduction, recurring in the coda) begins with a passage imitating horns, and that of K614, in 6/8 rhythm, retains something of a wind serenade atmosphere; K593 has a first movement in a style more spare in texture than the preceding quintets but polyphonically richer, particularly in the recapitulation where the exposition material is extended and elaborated. The Andante of K614 recalls the Romance style, with the recurrences increasingly complex in texture and the episodes representing development of the main theme; the K593 Adagio is altogether more intense with its chromaticisms, its dialogues between violin and cello across throbbing middle textures, and its great range of elaborations throughout every phase of the movement of the descending tetrachord figure heard at the start. The contrast of intensity persists. K614 has a ländler trio and a monothematic finale on a Haydn-like theme, including fugato treatment, while K593 has a sophisticated canonic minuet and a graceful dialogue-style trio, and a 6/8 finale whose main theme begins with a descending chromatic scale (the zigzag pattern long accepted was a publisher's emendation after Mozart's death) – it is contrapuntally developed, in light, open textures with a curiously cool, even astringent flavour.

The only other chamber works of the last years are of a more relaxed sort: a little Adagio and Rondo for musical glasses (or armonica), flute, oboe, viola and cello, of May 1791, and the Clarinet Quintet of autumn 1789, whose sensitive blend of a true chamber style and the concertante writing needed if the medium is to be effective far surpasses the earlier works for a wind instrument with strings. The necessary mixtures of dialogue and accompaniment, of homogeneous and heterogeneous textures, called forth a special quality and style of invention, as in the Piano and Wind Quintet K452.

Keyboard music of this period includes two sonatas, the relatively slight B♭ K570 and, written just after the Berlin journey and presumably intended for the Prussian princess, K576 in D. It is not exactly a 'leichte Klaviersonate' such as, Mozart wrote, seemed appropriate to her, for though light in texture it is often contrapuntal: in both outer movements the main secondary material is contrapuntally derived from the primary, and in the first there is much contrapuntal working in the development and the recapitulation. Among other keyboard works are a gigue K574 composed in Leipzig, and fancifully supposed to be a homage to Bach, and the unfinished G minor Allegro K312/590*d*; these last two may have been intended for further Prussian sonatas. Also from this period are the two fantasias K594 and 608, composed for mechanical organ, an instrument whose high-pitched pipes Mozart found objectionable; they are commonly played as piano duets or organ solos. It is interesting to see how Mozart, with no established design to follow, set about composing such pieces: one is made up of a sonata-allegro in F major, with much busy, quartet-like contrapuntal texture, framed by a chromatic F minor Adagio; the other is a fugue in F minor, introduced by material of a rhetorical kind (which recurs at climactic points), interrupted by an A♭ Andante, and resuming with increased pace and contrapuntal complexity. They show Mozart finding new and imaginative responses even to a challenge he did not relish.

The last two orchestral works were concertos, in B♭ K595 for piano and in A K622 for clarinet. K595 broadly follows the formal pattern of the 1784 concertos, but has an unusual abundance of ritornello material. Other special features include a marked tendency for the music to oscillate between major and minor, and a link between ritornello figuration and piano passage-work; also notable is the development section, beginning with a series of strange, disorientating modulations, followed by material closely based on the exposition, worked contrapuntally and with little piano virtuosity. After a long ternary Larghetto, with a main melody of extreme simplicity and beauty in Romance style, the finale is in the traditional 6/8 'hunting' rhythm, less ebullient and more rarefied than Mozart's other examples. His last instrumental work, the Clarinet Concerto for Anton Stadler, was originally to have been a basset-horn concerto in G, and the first movement was sketched in that form before he decided in favour of Stadler's 'basset clarinet' (a clarinet with a downwards extension of a major 3rd, probably also intended in K581). The work survives only in an adaptation by its original publisher, and not until the 1960s were attempts made to restore it and perform it on an extended instrument. The discovery that it was composed for basset clarinet explains several puzzling features in the text, and the extra compass makes the exploitation of the clarinet's contrasting registers even more striking than in its familiar form. The gentle-toned orchestra, with flutes, bassoons and horns but not oboes, doubtless reflects a preference for tone-colours to offset the clarinet as well as the factors touched on earlier (see chapter 5) regarding the orchestration of music in A major; and it helps impart to this graceful and lovingly written work a shading that it is tempting to regard as autumnal.

Mozart's large output of dance music ought not to be passed over. He composed, for dancing, about 120 minuets, more than 50 German dances or ländler and some 40 contredanses; nearly all the German dances and about one third of each of the other types postdate his court appointment. Some were composed each winter from 1787–8 to 1790–91. Most are 16 or 32 bars long, for strings (without viola) and varied wind. One is struck by the craftsmanship and the artistic invention he brought even to these humble pieces, and in particular by his capacity for overcoming the rhythmic monotony of 16-bar phrases, by the ingenious variety of colour, and above all by the melodic felicity that enabled him to offer piquant little surprises to those of the dancers who cared to listen.

22. Late vocal works

Chance dictated that Mozart, in his last months, should write works in three genres with which he had scarcely been occupied for almost a decade: Singspiel, *opera seria* and sacred music. The two theatrical forms, in particular, had undergone considerable change since the time of *Die Entführung* (1782) and *Idomeneo* (1781).

The first of the three to be composed was *Die Zauberflöte*, which was well under way by 11 June 1791, as a reference in a letter to Constanze makes clear, and probably complete in July but for three vocal items, the overture and the march. It has many sources. Schikaneder apparently drew its basic plot from Liebeskind's 'Lulu oder Die Zauberflöte', published in Wieland's collection of fairy tales, *Dschinnistan* (1786–9); this was a source for other operas given at the Freihaustheater and the rival Leopoldstädter-Theater, including several that Mozart knew, like Müller's *Kaspar der Fagottist* and Schack's *Der Stein der Weisen*, and which themselves may have provided ideas 'for Schikaneder and Mozart. Another source for the magical elements was Philipp Hafner's play *Megära* (1763). Many of the ritual elements are derived from Jean Terrasson's novel *Sethos* (1731), which has an ancient Egyptian setting, from contemporary free-masonry and possibly from other theatrical works of the time. The whole belongs firmly in the established traditions of Viennese popular theatre. Claims have been made on behalf of C. L. Giesecke, a poet and a member of the company, as author of the libretto, in the light of his own reported assertions about 30 years later; but they lack plausible support, and the arguments in favour of Schikaneder's authorship seem incontrovertible. The possibility that Giesecke, who put together Wranitzky's *Oberon* text, may have suggested ideas or helped over details cannot be ruled out.

Another hotly disputed point regarding *Die Zauberflöte* concerns a possible reshaping of the plot while composition was in progress. The opera begins as if a traditional tale of a heroic prince (Tamino) rescuing a beautiful princess (Pamina) at the bidding of her mother (the Queen of Night) from her wicked abductor (Sarastro) – like the basic plan of 'Lulu'. It soon transpires, however, that the abductor is beneficent and that it is the princess's mother who is wicked. One is tempted to think that this shift can only represent a change in plan by Schikaneder and Mozart; but the moral ambiguities that demand explanation if it does not – Sarastro's employment of the evil Monostatos, for example, or the Queen and her Ladies' gifts of the benevolently magical flute and bells to Tamino and Papageno, or Pamina's fear of Sarastro – are not out of line with Viennese popular theatrical traditions, nor with symbolic interpretations of the work.

Die Zauberflöte is distinguished from the bulk of contemporary Singspiels not merely by the quality of its music but also by the serious meanings that underlie what on the surface may seem childish pantomime or low comedy. In style it is diverse. The overture, in the 'masonic' key of E♭ (with three flats), embodies fugal writing, and it also at once implies masonic symbolism: the introduction sounds three chords, two of them twice, and thus signifies the number 3 (or possibly the masonic feminine number 5); it recurs with a less ambiguous three times three chords, and also appears in that form in the ritual scenes of Act 2. Papageno's strophic comic songs are in the same cheerful manner as those of other contemporary Singspiels, and close too to some of Mozart's own lieder of the preceding years. The songs for the serious characters, while rarely using the extended forms of Italian opera, are more Italianate, like Tamino's lyrical Portrait Aria, or the high coloratura ones that portray the Queen of Night with such fierce brilliance. Pamina's 'Ach ich fühl's' falls in between; its simple, intimate manner could not belong to a Countess or an Elvira in a like situation, and indeed reflects her more universal, idealized character as well as the different social ambience for which this opera was intended. The music for the Three Ladies is distinguished from that for the Three Boys in style and texture, the former intense and calling for vibrant tone, the latter cool and pellucid, representing at its height the element of serenity remarked earlier as characteristic of Mozart's late style.

The ritual music, including the songs for Sarastro, the choruses, certain ensembles and the cantus firmus 'chorale prelude' setting for the music of the Men in Armour, falls into yet another category. Stylistic parallels can be found, not surprisingly, in Mozart's masonic music, which includes four cantatas, among them one composed at the time of *Die Zauberflöte* and one just after, and which mostly contain songs and choral music in the solemn, exalted tone heard here; they share too the same masonic symbols in key, rhythm, instrumentation and other particulars. Most of the music in the two extended finales is of this kind.

Much has been written about freemasonry in *Die*

Zauberflöte (see particularly Nettl, 1957; Chailley, 1968; and Thomson, 1977). It has been suggested that the characters stood for people involved in the recent history of freemasonry – the Queen of Night for Maria Theresia, its oppressor, Tamino for Joseph II, Sarastro for the scientist Ignaz von Born or the Italian masonic martyr Cagliostro. Such particularizations are unlikely to have been in the authors' minds, and may seem to narrow the work, for the characters here, unlike those of the Da Ponte operas, are generalized and symbolic: for example Papageno and Papagena as children of nature, Tamino and Pamina as ideal beings seeking full realization and, especially, ideal union. In this *Die Zauberflöte* may be thought to pursue the theme of self-knowledge predicated in *Così fan tutte*. More broadly, it has been persuasively argued (Koenigsberger, 1975) that the opera is susceptible to interpretation in the light of the philosophical, cosmological and epistemological background of 18th-century freemasonry as an allegory about 'the quest of the human soul for both inner harmony and enlightenment', with the main characters 'joint participants in one being, one psyche, or one soul'. Such interpretations help explain how what may superficially seem a mixture of the sublime (musically) and the ridiculous (textually) melds into an opera not only theatrically effective but also of a philosophical or religious quality. Goethe tried to write a sequel to it; Bernard Shaw called it 'the music of my own church'.

Until the 1960s, Mozart scholars were inclined to dismiss *La clemenza di Tito* as an opera written hurriedly and with distaste. That it was written hurriedly, even if not as hurriedly as has been supposed, is probably true; but there is no reason to imagine that Mozart had reservations about composing it. Serious opera had always attracted him; and many composers were setting Metastasio's classical librettos modified to meet contemporary taste through the addition of ensembles and choruses. Mozart noted *Tito* in his catalogue as 'ridotto a vera opera' by Mazzolà, who removed 18 arias and added four, and supplied two duets, three trios and finale ensembles.

The opera was composed in a style more austere than that of the Da Ponte operas or *Die Zauberflöte*. This traditionally has been attributed to Mozart's alleged haste; but on other occasions he composed quickly and elaborately, and there is no reason to think that the opera would have been substantially different had he had longer. Its style is appropriate to its topic. The indebtedness of the original Metastasio libretto to French classical models has been pointed out (Moberly, 1974), and in its reduced form it may be seen as conforming to the neo-classical ideals then rapidly gaining ground in Germany. Mozart responded with restrained orchestral writing, smooth, broad vocal lines, and relatively brief numbers.

It is clear that the aria lengths were carefully planned. In Act 2 both the prima donna (Vitellia) and primo uomo (Sextus) have full-length rondò arias, Vitellia's being the movement, 'Non più di fiori', that may have been composed earlier. An interesting feature is the appearance of related material in the two sections; there is evidence that this was an afterthought. This aria has an obbligato part for basset-horn, and Sextus's Act 1 aria, 'Parto', has one for clarinet; these were composed for Stadler. Both Sextus's arias involve progressive increases of tempo, no doubt intended to represent the screwing up of his courage. The arias for the secondary characters, even Titus, are much shorter. The trios

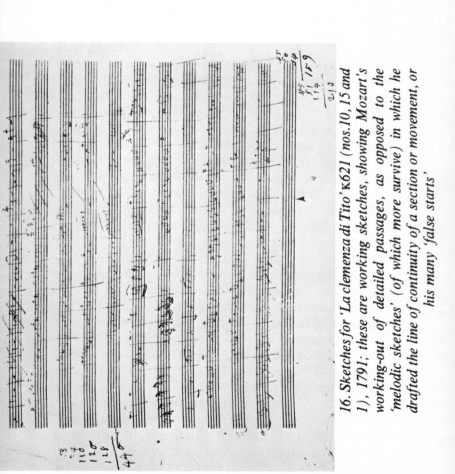

16. Sketches for 'La clemenza di Tito' K621 (nos.10, 15 and 1), 1791; these are working sketches, showing Mozart's working-out of detailed passages, as opposed to the 'melodic sketches' (of which more survive) in which he drafted the line of continuity of a section or movement, or his many 'false starts'

embody some degree of simultaneous representation of different emotions, as in the *opere buffe*. The Act 1 finale however moves in a sense opposite from that of the traditional, accelerating *opera buffa* ensemble of confusion: it starts Allegro and ends Andante, with the principals on the stage bewailing the betrayal of Titus while the groans of the populace are heard in the distance. *La clemenza di Tito*, compared with the preceding operas, is no less refined in craftsmanship, and it shows Mozart responding with music of restraint, nobility and warmth to a new kind of stimulus.

Mozart's last work was the Requiem. Besides the little funeral motet *Ave verum corpus*, of June 1791, it was his first sacred work since the abandoned C minor Mass of 1783 (though there is evidence, biographically unexplained, that he embarked on a number of sacred works in the late 1780s). It was, as we have seen, left unfinished. On his death Constanze, or someone acting for her, gave the score first to Joseph Eybler to complete, but he did little more than add orchestral parts in certain skeletal passages. Eventually Süssmayr undertook responsibility for its completion. He afterwards claimed that the Sanctus, Benedictus and Agnus Dei were wholly his own work. He adapted Mozart's music of the opening two movements for the 'Lux aeterna' and 'Cum sanctis tuis', and orchestrated all the movements from the 'Dies irae' to the 'Hostias', for most of which Mozart had left a figured bass and in several movements at least a top line to indicate the continuity (his customary mode of drafting a score). To what extent Süssmayr's claims were true must remain uncertain. The evidence is untrustworthy: it was in his interest to say that much of the work was his own, and in Constanze's to say that her husband had virtually completed it. She said that she passed sketch material to Süssmayr, who was close to Mozart in those last weeks and may have known the composer's detailed intentions; but one is bound to wonder why Constanze did not turn to him immediately. On the evidence embodied in the extant material – Mozart's manuscript with Eybler's additions, Süssmayr's copy, and a few inconclusive sketches – Mozart's contributions to the remaining movements must remain a matter for conjecture. Süssmayr's completion has however been criticized, as clumsy and untrue to Mozart, by Richard Strauss, Bruno Walter and many others; several other completions have been essayed, notably by Franz Beyer (1971) and Richard Maunder (1981).

The Requiem is less diverse in style than the C minor Mass. Its tone, in the form in which it survives (for Mozart might have orchestrated later movements differently), is determined by the sombre basset-horns and bassoons that comprise the woodwind section; there are also trumpets and timpani, and the traditional trombones of liturgical music, as well as strings and continuo. The increasingly contrapuntal style of Mozart's later years, too, and the plainer melodic writing, conduce to a greater consistency. Several of the solo movements, notably the 'Recordare', involve contrapuntal treatment, and even some of the dramatic choruses, for example the 'Confutatis' and the 'Rex tremendae majestatis', embody canonic writing. The most dramatic, the 'Dies irae', remains largely homophonic. Mozart followed established Austrian traditions in several choral numbers. The opening 'Requiem aeternam' and the 'Quam olim Abrahae' fugue are influenced by Michael Haydn's Requiem of 1771 (which also used plainchant at 'Te decet hymnus'), and the influence of Gassmann and others in the Austrian, Fuxian tradition has been noted. The fugue subject of the Kyrie, embodying a characteristic falling diminished 7th, has been cited as an example of the influence of Bach or Handel but this is a traditional phrase with obvious contrapuntal potentialities, used in various forms by many composers including Haydn and Mozart himself (K426). Here it is treated in a straightforward double fugue; the 'Quam olim Abrahae', with its chromatic subject, its awkward rhythms and its ostinato string accompaniments, is less conventional. To what extent Mozart's ideas may have been used in the movements claimed by Süssmayr cannot be deduced on stylistic grounds; commentators have often reckoned however that the perfunctory 'Osanna' settings are unlikely to be Mozart's (though his too are usually brief), that the Benedictus seems too characteristic to be wholly Süssmayr's, and that the sombre D minor music that begins the Agnus Dei could well incorporate Mozartian material. Whether Mozart intended the music of the opening movements to be used for the last ones it is impossible to say, but there is precedent in his earlier works (for example the Mass K317); and it at least ensures that the Requiem ends in fully authentic tones.

23. Appearance

There are surprisingly few descriptions of Mozart. Some observers commented on his small stature; as a child he was short, and in about 1785 an anonymous English traveller (quoted by King, 1973–4) set his height at 'not more than about five feet and four inches'. All agreed, too, on his slight build, and several noted his habitual pallor and his fine fair hair. His sister reported that, though handsome as a child, he suffered some disfigurement from smallpox and became sallow after visiting Italy. The English traveller and Hummel noted a melancholy expression, but Hummel, Kelly and others remarked on his bright eyes and animated countenance when aroused – 'as impossible to describe it, as it would be to paint sunbeams' (Kelly).

Most of the authentic portraits, engravings and the like are reproduced in Deutsch's *Mozart und seine Welt in zeitgenössischen Bildern* (1961). Of them, the earliest of any importance is the Verona portrait of 1770, probably by Saverio dalla Rosa (fig. 3). The Della Croce family portrait of about 1780 (fig. 7) was noted by Nannerl as giving a particularly good likeness; the one of Mozart as Knight of the Golden Spur (fig. 5) gives a similar, rather severe appearance. A softer, more pensive expression is shown on the famous unfinished portrait by Joseph Lange, husband of Mozart's sister-in-law Aloysia, probably from 1789 (fig. 17); also from his late years comes, besides various medallions, silhouettes and engravings, the sensitive silverpoint drawing by Doris Stock, done in Dresden in 1789 (fig. 13).

24. Mozart studies

To judge by the more than normally laudatory tone of the obituaries and other tributes, Mozart's reputation stood high in Vienna and throughout the German lands at the time of his death. Although his music was widely criticized as audacious, too highly flavoured, and too complex for the ordinary listener to follow, it was widely understood that he was an artist far out of the ordinary, on a par with the other great Viennese composer of the time, Haydn. His operas, led by *Die Zauberflöte* and *Don Giovanni*, and at first *La clemenza di Tito*, were widely performed (though often in corrupt versions) and published many times over in the last years of the 18th century and the first of the 19th. His main mature works, of which only a small proportion were printed in his lifetime, began to appear in print. In 1798 Spehr of Brunswick and Breitkopf & Härtel of Leipzig embarked on collected editions, the former of his keyboard works, the latter more comprehensive; several other sets with similar aims were inaugurated in the following decades. The André firm in Offenbach, who negotiated with Constanze over Mozart's manuscript material, also published many of his works, some in critical editions.

Early biographies include the obituary of Schlichtegroll (1793), which uses Nannerl's and J. A. Schachtner's recollections, and Niemetschek's important life (1798). Comparisons of Mozart and Haydn were published by I. F. Arnold (1810) and Stendhal (1814). In 1828 the substantial biography by Georg

Nikolaus Nissen, Constanze's second husband, was published; in the next year Constanze and Nannerl met Vincent and Mary Novello, in Salzburg on a Mozart pilgrimage, and talked to them about Mozart (see Medici and Hughes, 1955).

In the mid-19th century interest in Mozart grew along with the general growth of interest in music of the past; most writers on his music, viewing it in the context of Beethoven and the early Romantics, and Bach, tended to dwell on its purity, beauty and sweetness. Nissen's biography was the main source for others of the 1840s, like those of Oulibicheff (Ulïbïshev) and Holmes. The first substantial scholarly biography, embodying fresh research, appeared in the centenary year, 1856 – Otto Jahn's *W. A. Mozart*. Six years later came Ludwig von Köchel's chronological thematic catalogue of Mozart's works, which, ahead of its time in scholarly method, gave the fullest possible source information; and Köchel was influential in the publication of the Breitkopf & Härtel collected edition, which began in 1877 and was largely finished in six years.

In the early decades of the 20th century Mozart scholarship made particular progress, with the beginning in 1912 of Wyzewa and Saint-Foix's highly schematic analytical and stylistic study of his works, the appearance in 1913 and 1914 of Dent's study of the operas and Schiedermair's critical edition of the letters, and the publication in 1919–21 of Hermann Abert's substantial revision of Jahn's biography. The first series of Mozart yearbooks began in the 1920s, lasting only three issues, like the second series in 1941–3, but including research more solid than the *Mitteilungen* of the leading Mozart societies, those in Berlin, Salzburg and Vienna. Mozart studies in England in the 1930s were stimulated by the scholarly and collecting activities of C. B. Oldman and later A. H. King, by the coming to England of Paul Hirsch and his Mozart collection, and by the appearance in 1938 of Emily Anderson's translation of the letters, the most complete edition then to be had. In 1937 Einstein published the third edition of the Köchel catalogue, following up Paul Graf von Waldersee's revision of 1905 with a more radical one involving much renumbering for his new chronology, which was based as much on stylistic argument as on source studies; there was a reprint with a supplement in 1947. Einstein's deeply perceptive if over-romantic book on the composer appeared in 1945.

The range of Mozart's works familiar to the musical public had not been large in the 19th century; in the 20th it greatly increased, with performances of more of the piano concertos and symphonies in particular, and the revival of *Idomeneo* and *Così fan tutte*, which entered the repertory only from the 1950s; by the 1970s, with the more general acceptance of *opera seria* conventions, a reconsideration of the dramatic viability of *La clemenza di Tito* was under way, and the earlier operas too had occasional revivals. Mozart's operas have occupied a specially prominent role at the Salzburg Festival and at the small opera house at Glyndebourne, Sussex (founded in 1934). The influence of the gramophone in the dissemination of his music, with the appearance, in the 1960s and 1970s of complete recordings of many entire categories of his works, has been profound.

All these developments were much encouraged by the bicentenary celebrations of 1956, which themselves came early in a new wave of Mozart scholarship. A third yearbook series had been instituted in 1950, by the

17. Mozart: unfinished portrait (probably 1789) by Joseph Lange

Internationale Stiftung Mozarteum in Salzburg, and the early 1950s also saw the foundation of a new series of *Mitteilungen* from the Mozarteum and of *Acta Mozartiana*. Still more crucial was the institution in 1955 of the Neue Mozart-Ausgabe, published by Bärenreiter, a new critical edition of all Mozart's works, with full prefaces and (eventually) critical commentaries. Its work was however hampered by the removal in World War II and the unavailability until 1980 of most of the largest single collection of Mozart autographs, that of the Prussian State Library, Berlin.

The most important individual Mozart scholar in the mid-20th century was O. E. Deutsch, who prepared, in association with the Neue Mozart-Ausgabe, a documentary biography (1961, supplement in 1978), a pictorial study of Mozart's life (1961) and, with W. A. Bauer and J. H. Eibl, a complete, critical edition of the family correspondence, richly annotated. The huge growth in Mozart studies is shown in Schneider and Algatzy's valuable *Mozart-Handbuch* of 1962, which contains a bibliography of nearly 4000 items, and by Angermüller and Schneider's even larger bibliography in the *Mozart-Jahrbuch 1975* (supplement in 1978). In 1964 the sixth edition of the Köchel catalogue appeared, with adjustments to the chronology, generally based on more exact palaeographic methods than Einstein's, with further revisions to the numbering system and a more rationally organized series of appendices dealing with unauthentic or doubtful works and arrangements. The work of the Neue Mozart-Ausgabe, in association with the 'Mozart towns' Augsburg, Salzburg and Vienna, has provoked a new wave of textual and source scholarship, typified by the detailed autograph studies of Wolfgang Plath, which along with Alan Tyson's paper studies (given a new lease of life by the availability in Kraków of the autographs from Berlin) have involved a re-examination of matters of dating and authenticity. Mozart's methods of composition, which have fascinated commentators since the time of Niemetschek and Rochlitz – particularly the semi-myth of his conceiving works entire in his head before committing anything to paper – have also been the subject of recent research.

WORKS

Editions: *W. A. Mozarts Werke*, ed. L. von Köchel and others (Leipzig, 1877–83, suppls. 1877–1910/*R* with changes) [MW]
W. A. Mozart: Neue Ausgabe sämtlicher Werke, ed. E. F. Schmid, W. Plath and W. Rehm, Internationale Stiftung Mozarteum Salzburg (Kassel, 1955–) [NMA; nos. shown, e.g. Werkgruppe (3)/Abteilung (2)/Band (i), page (273) – IV:3/2/i, 273; Abteilung and Band nos. not always applicable]

Catalogue: *Chronologisch-thematisches Verzeichnis sämtlicher Tonwerke Wolfgang Amade Mozarts*, ed. L. von Köchel (Leipzig, 1862; 2/1905 ed. P. Graf von Waldersee; 3/1937 ed. A. Einstein, with suppl. 1947; 6/1964 ed. F. Giegling, A. Weinmann and G. Sievers)

K – *no. in Köchel, 1862; for items not in 1862*
    edn. no. from 2/1905 or 3/1937 given
K⁶ – *no. in Köchel, 6/1964: nos. preceded by A. B or C*
    in appendices
sk – *associated sketch, draft or frag. material*

A – *Anhang* [appx]: *applicable only to edns. of Köchel before 6/1964*
BH – *no. in Breitkopf edn*
(D) – *date from MS of work (not always clear)*
(L) – *date from Mozart's letters*
(C) – *date from Mozart: Verzeichnüss aller meiner Werke (1784–91)*

Editions published in Mozart's lifetime are noted in the Remarks column, excluding arrangements, and, generally, pf reductions; references to movements are shown in small roman, e.g. k320/iii.

Items are arranged in each category by order of K⁶ numbers.
Numbers in the right-hand column denote references in the text.

MASSES, MASS MOVEMENTS, REQUIEM

K	K⁶	Title	Key	Scoring	Composition	MW	NMA	Remarks	
33	33	Kyrie	F	SATB, str	Paris, 12 June 1766 (D)	III/i, 2			
139	47a	Missa solemnis	c	S, A, T, B, SATB, 2 ob, 4 tpt, 3 trbn, timp, str, org	?Vienna, aut. 1768	I/i, 117	I:1/1/i, 37	'Waisenhausmesse'; perf. orphanage in Rennweg, Vienna, 7 Dec 1768	12, 30
49	47d	Missa brevis	G	S, A, T, B, SATB, [3 trbn,] str, org	Vienna, Oct–Nov 1768 (D)	I/i, 1	I:1/1/i, 3	frag. alternative settings of Gloria and Credo, kA20a/6266,25	30
65	61a	Missa brevis	d	S, A, T, B, SATB, str, org	Salzburg, 14 Jan 1769 (D)	I/i, 33	I:1/1/i, 159	perf. Salzburg, collegiate church, 5 Feb 1769	30
66	66	Missa	C	S, A, T, B, SATB, 2 ob, 2 hn, 2 [+2] tpt, [3 trbn,] timp, str	Salzburg, Oct 1769 (D)	I/i, 49	I:1/1/i, 185	'Dominicus' Mass; perf. Salzburg, St Peter, 15 Oct 1769, for Cajetan Hagenauer; extra wind pts. by Mozart and Leopold	13, 30, 37

	C 1.12								
140	140	Missa brevis	G	S, A, T, B, SATB, 2 vn, b	?Salzburg, 1773	—	I:1/I/i, 285	doubtful; incl. in K³ as 235d; MS pts. have autograph corrections	
167	167	Missa	C	SATB, 2 ob, 4 tpt, [3 trbn,] timp, 2 vn, b, org	Salzburg, June 1773 (D)	I/i, 179	I:1/I/ii, 3	'In honorem Ssmae Trinitatis'	42
192	186f	Missa brevis	F	S, A, T, B, SATB (2 tpt,) [3 trbn,] 2 vn, b, org	Salzburg, 24 June 1774 (D)	I/i, 239	I:1/I/ii, 75	tpts added later by Mozart (tpt 2 = K626b,20)	42, 43, 52
194	186h	Missa brevis	D	S, A, T, B, SATB, [3 trbn,] 2 vn, b, org	Salzburg, 8 Aug 1774 (D)	I/i, 265	I:1/I/ii, 121	sk K91/186i, MW, XXIV, no.32	42
220	196b	Missa brevis	G	S, A, T, B, SATB, 2 tpt [3 trbn,] timp, 2 vn, b, org	1775-6	I/i, 291	I:1/I/ii, 163	'Spatzenmesse'	52
262	246a	Missa [longa]	C	S, A, T, B, SATB, 2 ob, 2 hn, 2 tpt, [3 trbn, timp,] 2 vn, b, org	Salzburg, 1775	I/ii, 119	I:1/I/ii, 197		52
257	257	Missa	C	S, A, T, B, SATB, 2 ob, 2 tpt, [3 trbn,] timp, 2 vn, b, org	Salzburg, Nov 1776 (D)	I/ii, 1	I:1/I/iii, 3	'Credo'	52
258	258	Missa brevis	C	S, A, T, B, SATB, 2 tpt, timp, 2 vn, b, org	Salzburg, Dec 1776 (D)	I/ii, 55	I:1/I/iii, 115	'Spaur'	52
259	259	Missa brevis	C	S, A, T, B, SATB, 2 tpt, timp, 2 vn, b, org	Salzburg, Dec 1776 (D)	I/ii, 89	I:1/I/iii, 195	'Organ solo'	52
275	272b	Missa brevis	B♭	S, A, T, B, SATB, 2 vn, b, org	Salzburg, late 1777	I/ii, 183	I:1/I/iv	perf. Salzburg, St Peter, 21 Dec 1777	53
317	317	Missa	C	S, A, T, B, SATB, 2 ob, 2 hn, 2 tpt, 3 trbn, timp, 2 vn, b, org	Salzburg, 23 March 1779 (D)	I/ii, 207	I:1/I/iv	'Coronation'	70
337	337	Missa solemnis	C	S, A, T, B, SATB, 2 ob, 2 bn, 2 tpt, [3 trbn,] timp, 2 vn, b, org	Salzburg, March 1780 (D)	I/ii, 255	I:1/I/iv	frag. of different Credo in MW, XXIV, no.135	70
341	368a	Kyrie	d	SATB, 2 fl, 2 ob, 2 cl, 2 bn, 4 hn, 2 tpt, timp, str, org	?Munich, 1780-81	III/i, 31			89

K	K⁶	Title	Key	Scoring	Composition	MW	NMA	Remarks	
427	417a	Missa	c	2 S, T, B, SSAATTBB, fl, 2 ob, 2 bn, 2 hn, 2 tpt, 3 trbn, timp, str, org	Vienna, c July 1782–May 1783	XXIV, no.29	I:1/I/v	Credo inc., Agnus Dei not composed; Kyrie, Gloria perf. Salzburg, St Peter, 26 Oct 1783; see Davide penitente K496	84, 89, 90, 164, 165
626	626	Requiem	d	S, A, T, B, SATB, 2 basset hn, 2 bn, 2 tpt, 3 trbn, timp, str, org	Vienna, late 1791	XXIV, no.1	I:1/2/i–ii	inc.; completed by F. X. Süssmayr	30, 165

Kyrie frags.: C (49 bars), KA18/166f; D (12 bars), KA18/166f; 11: KA12/296b, lost; C (37 bars), K323, ?1788–9, MW, III/i, 22; D (11 bars), KA14/422a, ?1783, Gloria frag.: C (26 bars), KA20/323a, ?early 1778, MW, III/i, 11: KA12/296b, lost; C (37 bars), K323, ?1788–9, MW, III/i, 22; D (11 bars), KA14/422a, ?1783, Gloria frag.: C (26 bars), KA20/323a, ?1788–9. Sanctus/Benedictus frag.: E♭ (18 bars), K296c. Osanna frag.: C (21 bars), K223/166e, ?1772.

Doubtful and spurious masses (selective list): d, K90 (Kyrie), ?copy of another composer's work, MQ, xxvii (1951), 1: C, K115/166d, MW, XXIV, no.28, inc., ?by Leopold; F, K116/90a, MW, XXIV, no.33 with 417B (Quoniam), by Leopold (see Plath, MJb 1971–2, 21), C, KA185/C1.01, Novello no.17; E♭, KA235/C1.02, by B. Schack, in Periodical Collection of Sacred Music, no.4 (May 1831), ?additions by Mozart'; E♭ KA186/C1.03, Novello nos.13, 16; G, KA232/C1.04, Novello no.12 ('Twelfth Mass'); B♭, KA233/C1.06, Novello no.7; G, K140/C1.12, see above; G ('Missa solemnis pastorita'), kdeest/C1.18 (Munich, 1946); d ('Requiem brevis'), KA237/C1.90, Novello no.18: Kyrie, C, K340/C3.06: Kyrie, C, K221/A1, MW, XXIV, no.34, by Eberlin

LITANIES, VESPERS, VESPER PSALMS

K	K⁶	Title	Key	Scoring	Composition	MW	NMA		
109	74e	Litaniae Lauretanae BVM	B♭	S, A, T, B, SATB, [3 trbn,] 2 vn, b, org	Salzburg, May 1771 (D)	II, 1	I:2/i, 3		31, 43
125	125	Litaniae de venerabili altaris sacramento	B♭	S, A, T, B, SATB, 2 ob/fl, 2 hn, 2 tpt, [3 trbn,] str, org	Salzburg, March 1772 (D)	II, 13	I:2/i, 23		31
195	186d	Litaniae Lauretanae BVM	D	S, A, T, B, SATB, 2 ob, 2 hn, [3 trbn,] str, org	Salzburg, May 1774 (D)	II, 63	I:2/i, 135		43
193	186g	Dixit Dominus, Magnificat	C	S, T, SATB, 2 tpt, 3 trbn, 2 vn, b, org	Salzburg, July 1774 (D)	II, 169	I:2/ii, 1		43
243	243	Litaniae de venerabili altaris sacramento	E♭	S, A, T, B, SATB, 2 ob/fl, 2 bn, 2 hn, 3 trbn, str, org	Salzburg, March 1776 (D)	II, 109	I:2/i, 251		53
321	321	Vesperae de Dominica	C	S, A, T, B, SATB, [bn,] 2 tpt, [3 trbn,] timp, 2 vn, b, org	Salzburg, 1779	II, 193	I:2/ii, 33		71

71									
339	339	Vesperae solennes de confessore	C	S, A, T, B, SATB, [bn,] 2 tpt, [3 trbn,] timp, 2 vn, b, org	Salzburg, 1780 (D)	II, 237	I:2/ii, 101		29

Frag.: Magnificat, C, K321a. NMA. I:2/ii. 18 (7 bars)

SHORT SACRED WORKS

20	20	God is our refuge	g	SATB	London, July 1765	III/i, 47	III:9, 2	motet; autograph (partly in Leopold's hand) given to *GB-Lbm*, July 1765	29
33c	33c	Stabat mater		SATB	Paris and Salzburg, 1766			lost; in LC	
34	34	Scande coeli limina	C	S, SATB, 2 tpt, timp, 2 vn, b, org	Kloster Seeon, Bavaria, early 1767	III/ii, 1	I:3, 3	offertory	31
47	47	Veni Sancte Spiritus	C	S, A, T, B, SATB, 2 ob, 2 hn, 2 tpt, timp	Vienna, aut. 1768	III/i, 48	I:3, 12		
	47b	—		—	Vienna, late 1768			'lost; 'grand offertory' perf. at Waisenhauskirche, Vienna, 7 Dec 1768; offertory; ? = 47b	
117	66a	Benedictus sit Deus	C	S, SATB, 2 fl, 2 hn, 2 tpt, timp, str, org	Salzburg, 1769	III/ii, 21	I:3, 25		31
141	66b	Te Deum	C	SATB, 4 tpt, [timp,] 2 vn, b, org	Salzburg, end 1769	III/i, 133	I:3, 43		
143	73a	Ergo interest	G	S, str, org	Salzburg, late 1773	III/ii, 37	I:3, 62	motet; last 3 verses ?incorrectly attrib. J. André in one MS	
85	73s	Miserere	a	ATB, b	Bologna, July–Aug 1770	III/i, 58	I:3, 69		
44	73u	Cibavit eos	a	SATB, org	1770	XXIV, no.31		antiphon, doubtful; see Federhofer, *MJb 1960–61*, 43	
86	73v	Quaerite primum	d	SATB	Bologna, 9 Oct 1770	III/i, 62	I:3, 73	antiphon; exercise for Accademia Filarmonica, Bologna	16
108	74d	Regina coeli	C	S, SATB, 2 ob/fl, 2 hn, 2 tpt, timp, str, org	Salzburg, May 1771	III/i, 63	I:3, 74		31

K	K⁶	Title	Key	Scoring	Composition	MW	NMA	Remarks	
72	74f	Inter natos mulierum	G	SATB, 2 vn, b, org	Salzburg, May–June 1771	III/ii, 9	I:3, 9	offertory; for feast of St John the Baptist, 24 June	
127	127	Regina coeli	B♭	S, SATB, 2 ob/fl, 2 hn, str, org	Salzburg, May 1772	III/i, 87	I:3, 120		20, 31
165	158a	Exsultate, jubilate	F	S, 2 ob, 2 hn, str, org	Milan, Jan 1773	III/ii, 43	I:3, 157	motet, for Rauzzini; perf. Milan, 17 Jan 1773	
197	C3.05	Tantum ergo	D	SATB, 2 tr, str, org	?Salzburg, 1774	III/i, 149	I:3, 276	doubtful; see Münster, Acta Mozartiana, x (1963), 54	
198	C3.08	Sub tuum praesidium	F	S, T, str, org	?Salzburg, 1774	III/ii, 73	I:3, 177	offertory, doubtful, incl. in K³ as 158b; ?adaptation of secular work	
222	205a	Misericordias Domini	d	SATB, 2 vn, [va], b, org	Munich, early 1775	III/ii, 77	I:3, 182	offertory	45
260	248a	Venite populi	D	SSAATTBB, 2 vn ad lib, b, org	Salzburg, mid-1776	III/ii, 91	I:3, 199		
277	272a	Alma Dei creatoris	F	S, A, T, SATB, 2 vn, b, org	Salzburg, 1777	III/ii, 111	I:3, 223	offertory	
273	273	Sancta Maria, mater Dei	F	SATB, str, org	Salzburg, 9 Sept 1777 (D)	III/ii, 103	I:3, 234	gradual, for feast of BVM, 12 Sept	
A1	297a	Miserere (8 movts)		SATB, orch	Paris, March–April 1778	—	—	for work by Holzbauer; lost; see letter, 5 April 1778	
146	317b	Kommet her, ihr frechen Sünder	B♭	S, str, org	Salzburg, ?March–April 1779	VI/i, 81	I:4/iv, 33	aria	
276	321b	Regina coeli	C	S, A, T, B, SATB, 2 ob, 2 tpt, timp, 2 vn, b, org	Salzburg, ?1779	III/i, 118	I:3, 243		
343	336c	O Gottes Lamm; Als aus Aegypten	F; C	S, b	Prague, or Vienna, ?early 1787	III/i, 154	III:8, 30	Ger. sacred songs	
618	618	Ave verum corpus	D	SATB, str, org	Baden, 17 June 1791 (D)	III/ii, 123	I:3, 261	motet	138, 164

Frag.: In te Domine speravi, C, k.A23/[166f] (34 bars), 1774
Doubtful or spurious works (selective list):
copied by Mozart: Lacrimosa, c, k.A21/A2, MW, XXIV, no.30, by Eberlin; Justum deduxit (hymn), k326/A4, MW, III/ii, 117, by Eberlin; Adoramus te (hymn), k327/A10, MW, III/ii, 121, by Q. Gasparini; De profundis (psalm), k93/A22, MW, III/ii, 18, by G. von Reutter (ii); Memento Domine David (psalm), by Reutter
others: Salve regina, k92/C3.01; Salus infirmorum (hymn), k324/C3.02; Sancta Maria (hymn), k325/C3.03; Tantum ergo, B♭, k142/C3.04, MW, iii/1, 144, and NMA, I:3, 270 (?by J. Zach; see Münster, Acta Mozartiana, x (1963), 54: xii (1965), 9); Convertentur sedentes (offertory), k177 and 342/C3.09, MW, III/ii, 59, by Leopold: Venti, fulgura, procellae (motet). kdeest (see de Nys, Acta Mozartiana, xviii (1971), 7, and MJb 1971–2, 37)

CHURCH SONATAS

K	K⁶	Key	Scoring	Composition	MW	NMA
67	41h	E♭	2 vn, b, org	Salzburg, 1772	XXIII, 1	VI:16, 2
68	41i	B♭	2 vn, b, org	Salzburg, 1772	XXIII, 3	VI:16, 4
69	41k	D	2 vn, b, org	Salzburg, 1772	XXIII, 5	VI:16, 6
144	124a	D	2 vn, b, org	Salzburg, 1774	XXIII, 7	VI:16, 8
145	124b	F	2 vn, b, org	Salzburg, 1774	XXIII, 9	VI:16, 11
212	212	B♭	2 vn, b, org	Salzburg, July 1775 (D)	XXIII, 11	VI:16, 13
241	241	G	2 vn, b, org	Salzburg, Jan 1776 (D)		VI:16, 16
224	241a	F	2 vn, b, org	Salzburg, early 1780	XXIII, 14	VI:16, 18
225	241b	A	2 vn, b, org	Salzburg, early 1780	XXIII, 18	VI:16, 22
244	244	F	2 vn, b, org [solo]	Salzburg, April 1776 (D)	XXIII, 21	VI:16, 25
245	245	D	2 vn, b, org [solo]	Salzburg, April 1776 (D)	XXIII, 24	VI:16, 28
263	263	C	2 tpt, 2 vn, b, org [solo]	Salzburg, Dec 1776	—	VI:16, 32
274	271d	G	2 vn, b, org	Salzburg, 1777 (D)	XXIII, 27	VI:16, 36
278	271e	C	2 ob, 2 tpt, timp, 2 vn, b, org	Salzburg, March–April 1777	XXIII, 30	VI:16, 39
329	317a	C	2 ob, 2 hn, 2 tpt, timp, 2 vn, b, org [solo]	Salzburg, ?March 1779	XXIII, 41	VI:16, 49
328	317c	C	2 vn, b, org [solo]	Salzburg, ?early 1779	XXIII, 36	VI:16, 60
336	336d	C	2 vn, b, org [solo]	Salzburg, March 1780	XXIII, 51	VI:16, 65

Frag.: D, ĸA65a/124A

ORATORIOS, SACRED DRAMAS, CANTATAS

K	K⁶	Title (description, libretto)	Scoring	Composition	MW	NMA	Remarks	
35	35	Die Schuldigkeit des ersten Gebots (pt i of sacred drama, 3, I. A. Weiser)	3 S, 2 T, 2 ob/fl, 2 bn, 2 hn, trbn, str	Salzburg, early 1767	V/i	I:4/i	perf. Salzburg, 12 March 1767; pt ii by J. M. Haydn, pt iii by A. C. Adlgasser	10, 11, 32, 34, 35
42	35a	Grabmusik (cantata)	S, B, SATB, [2 ob,] 2 hn, str	Salzburg, 1767	IV/1, 1	I:4/iv, 1	?perf. Salzburg Cathedral, 7 April 1767; final recit and chorus added c1773	
118	74c	La Betulia liberata (oratorio, 2, Metastasio)	4 S, T, B, SATB, 2 ob/fl, 2 bn, 4 hn, 2 tpt, str	Italy and Salzburg, March–July 1771	IV/2, 1	I:4/ii	commissioned in Padua, apparently not perf.	18, 34, 35, 40
429	468a	Dir, Seele des Weltalls (cantata, L. L. Haschka)	T, TTB, fl, 2 ob, cl, 2 hn, bn, str	Vienna, 1785	XXIV, no.36a–b	I:4/iv, 96	inc.; partly completed M. Stadler	

K	K*	Title (description, libretto)	Scoring	Composition	MW	NMA	Remarks	
469	469	Davidde penitente (oratorio, 3, ?Da Ponte)	2 S, T, SATB, 2 fl, 2 ob, 2 cl, 2 bn, 2 hn, 3 trbn, timp, str	Vienna, March 1785	IV/2, 1		music from Mass k427/417a except for 2 arias, 6 and 11 March 1785 (C); perf. Burgtheater, 13 March	91
471	471	Die Maurerfreude (cantata, F. Petran)	T, TTB, 2 ob, cl, 2 hn, str	Vienna, 20 April 1785 (C)	IV/1, 24	I:4/iv, 35	perf. Lodge 'Zur gekrönten Hoffnung', 24 April 1785 (Vienna, 1785)	
619	619	Die ihr des unermesslichen Weltalls Schöpfer ehrt (cantata, F. H. Ziegenhagen)	S, pf	Vienna, July 1791 (C)	VII/1, 82	I:4/iv, 59		
623	623	Laut verkünde unsre Freude (cantata, E. Schikaneder)	2 T, B, fl, 2 ob, 2 hn, str	Vienna, 15 Nov 1791 (C)	IV/1, 40	I:4/iv, 65	perf. Lodge 'Zur neugekrönten Hoffnung', 18 Nov 1791	
623	623a	Lasst uns mit geschlungen Händen	S, ?	Vienna, ?Nov 1791			frag. of 32 bars, appended to 1st edn. of k623, pubd 1792; ?spurious	

OPERAS, MUSICAL PLAYS, DRAMATIC CANTATAS

K	K*	Title (description, libretto)	Scoring	First perf.	MW	NMA	Remarks	
38	38	Apollo et Hyacinthus (Lat. intermezzo, 3, ?P. F. Widl)	2 S, 2 A, T, B, 2 ob, 2 hn, str	Salzburg University, 13 May 1767	V/ii	II:5/i	perf. with Widl's Lat. play, Clementia Croesi	10, 23, 33
51	46a	La finta semplice (opera buffa, 3, M. Coltellini after Goldoni)	3 S, 2 T, 2 B, 2 fl/eng hn, 2 ob, 2 bn, 2 hn, str	Salzburg, Archbishop's palace, 1 May 1769	V/iv	II:5/ii	composed Vienna, mid-1768	12, 13, 23, 33, 34
50	46b	Bastien und Bastienne (Singspiel, 1, F. W. Weiskern and J. A. Schachtner after J. J. Rousseau: Le devin du village and C. S. Favart: Les amours de Bastien et Bastienne)	S, T, B, 2 ob/fl, 2 hn, str	Vienna, F. A. Mesmer's house, ?Sept–Oct 1768	V/iii	II:5/iii		12, 34

87	74a	Mitridate, rè di Ponto (opera seria, 3, V. A. Cigna-Santi after G. Parini and Racine)	4 S, A, 2 T, 2 fl, 2 ob, 2 bn, 4 hn, str	Milan, Regio Ducal Teatro, 26 Dec 1770	V/v	II:5/iv		16, 24, 34
111	111	Ascanio in Alba (festa teatrale, 2, Parini)	4 S, T, SATB, 2 fl, 2 ob/eng hn/serpentini, 2 bn, 2 hn, 2 tpt/hn, timp, str	Milan, Regio Ducal Teatro, 17 Oct 1771	V/vi	II:5/v	for wedding of Archduke Ferdinand of Austria and Maria Ricciarda Berenice of Modena	18, 35
126	126	Il sogno di Scipione (serenata, 1, Metastasio)	2 S, 3 T, 2 fl, 2 ob, 2 bn, 2 hn, 2 tpt, timp, str	Salzburg, Arch-bishop's palace, cMay 1772	V/vii	II:5/vi	? for installation of Colloredo as Prince-Archbishop of Salzburg	19, 35
135	135	Lucio Silla (opera seria, 3, G. de Gamerra)	4 S, 2 T, SATB, 2 ob/fl, 2 bn, 2 hn, 2 tpt, timp, str	Milan, Regio Ducal Teatro, 26 Dec 1772	V/viii	II:5/vii		19, 35
196	196	La finta giardiniera (opera buffa, 3, ?Calzabigi rev. Coltellini)	4 S, 2 T, B, 2 fl, 2 ob, 2 bn, 2 hn, 2 tpt/hn, timp, str	Munich, Assembly Rooms, 13 Jan 1775	V/ix	II:5/viii	perf. as Singspiel, Die verstellte Gärtnerin, Augsburg, 1 May 1780	44, 47, 52
208	208	Il rè pastore (dramma per musica, 2, after Metastasio)	3 S, 2 T, 2 fl, 2 ob/eng hn, 2 bn, 2 hn, 2 tpt/hn, str	Salzburg, Arch-bishop's palace, 23 April 1775	V/x	II:5/ix		47, 48, 50
A11	315e	Semiramis (duodrama, O. von Gemmingen)		?Mannheim, Nov 1778	—	—	lost; ?never started	71
345	336a	Thamos, König in Ägypten (play with music, 5, T. P. Gebler)	B, SATB, 2 fl, 2 ob, 2 bn, 2 hn, 2 tpt, 3 trbn, timp, str	Salzburg, ?1776–9	V/xii	II:6/i	? 2 choruses composed Vienna, 1773; final version ?1776–9	72
344	336b	Zaide (Singspiel, 2, Schachtner, after F. J. Sebastiani: Das Serail)	S, 2/3 T, 2 B, 2 fl, 2 ob, 2 bn, 2 hn, 2 tpt, timp, str	Salzburg, 1779–80	V/xi	II:5/x	inc.; lacks ov. and final chorus	61, 71, 88
366	366	Idomeneo, rè di Creta (opera seria, 3, G. Varesco after A. Danchet: Idoménée)	3 S, 3 T, B, SATB, 2 fl, 2 ob, 2 cl, 2 bn, 2 hn, 2 tpt, timp, str	(i) Munich, Hoftheater, 29 Jan 1781 (ii) Vienna, Auersperg Palace, March 1786	V/xiii	II:5/xi	with ballet, K367 perf. with K489, 490, both composed by 10 March 1786 (C)	71, 74, 76, 87, 89, 97, 109, 158, 170
384	384	Die Entführung aus dem Serail (Singspiel, 3, J. G. Stephanie jr after C. F. Bretzner: Belmonte und Constanze)	2 S, 2 T, B, SATB, 2 fl/pic, 2 ob, 2 cl/basset hn, 2 bn, 2 hn, 2 tpt, timp, str	Vienna, Burgtheater, 16 July 1782	V/xv	II:5/xii	vocal score (Vienna, 1785); for addl march see Croll, Mitteilungen der Internationalen Stiftung Mozarteum, xxviii/1–2 (1980), 2	72, 79, 80, 86, 87, 88, 107, 109, 115, 134, 147, 158

K	Kᵉ	Title (description, libretto)	Scoring	First perf.	MW	NMA	Remarks	
422	422	L'oca del Cairo (opera buffa, 2, Varesco)	3 S, 2 T, 2 B, [chorus,] 2 ob, 2 bn, 2 hn, str	—	XXIV, no.37	II:5/xiii	Salzburg and Vienna, late 1783, inc.; 1 trio complete, 6 nos. sketched; see Holschneider, Mf, xv (1962), 231	88
430	424a	Lo sposo deluso (opera buffa, 2, ?Da Ponte)	2 S, 2 T, 2 fl, 2 ob, 2 bn, 2 hn, 2 tpt, timp, str	—	XXIV, no.38	II:5/xiv	?begun 1783; only ov., trio and qt completed, 2 other nos. sketched	88
486	486	Der Schauspieldirektor (Singspiel, 1, Stephanie jr)	2 S, T, B, 2 fl, 2 ob, 2 cl, 2 bn, 2 hn, 2 tpt, timp, str	Schönbrunn Palace, Orangery, 7 Feb 1786	V/xvi	II:5/xv	completed Vienna, 3 Feb 1786 (C), see Kunze, MJb 1962–3, 156	109
492	492	Le nozze di Figaro (opera buffa, 4, Da Ponte after Beaumarchais)	5 S, 1/2 T, 3/4 B, SATB, 2 fl, 2 ob, 2 cl, 2 bn, 2 hn, 2 tpt, timp, str	(i) Vienna, Burgtheater, 1 May 1786 (ii) Vienna, Burgtheater, 29 Aug 1789	V/xvii	II:5/xvi	completed Vienna, 29 April 1786 (D); excerpts, vocal score (Berlin, 1790) with arias K577, 579	26, 70, 71, 95, 109, 110, *111*, 112, 113, 115, 124, 125, 128, 133, 135, 138, 143, 145, 146, 147, 148
527	527	Il dissoluto punito, ossia Il Don Giovanni (opera buffa, 2, Da Ponte)	3 S, T, 4 B, SATB, 2 fl, 2 ob, 2 cl, 2 bn, 2 hn, 2 tpt, 3 trbn, timp, mand, str	(i) Prague, National Theatre, 29 Oct 1787 (ii) Vienna, Burgtheater, 7 May 1788	V/xviii	II:5/xvii (concert version of ov., IV: 11/x, 23	Prague, 28 Oct 1787 (C); excerpts, vocal score (Speyer, 1788) and (Vienna, 1790–91) with addns K540a, b, c	112, 113, 115, 133, 135, 140, 143, 144, 145, 146, 148, 150, 151, 168
588	588	Così fan tutte, ossia La scuola degli amanti (opera buffa, 2, Da Ponte)	3 S, T, 2 B, SATB, 2 fl, 2 ob, 2 cl, 2 bn, 2 hn, 2 tpt, timp, str	Vienna, Burgtheater, 26 Jan 1790	V/xix	II:5/xviii	Jan 1790 (C); excerpts, vocal score (Vienna, 1790)	135, 143, 144, 148, 151, 161, 170
620	620	Die Zauberflöte (Singspiel, 2, E. Schikaneder)	7 S, 2 A, 4 T, 5 B, SATB, 2 fl/pic, 2 ob, 2 cl/basset hn, 2 bn, 2 hn, 2 tpt, 3 trbn, timp, glock, str	Vienna, Theater auf der Wieden, 30 Sept 1791	V/xx	II:5/xix	vocal nos. begun July 1791 (C), ov. and march completed 28 Sept 1791 (C); excerpts, vocal score (Vienna, 1791–2)	72, 139, 140, 158, 159, 160, 161, 162, 168
621	621	La clemenza di Tito (opera seria, 2, C. Mazzolà after Metastasio)	4 S, T, B, SATB, 2 fl, 2 ob, 2 cl/basset hn, 2 bn, 2 hn, 2 tpt, timp, str	Prague, National Theatre, 6 Sept 1791	V/xxi	II:5/xx	for Prague coronation of Leopold II; completed 5 Sept 1791 (C); plain recits ?not by Mozart; see Giegling, MJb 1967, 121; Plath, MJb 1971–2, 34	139, 140, 161, 162, *163*, 164, 168, 170

BALLET MUSIC

K	K⁶	Title	Scoring	Composition	MW	NMA	Remarks
A207	C27.06	[?for Ascanio in Alba]		?Milan, late 1771	—		9 nos. only extant, arr. pf; see Plath, *MJb 1964*, 111
A109	135a	Le gelosie del serraglio [for Lucio Silla]		?Milan, late 1772	—		?doubtful; autograph incipits for ballet of 32 nos., 6 from J. Starzer: Le cinque soltane; see Senn, *Acta Mozartiana*, xxxiii (1961), 169
A10	299b	Les petits riens	2 fl, 2 ob, 2 cl, 2 bn, 2 hn, 2 tpt, timp, str	Paris, May–June 1778	XXIV, no.10a	II:6/ii, 13	perf. 11 June 1778, Opéra, Paris, 66 after Piccinni: Le finte gemelle; 20 movts, ov. and 13 (of 20) by Mozart
A103	299d	La chasse (rondo)	2 fl, 2 ob, 2 bn, 2 hn	?Salzburg, 1778		II:6/ii, 112	1 movt
300	300	[Gavotte]	2 ob, 2 bn, 2 hn, str	?Paris, early 1778		II:6/ii, 46	?discarded movt of Les petits riens
367	367	[Ballet for Idomeneo]					see 'Operas'
446	416d	[Pantomime]	str	Vienna, Feb 1783	XXIV, no.18	II:6/ii, 120	perf. Vienna, Hofburg, 3 March 1783; only 5 of at least 15 nos. extant

Frag.: sketches K299c, for a ballet of 27 nos., ?Paris, early 1778

DUETS AND ENSEMBLES FOR SOLO VOICES AND ORCHESTRA

K	K⁶	First words (author)	Voices	Accompaniment	Composition	MW	NMA	Remarks
389	384A	Welch ängstliches Beben (Bretzner)	T, T	fl, ob, bn, 2 hn, str	Vienna, April–May 1782	XXIV, no.42		intended for Die Entführung aus dem Serail K384; inc.
479	479	Dite almeno in che mancai (G. Bertati)	S, T, B, B	2 ob, 2 cl, 2 bn, 2 hn, str	Vienna, 5 Nov 1785 (C)	VI/ii, 70	II:7/iii, 101	for F. Bianchi: La villanella rapita, perf. Burgtheater, 28 Nov 1785
480	480	Mandina amabile (Bertati)	S, T, B	2 fl, 2 ob, 2 cl, 2 bn, 2 hn, str	Vienna, 21 Nov 1785 (C)	VI/ii, 87	II:7/iii, 143	as 479 (Paris, 1789–90)

K	K*	First words (author)		Accompaniment	Composition	MW	NMA	Remarks
434	480b	Del gran regno delle amazzoni (G. Petrosellini: Il regno delle amazoni)	T, B, B	2 ob, 2 bn, 2 tpt, str	?Vienna, end 1785	XXIV, no.44	II:7/iv, 154	106 bars, inc., sketch; sk K626b/32-3
489	489	Spiegarti non poss'io	S, T	2 ob, 2 bn, 2 hn, str	Vienna, 10 March 1786 (C)	V/xiii	II:5/xi, 376	for Idomeneo K366
540b	540b	Per queste due manine (Da Ponte)	S, B	2 fl, 2 ob, 2 bn, 2 tpt, str	Vienna, 28 April 1788 (C)	V/xviii	II:5/xvii, 497	addn to Don Giovanni K527
625 615	592a 615	Nun liebes Weibchen Viviano felici (T. Grandi: Le gelosie villane)	S, B S, A, T, B		Vienna, 20 April 1791 (C)	—	—	see 'Arrangements' lost; known only from Mozart's catalogue; for perf. of Sarti: Le gelosie villane
VOCAL ENSEMBLES WITH PIANO OR ENSEMBLE								
A24a	43a	Ach, was müssen wir erfahren	S, S	pf	?Vienna, Oct 1767	—	III:9, 51	
436	436	Ecco quel fiero istante (Metastasio: Canzonette)	S, S, B	3 basset hn	?Vienna, 1783–6	VI/ii, 65	III:9, 31	notturno; ?partly by G. von Jacquin; see Plath, MJb 1971–2, 35
437	437	Mi lagnerò tacendo (Metastasio: Siroe)	S, S, B	2 cl, basset hn	?Vienna, 1783–6	VI/ii, 67	III:9, 35	as 436
438	438	Se lontan ben mio (Metastasio: Strofe per musica)	S, S, B	2 cl, basset hn	?Vienna, 1783–6	XXIV, no.46	III:9, 29	as 436
439	439	Due pupille amabili	S, S, B	3 basset hn	?Vienna, 1783–6	—	III:9, 26	as 436
346	439a	Luci care, luci belle	S, S, B	3 basset hn	?Vienna, 1783–6	—	III:9, 42	as 436
441	441	Liebes Mandel, wo is's Bandel (?Mozart)	S, T, B	str	Vienna, ?1783	VII/1, 25	III:9, 7	
532	532	[Grazie agl'inganni tuoi] (Metastasio: La libertà di Nice)	S, T, B	fl, cl, 2 hn, 2 bn, b	?Vienna, 1787	VII/1, 73	III:9, 62	26 bars without words based on M. Kelly's duet, 'Grazie agl'inganni tuoi'
549	549	Più non si trovano (Metastasio: L'Olimpiade)	S, S, B	3 basset hn	Vienna, 16 July 1788 (C)	VI/ii, 185	III:9, 44	authenticity of acc. doubtful

| A5 | 571a | Caro mio Druck und Schluck (Mozart) | S, T, T, B | ?pf | ?Vienna, 1789 | XXIV, no.50 | III:9, 64 | inc. |

Doubtful: Liebes Mädchen, S, S, B, K441c/C9.04, also ascribed to Haydn

ARIAS AND SCENES FOR VOICE AND ORCHESTRA

K	K⁶	First words (author)	Accompaniment	Composition	MW	NMA	Remarks
				for soprano			
23	23	Conservati fedele (Metastasio: Artaserse)	str	The Hague, Oct 1765	VI/i, 9; XXIV, no.54	II:7/i, 13	rev. Jan 1766; ? earlier version; ?(The Hague, 1766)
70	61c	A Berenice … Sol nascente	2 ob, 2 hn, str	Salzburg, ?Dec 1766	VI/i, 23	II:7/i, 47	?licenza for Sarti: Vologeso, Salzburg, 28 Feb 1767, or for perf. March 1769 — 32
78	73b	Per pietà, bell'idol mio (Metastasio: Artaserse)	2 ob, 2 hn, str	c1766	VI/i, 49	II:7/i, 17	
—	—	Quel destrier (Metastasio: L'Olimpiade)		c1766			lost; Constanze owned MS, 1799
—	73A	Cara se le mie pene (Metastasio: Demetrio)	2 hn, vn, va, b	Salzburg, c1769	—	II:7/i, 59	
A2		Misero tu non sei (Metastasio: Demetrio)		Milan, 26 Jan 1770 (L)	—	—	lost; known only from letter, 26 Jan 1770
88	73c	Fra cento affani (Metastasio: Artaserse)	2 ob, 2 hn, 2 tpt, str	Milan, Feb–March 1770	VI/i, 66	II:7/i, 65	15
79	73d	O temerario Arbace … Per quel paterno amplesso (Metastasio: Artaserse)	2 ob, 2 bn, 2 hn, str	c1766	VI/i, 54	II:7/i, 23	
77	73e	Misero me … Misero pargoletto (Metastasio: Demofoonte)	2 ob, 2 bn, 2 hn, str	Milan, March 1770	VI/i, 33	II:7/i, 83	15
82	73o	Se ardire, e speranza (Metastasio: Demofoonte)	2 fl, 2 hn, str	Rome, 25 April 1770 (D)	XXIV, no.48a	II:7/i, 103	
83	73p	Se tutti i mali miei (Metastasio: Demofoonte)	2 ob, 2 hn, str	Rome, April–May 1770	VI/i, 60	II:7/i, 115, 177	2 versions
74b	74b	Non curo l'affetto (Metastasio: Demofoonte)	2 ob, 2 hn, str	Milan or Pavia, early 1771	—	II:7/i, 125	

K	K*	First words (author)	Accompaniment	Composition	MW	NMA	Remarks	
217	217	Voi avete un cor fedele (after Goldoni: Le nozze di Dorina)	2 ob, 2 hn, str	Salzburg, 26 Oct 1775 (D)	VI/i, 93	II:7/i, 147	? for Galuppi: Le nozze di Dorina	
272	272	Ah, lo prevdi...Ah, t'invola agl'occhi miei (V. A. Cigna-Santi: Andromeda)	2 ob, 2 hn, str	Salzburg, Aug 1777 (D)	VI/i, 119	II:7/ii, 23		
294	294	Alcandro lo confesso... Non sò d'onde viene (Metastasio: L'Olimpiade)	2 fl, 2 cl, 2 bn, 2 hn, str	Mannheim, 24 Feb 1778 (D)	VI/i, 134	II:7/ii, 41, 151	2 versions	70
486a	295a	Basta vincesti... Ah, non lasciarmi (Metastasio: Didone abbandonata)	2 fl, 2 bn, 2 hn, str	Mannheim, 27 Feb 1778 (D)	XXIV, no.61	II:7/ii, 77	see Plath, Festschrift Walter Senn (Munich and Salzburg, 1975), 174	
316	300b	Popoli di Tessaglia...Io non chiedo (Calzabigi: Alceste)	ob, bn, 2 hn, str	Paris, July 1778; Munich, 8 Jan 1779 (D)	VI/i, 164	II:7/ii, 85		70
A3	315b	[Scena]	ob, 2 cl, 3 hn, pf, str	St Germain, Aug 1778	—	—	lost; for Tenducci; see Oldman, ML, xlii (1961), 44	
A11a	365a	Warum, o Liebe... Zittre, töricht Herz (?F. A. C. Werther)		Munich, Nov 1780	—	—	lost; sung in Gozzi: Le due notti affannose, trans. Werther (Salzburg, 1 Dec 1780)	
368	368	Ma che vi fece...Sperai vicino (Metastasio: Demofoonte)	2 fl, 2 bn, 2 hn, str	Salzburg, 1779-80	VI/i, 183	II:7/ii, 107		
369	369	Misera! dove son...Ah! non son io (Metastasio: Ezio)	2 fl, 2 hn, str	Munich, 8 March 1781 (D)	VI/i, 198	II:7/ii, 125		
374	374	A questo seno...Or che il cielo (G. de Gamerra: Sismano nel Mogol)	2 ob, 2 hn, str	?Vienna, April 1781 (L)	VI/i, 206	II:7/ii, 135		78
119	382h	Der Liebe himmlisches Gefühl	[2 ob, 2 hn, str]	?Vienna, 1782	XXIV, no.40	II:7/ii, 203	acc. extant only in kbd red.	
383	383	Nehmt meinen Dank	fl, ob, bn, str	Vienna, 10 April 1782 (D)	VI/i, 217	II:7/iii, 3		
416	416	Mia speranza adorata... Ah, non sai qual pena (G. Sertor: Zemira)	2 ob, 2 bn, 2 hn, str	Vienna, 8 Jan 1783 (D)	VI/ii, 2	II:7/iii, 11		89

					XXIV, no.41	II:7/iii, 210	
178	417e	Ah, spiegarti, oh Dio		?Vienna, June 1783	XXIV, no.41	II:7/iii, 210	acc. extant only in kbd red., ?version of K418
418	418	Vorrei spiegarvi, oh Dio	2 ob, 2 bn, 2 hn, str	Vienna, 20 June 1783 (D)	VI/ii, 11	II:7/iii, 25	for Anfossi: Il curioso indiscreto, Burgtheater, 30 June 1783
419	419	No, che non sei capace	2 ob, 2 hn, 2 tpt, timp, str	Vienna, June 1783 (D)	VI/ii, 21	II:7/iii, 37	as K418
490	490	Non più, tutti ascoltai… Non temer, amato bene	2 cl, 2 bn, 2 hn, vn solo, str	Vienna, 10 March 1786 (C)	V/xiii	II:5/xi, 192	for Idomeneo K366
505	505	Ch'io mi scordi di te … Non temer, amato bene	2 cl, 2 bn, 2 hn, pf, str	Vienna, 26 Dec 1786 (D)	VI/ii, 100	II:7/iii, 175	text from 1786 addn to Idomeneo K490
528	528	Bella mia fiamma … Resta, o cara (D. M. Scarcone: Cerere placata)	fl, 2 ob, 2 bn, 2 hn, str	Prague, 3 Nov 1787 (DC)	VI/ii, 146	II:7/iv, 37	for Josefa Dušek 114
538	538	Ah se in ciel, benigne stelle (Metastasio: L'eroe cinese)	2 ob, 2 bn, 2 hn, str	Vienna, 4 March 1788 (DC)	VI/ii, 161	II:7/iv, 57	
540c	540c	In quali eccessi … Mi tradì (Da Ponte)	fl, 2 cl, bn, 2 hn, str	Vienna, 30 April 1788 (DC)	V/xviii	II:5/xvii, 511	addn to Don Giovanni K527
569	569	Ohne Zwang, aus eignem Triebe	2 ob, 2 bn, 2 hn, str	Vienna, Jan 1789 (C)	—	—	lost; Mozart's catalogue: 'Eine teutsche Aria'
577	577	Al desio di chi t'adora (?Da Ponte)	2 basset hn, 2 bn, 2 hn, str	Vienna, July 1789 (DC)	V/xvii	II:5/xvi, 602	addn to Le nozze di Figaro K492
578	578	Alma grande e nobil core (G. Palomba)	2 ob, 2 bn, 2 hn, str	Vienna, Aug 1789 (DC)	VI/ii, 187	II:7/iv, 91	insertion in Cimarosa: I due baroni, Burgtheater, Sept 1789
579	579	Un moto di gioia (?Da Ponte)	fl, ob, bn, 2 hn, str	Vienna, Aug 1789 (DC)	VII/1	II:5/xvi, 597	addn to Le nozze di Figaro K492
580	580	Schon lacht der holde Frühling	2 cl, 2 bn, 2 hn, str	Vienna, 17 Sept 1789 (DC)	XXIV, no.48	II:7/iv, 168	insertion for Ger. version of Paisiello: Il barbiere di Siviglia, not used; orch inc.
582	582	Chi sa qual sia (?Da Ponte)	2 cl, 2 bn, 2 hn, str	Vienna, Oct 1789 (DC)	VI/ii, 195	II:7/iv, 105	for Martin y Soler: Il burbero di buon cuore, Burgtheater, 9 Nov 1789
583	583	Vado, ma dove? (?Da Ponte)	2 cl, 2 bn, 2 hn, str	Vienna, Oct 1789 (DC)	VI/ii, 203	II:7/iv, 115	as 582

Frags.: Per quel paterno amplesso (Metastasio: Artaserse), K73D, 3 bars only, c1766; In te spero (Metastasio: Demofoonte), K440/383h, MW, XXIV, no.47, 81 bars, v and b only

According to LC, c10 other arias (not necessarily for S) composed 1764–6; 5 Metastasio settings, Vienna, late sum.–aut. 1768

K	K*	First words (author)	Accompaniment	Composition	MW	NMA	Remarks
				for alto			
255	255	Ombra felice ... Io ti lascio	2 ob, 2 hn, str	Salzburg, Sept 1776 (D)	VI/i, 103	II:7/ii, 3	text from M. Mortellari: Arsace (Padua, 1775)
				for tenor			
21	19c	Va dal furor portata (Metastasio: Ezio)	2 ob, 2 bn, 2 hn, str	London, 1765	VI/i, 1	II:7/i, 3, 163	2 versions, 1 ed. Leopold 32
36	33i	Or che il dover ... Tali e cotanti sono	2 ob, 2 bn, 2 hn, 2 tpt, timp, str	Salzburg, Dec 1766	VI/i, 13	II:7/i, 33	licenza perf. anniversary of Archbishop Sigismund's consecration, 21 Dec 1766
71	71	Ah più tremar non voglio (Metastasio: Demofoonte)	2 ob, 2 hn, str	Salzburg, late 1769–early 1770	XXIV, no.39	II:7/iv, 145	only 48 bars extant
209	209	Si mostra la sorte	2 fl, 2 hn, str	Salzburg, 19 May 1775 (D)	VI/i, 83	II:7/i, 131	
210	210	Con ossequio, con rispetto	2 ob, 2 hn, str	Salzburg, May 1775 (D)	VI/i, 87	II:7/i, 139	
256	256	Clarice cara	2 ob, 2 hn, str	Salzburg, Sept 1776 (D)	VI/i, 113	II:7/i, 15	
295	295	Se al labbro mio non credi	2 fl, 2 ob, 2 bn, 2 hn, str	Mannheim, 27 Feb 1778 (D)	VI/i, 148	II:7/ii, 59, 167	2 versions; text from Hasse: Artaserse
435	416b	Müsst'ich auch durch tausend Drachen	fl, ob, cl, 2 bn, 2 hn, 2 tpt, timp, str	?Vienna, 1783	XXIV, no.45	II:7/iv, 162	orch inc.
420	420	Per pietà non ricercate	2 cl, 2 bn, 2 hn, str	Vienna, 21 June 1783 (D)	VI/ii, 31	II:7/iii, 51	for Anfossi: Il curioso indiscreto, not perf.
431	425b	Misero! o sogno ... Aura che intorni spiri	2 fl, 2 bn, 2 hn, str	?Vienna, Dec 1783	VI/ii, 39	II:7/iii, 81	
540a	540a	Dalla sua pace (Da Ponte)	fl, 2 ob, 2 bn, 2 hn, str	Vienna, 24 April 1788 (DC)	V/xviii	II:5/xviii, 489	addn to Don Giovanni K527
				for bass			
432	421a	Così dunque tradisci ... Aspri rimorsi atroci (Metastasio: Temistocle)	2 fl, 2 ob, 2 bn, 2 hn, str	?Vienna, 1783	VI/ii, 55	II:7/iii, 67	
512	512	Alcandro, lo confesso ... Non sò d'onde viene (Metastasio: L'Olimpiade)	fl, 2 ob, 2 bn, 2 hn, str	Vienna, 19 March 1787 (D)	VI/ii, 120	II:7/iv, 3	

K	K⁶	Title		Composition	VI/ii	II:7/iv	Remarks
513	513	Mentre ti lascio (Angioli–Morbilli: La disfatta di Dario)	fl, 2 cl, 2 bn, 2 hn, str	Vienna, 23 March 1787 (DC)	VI/ii, 133	II:7/iv, 19	
539	539	Ich möchte wohl der Kaiser sein (J. W. L. Gleim)	pic, 2 ob, 2 bn, 2 hn, perc, str	Vienna, 5 March 1788 (DC)	VI/ii, 177	II:7/iv, 79	Ger. warsong for F. Baumann, Leopoldstädter-Theater, 7 March 1788
541	541	Un bacio di mano (?Da Ponte)	fl, 2 ob, 2 bn, 2 hn, str	Vienna, May 1788 (C)	VI/ii, 180 ·	II:7/iv, 83	for Anfossi: Le gelosie fortunate, Burgtheater, 2 June 1788 128
584	584	Rivolgete a lui lo sguardo (Da Ponte)	2 ob, 2 bn, 2 tpt, timp, str	Vienna, Dec 1789 (C)	VI/ii, 209	II:7/iv, 123	for Così fan tutte K588; replaced by 'Non siate ritrosi'
612	612	Per questa bella mano	fl, 2 ob, 2 bn, 2 hn, db solo, str	Vienna, 8 March 1791 (DC)	VI/ii, 224		
A245	621a	Io ti lascio	str	?Prague, Sept 1791		II:7/iv, 139	?only vn pts by Mozart, rest by Jacquin; see Kunze, MJb 1967, 205; Plath, MJb 1971–2, 35

Frags.: Un dente guasto, k209a, 16 bars extant, sum. 1772; Männer suchen stets zu naschen, k433/416c, ?1783, MW, XXIV, no.43, orch barely sketched

SONGS

(pf acc. unless otherwise stated)

K	K⁶	Title	First words	Key	Author	Composition	MW	NMA	Remarks
53	47e	An die Freude	Freude, Königin der Weisen	F	J. P. Uz	Vienna, aut. 1768	VII/1, 2	III:8, 2	(Vienna, c1768)
147	125g		Wie unglücklich bin ich nit	F		Salzburg, ?1775–6	VII/1, 4	III:8, 4	
148	125h	Lobgesang auf die feierliche Johannisloge	O heiliges Band der Freundschaft	D	L. F. Lenz	Salzburg, ?1775–6	VII/1, 5	III:8, 4	
307	284d	Ariette	Oiseaux, si tous les ans	C	A. Ferrand	Mannheim, wint. 1777–8	VII/1, 12	III:8, 6	
308	295b	Ariette	Dans un bois solitaire	Ab	A. H. de la Motte	Mannheim, wint. 1777–8	VII/1, 14	III:8, 8	
343	336c	[2 Ger. church songs]							see 'Short sacred works'

K	K*	Title	First words	Key	Author	Composition	MW	NMA	Remarks
392	340a		Verdankt sei es dem Glanz	F	J. T. Hermes	Vienna, 1781–2	VII/1, 24	III:8, 15	
391	340b	[An die Einsamkeit]	Sei du mein Trost	B♭	Hermes	Vienna, 1781–2	VII/1, 23	III:8, 16	
390	340c	[An die Hoffnung]	Ich würd' auf meinem Pfad	d	Hermes	Vienna, 1781–2	VII/1, 22	III:8, 17	
349	367a	Die Zufriedenheit	Was frag ich viel	G	J. M. Miller	Munich, wint. 1780–81	VII/1, 18	III:8, 12	2 versions, one with mand acc.
351	367b		Komm, liebe Zither	C		Munich, wint. 1780–81	VII/1, 21	III:8, 14	mand acc.
A25	386d	[Gibraltar]	O Calpe!	D	J. N. C. M. Denis	Vienna, end 1782(L)	—	III:8, 72	only pf pt. sketched
178	417e		Ah, spiegarti, o Dio						see 'Arias and Scenes . . .' (soprano)
468	468	Lied zur Gesellenreise	Die ihr einem neuen Grade	B♭	J. F. von Ratschky	Vienna, 26 March 1785 (C)	VII/1, 34	III:8, 18	acc.: org in autograph, pf in Mozart's catalogue (Vienna, 1788)
472	472	Der Zauberer	Ihr Mädchen, flieht Damöten ja!	g	C. F. Weisse	Vienna, 7 May 1785 (C)	VII/1, 36	III:8, 20	
473	473	Die Zufriedenheit	Wie sanft, wie ruhig	B♭	Weisse	Vienna, 7 May 1785 (C)	VII/1, 38	III:8, 22	
474	474	Die betrogene Welt	Der reiche Tor	G	Weisse	Vienna, 7 May 1785 (C)	VII/1, 40	III:8, 24	(Vienna, 1788)
476	476	Das Veilchen	Ein Veilchen	G	J. W. von Goethe	Vienna, 8 June 1785 (C)	VII/1, 42	III:8, 26	(Vienna, 1789)
483	483		Zerfliesset heut', geliebte Brüder	B♭	A. V. von Schlittersberg	Vienna, end 1785	VII/1, 44	III:9, 20	masonic song, with male chorus
484	484		Ihr unsre neuen Leiter	G	Schlittersberg	Vienna, end 1785	VII/1, 46	III:9, 22	masonic song, with male chorus
506	506	Lied der Freiheit	Wer unter eines Mädchens Hand	F	J. A. Blumauer	Vienna, ? end 1785	VII/1, 48	III:8, 28	(Vienna, 1786)
517	517	Die Alte	Zu meiner Zeit	e	F. von Hagedorn	Vienna, 18 May 1787 (C)	VII/1, 50	III:8, 32	(Vienna, 1788)
518	518	Die Verschweigung	Sobald Damötas Chloen sieht	F	Weisse	Vienna, 20 May 1787 (C)	VII/1, 52	III:8, 34	(Vienna, 1788)
519	519	Das Lied der Trennung	Die Engel Gottes weinen	f	K. E. K. Schmidt	Vienna, 23 May 1787 (C)	VII/1, 54	III:8, 36	(Vienna, 1789)

				C			VII/1, 58	III:8, 40	
520	520	Als Luise die Briefe	Erzeugt von heisser Phantasie	C	G. von Baumberg	Vienna, 26 May 1787 (DC)	VII/1, 58	III:8, 40	
	523	Abendempfindung	Abend ist's	F	?J. H. Campe	Vienna, 24 June 1787 (C)	VII/1, 60	III:8, 42	(Vienna, 1789)
	524	An Chloe	Wenn die Lieb' aus deinen blauen	Eb	J. G. Jacobi	Vienna, 24 June 1787 (C)	VII/1, 64	III:8, 46	(Vienna, 1789)
	529	Des kleinen Friedrichs Geburtstag	Es war einmal, ihr Leutchen	F	J. E. F. Schall	Prague, 6 Nov 1787 (C)	VII/1, 68	III:8, 50	(Vienna, 1788)
	530	Das Traumbild	Wo bist du, Bild	Eb	L. H. C. Hölty	Prague, 6 Nov 1787	VII/1, 70	III:8, 52	
	531	Die kleine Spinnerin	Was spinnst du	C		Vienna, 11 Dec 1787 (C)	VII/1, 72	III:8, 54	(Vienna, 1787)
	552	Beim Auszug in das Feld	Dem hohen Kaiser-Worte treu	A		Vienna, 11 Aug 1788 (C)	—	III:8, 56	(Vienna, 1788)
	596	Sehnsucht nach dem Frühlinge	Komm, lieber Mai	F	C. A. Overbeck	Vienna, 14 Jan 1791 (C)	VII/1, 77	III:8, 58	(Vienna, 1791)
	597	Im Frühlingsanfang	Erwacht zum neuen Leben	Eb	C. C. Sturm	Vienna, 14 Jan 1791 (C)	VII/1, 78	III:8, 59	(Vienna, 1791)
	598	Das Kinderspiel	Wir Kinder	A	Overbeck	Vienna, 14 Jan 1791 (C)	VII/1, 80	III:8, 60	(Vienna, 1791)
	619	Die ihr des unermess-lichen Weltalls							see 'Oratorios'

Frags.: Ja! grüss dich Gott, K441a, 20 bars, ?Vienna, 1783; Einsam bin ich, K26/475a, 8 bars, ?Vienna, 1785

Lost: Per la ricuperata salute di Ophelia (Da Ponte), K411a/477a (set by Mozart, Salieri and 'Cornetti', mentioned in *Wienerblättchen*, 26 Sept 1785); Des Todes Werk und Vollbracht ist die Arbeit der Meister (G. Leon), Kdeest. 1786–90, see NMA, III:8, 78

Doubtful and spurious:

K52/46c: Daphne deine Rosenwangen, arr. by Leopold of Meiner Liebsten schöne Wangen (Bastien und Bastienne K51/46b) with new text, MW, VII/1, 1; NMA, II:5/iii, 90

K149/125d, Ich hab' es längst (Die grossmütige Gelassenheit), 1 by Leopold; MW, VII/1, 6; see Ballin, *Acta Mozartiana*, viii (1961), 18

K150/125e, Was ich in Gedanken küsse (Geheime Liebe), MW, VII/1, 7; as 149

K151/125f, Ich trachte nicht (Die Zufriedenheit), MW, VII/1, 8; as 149

K152/210a, Ridente la calma (canzonetta), adapted arr. ?by Mozart, of aria by Myslivecek, see MW, VII/1, 9; Flothuis, *MJb 1971–2*, 241

K350/C.8.48, Wiegenlied, by B. Flies, MW, VII/1, 20

CANONS

K	K⁶	Work and type	Key	Composition	MW	NMA	Remarks, alternative texts
89aI	73i	canon 4 in 1	A	1772	—	III:10, 71	
89	73k	Kyrie, 5 in 1	G	1772	III/i, 5	III:10, 3	
89aII	73r	1 Incipe Menalios, 3 in 1	F	1772	—	III:10, 73	
		2 Cantate Domino, 8 in 1	G				
		3 Confitebor, 2 in 1 (+1)	C				
		4 Thebana bella cantus, 6 in 2	B♭				
A109d	73x	14 canonic studies		1772			
—	—	canon 8 in 1	a	?Italy or Salzburg, 1770–71	—	—	see Zaslaw, MJb 1971–2, 419
229	382a	canon 3 in 1	c	?Vienna, c1782	VII/2, 2	III:10, 80	Sie ist dahin (Hölty)
230	382b	canon 2 in 1	c	?Vienna, c1782	VII/2, 4	III:10, 83	Selig, selig (Hölty)
231	382c	Leck mich im Arsch (Mozart), 6 in 1	B♭	?Vienna, c1782	VII/2, 5	III:10, 11	Lasst froh uns sein (Breitkopf)
233	382d	Leck mir den Arsch (Mozart), 3 in 1	B♭	?Vienna, c1782	VII/2, 11	III:10, 17	Nichts labt mich mehr (Härtel)
234	382e	Bei der Hitz' im Sommer ess ich (Mozart), 3 in 1	G	?Vienna, c1782	VII/2, 13	III:10, 20	Essen, trinken (Breitkopf)
347	382f	canon 6 in 1	D	?Vienna, c1782	VII/2, 15	III:10, 84	Wo der perlende Wein (Breitkopf): Lasst uns ziehn (Köchel)
348	382g	V'amo di core teneramente, 12 in 3	G	?Vienna, c1782	VII/2, 16	III:10, 24	
507	507	canon 3 in 1	F	Vienna, after 3 June 1786	VII/2, 18	III:10, 86	Heiterkeit und leichtes Blut (Härtel)
508	508	canon 3 in 1	F	Vienna, after 3 June 1786	VII/2, 18	III:10, 88	Auf das Wohl aller Freunde (Härtel)
—	508A	canon 3 in 1	C	Vienna, after 3 June 1786	—		
508a, 1–2	508a, 1–2	2 canons 3 in 1	F	Vienna, after 3 June 1786	—	III:10, 89	
508a, 3–8	508a, 3–8	6 canons 2 in 1	F	Vienna, after 3 June 1786	—	III:10, 90	
—	—	8 canons 2 in 1	F	Vienna, after 3 June 1786	—	III:10, 90	
—	—	canon 4 in 1	F	Vienna, ?sum. 1786	—	III:10, 97	
232	509a	Lieber Freistädtler, lieber Gaulimauli (Mozart), 4 in 1	G	Vienna, after 4 July 1787	VII/2, 8; XXIV, no.52	III:10, 27	Wer nicht liebt Wein (Härtel)
283	515b	canon 4 in 2	F	Vienna, 24 April 1787 (D)	VII/2, 1	III:10, 96	Ach! zu kurz (Härtel)

K	K⁶	BH	Key	Mvts	Scoring		Composition	MW	NMA	Remarks
553	553				Alleluia, 3 in 1	C	Vienna, 2 Sept 1788 (C)	VII/2, 19	III:10, 32	
554	554				Ave Maria, 4 in 1	F	Vienna, 2 Sept 1788 (C)	VII/2, 20	III:10, 34	
555	555				Lacrimoso son'io, 4 in 1	a	Vienna, 2 Sept 1788 (C)	VII/2, 21	III:10, 36	text earlier set by Caldara; Ach zum Jammer (Breitkopf)
556	556				Grechtel's enk (Mozart), 4 in 1	G	Vienna, 2 Sept 1788 (C)	VII/2, 23	III:10, 38	Alles Fleisch (Breitkopf)
557	557				Nascoso e il mio sol, 4 in 1	f	Vienna, 2 Sept 1788 (C)	VII/2, 25	III:10, 40	text earlier set by Caldara
558	558				Gehn wir im Prater (Mozart), 4 in 1	Bb	Vienna, 2 Sept 1788 (C)	VII/2, 27	III:10, 43	Alles ist eitel hier (Breitkopf)
559	559				Difficile lectu mihi mars (Mozart), 3 in 1	F	Vienna, 2 Sept 1788 (C)	VII/2, 29	III:10, 47	Nimm, ist's gleich warm (Breitkopf)
560a	559a				O du eselhafter Peierl! (Mozart), 4 in 1	F	Vienna, 2 Sept 1788 (C)	VII/2, 36	III:10, 49, 55	versions K560, MW, VII, 2, 31, in F or G with slightly different words; Gähnst du (Breitkopf)
561	561				Bona nox! bist a rechta Ox (Mozart), 4 in 1	A	Vienna, 2 Sept 1788 (C)	VII/2, 37	III:10, 62	Gute Nacht (Breitkopf)
562	562				Caro bell'idol mio, 3 in 1	A	Vienna, 2 Sept 1788 (C)	VII/2, 39	III:10, 65	text earlier set by Caldara; Ach süsses teures Leben (Breitkopf)
562a	562a				canon 4 in 1	Bb	?Vienna	—	III:10, 98	
A191	562c				[? for 2 vn, va, b] 4 in 1	C	?Vienna	XXIV, no.51	III:10, 68	

SYMPHONIES, SYMPHONY MOVEMENTS

K	K⁶	BH	Key	Mvts	Scoring		Composition	MW	NMA	Remarks	
16	16	1	Eb	3	2 ob, 2 hn, str		London, 1764 5, ?London, 1765	VIII/i, 1	IV:11/i		22, 25
A220	16a		a/?A					—	—	lost; in Breitkopf catalogue	
19	19	4	D	3	2 ob, 2 hn, str		London, 1765, ?London, 1765	VIII/i, 37	IV:11/i		22
A223	19a		F	3	2 ob, 2 hn, str		?London, 1765	—	IV:11/i		redescovered 1981 (Kassel, 1981)
A222	19b		C				?London, 1765	—	—	lost; in Breitkopf catalogue	
22	22	5	Bb	3	2 ob, 2 hn, str		The Hague, Dec 1765	VIII/i, 47	IV:11/i		22

K	K*	BH	Key	Movts	Scoring	Composition	MW	NMA	Remarks	
76	42a	43	F	4	2 ob, 2 bn, 2 hn, str	?Vienna, 1767	XXIV, no.3	IV:11/i	?doubtful	23, 33
43	43	6	F	4	2 ob/fl, 2 hn, str	Vienna, 1767	VII/i, 56	IV:11/i		23
45	45	7	D	4	2 ob, 2 hn, 2 tpt, timp, str	Vienna, 16 Jan 1768 (D)	VIII/i, 69	IV:11/i	adapted as ov. to La finta semplice	
A221	45a		G	3	2 ob, 2 hn, str	The Hague, late 1765–early 1766	—	IV:11/i	'Lambach'	
A214	45b	8	B♭	4	2 ob, 2 hn, str	?Vienna, 1768	—	IV:11/i		
48	48		D	4	2 ob, 2 hn, 2 tpt, timp, str	Vienna, 13 Dec 1768 (D)	VIII/i, 81	IV:11/i		23
A215	66c		D	4	2 ob, 2 bn, 2 hn, str	?Salzburg, ?1769	—	—	lost; incipit in Breitkopf catalogue	
A217	66d		B♭		2 fl, 2 hn, str	?Salzburg, ?1769	—	—	lost; see 66c	
A218	66e		B♭		2 fl, 2 ob, 2 bn, 2 hn, str	?Salzburg, ?1769	—	—	lost; see 66c	24
73	73	9	C	4	2 ob/fl, 2 hn, 2 tpt, timp, str	Salzburg, early sum. 1772	VIII/i, 97	IV:11/i		24
81	73l	44	D	3	2 ob, 2 hn, str	Rome, April 1770	XXIV, no.4	IV:11/i	also attrib. Leopold	24
97	73m	47	D	4	2 ob, 2 hn, 2 tpt, timp, str	Rome, April 1770	XXIV, no.4	IV:11/i		24
95	73n	45	D	4	2 fl, 2 tpt, str	Rome, April 1770	XXIV, no.5	IV:11/ii		24
84	73q	11	D	3	2 ob, 2 hn, str	Milan or Bologna, 1770	VII/i, 121	IV:11/ii	also attrib. Leopold, Dittersdorf and others; see LaRue, MJb 1971–2, 48	24
74 A216	74 C11.03	10 —	G B♭	3 4	2 ob, 2 hn, str 2 ob, 2 hn, str	Milan, 1770 Milan or Salzburg, 1770–71	VIII/i, 110 —	IV:11/ii —	K²74g, doubtful; see Allroggen, AnMc, no. 18 (1978), 237	24
75	75	42	F	4	2 ob, 2 hn, str	Salzburg, 1771	XXIV, no.2	IV:11/ii		24
110	75b	12	G	4	2 ob/fl, 2 bn, 2 hn, str	Salzburg, July 1771 (D)	VIII/i, 135	IV:11/ii		24
120	111a		D	1	2 fl, 2 ob, 2 hn, 2 tpt, timp, str	Milan, Oct–Nov 1771	XXIV, no.9	IV:11/ii	finale, to form sym. with ov. Ascanio in Alba K111	26
96	111b	46	C	4	2 ob, 2 hn, 2 tpt, timp, str	Milan, Oct–Nov 1771	XXIV, no.6	IV:11/ii		24
112	112	13	F	4	2 ob, 2 hn, str	Milan, 2 Nov 1771 (D)	VIII/i, 149	IV:11/ii		24
114	114	14	A	4	2 fl/ob, 2 hn, str	Salzburg, 30 Dec 1771 (D)	VIII/i, 161	IV:11/ii		24, 26

K	K⁶	No.	Key	Movts	Scoring	Composed	NMA	IV:11	Remarks	Page
124	124	15	G	4	2 ob, 2 hn, str	Salzburg, 21 Feb 1772 (D)	VIII/i, 175	IV:11/ii		25
128	128	16	C	3	2 ob, 2 hn, str	Salzburg, May 1772 (D)	VIII/i, 187	IV:11/iii, 1		25
129	129	17	G	3	2 ob, 2 hn, str	Salzburg, May 1772 (D)	VIII/i, 199	IV:11/iii, 15		25
130	130	18	F	4	2 fl, 4 hn, str	Salzburg, May 1772 (D)	VIII/i, 215	IV:11/iii, 31		25, 130
132	132	19	Eb	4	2 ob, 4 hn, str	Salzburg, July 1772 (D)	VIII/i, 233	IV:11/iii, 52	alternative slow movts; see Plath, Mf, xxvii (1974), 93	25
133	133	20	D	4	fl, 2 ob, 2 hn, 2 tpt, str	Salzburg, July 1772 (D)	VIII/i, 252	IV:11/iii, 78		26
134	134	21	A	4	2 fl, 2 hn, str	Salzburg, Aug 1772 (D)	VIII/i, 271	IV:11/iii, 102		26
161, 163	141a	50	D	3	2 fl, 2 ob, 2 hn, 2 tpt, timp, str	Salzburg, 1773–4	XXIV, no.10 [163 only]	IV:11/iii, 123	movts K161 from ov. Il sogno di Scipione K126 with finale K163	26
184	161a	26	Eb	3	2 fl, 2 ob, 2 bn, 2 hn, 2 tpt, str	Salzburg, 30 March 1773 (D)	VIII/ii, 58	IV:11/iv, 15		40
199	161b	27	G	3	2 fl, 2 hn, str	Salzburg, 10 [?16] April 1773 (D)	VIII/ii, 79	IV:11/iv, 37		40
162	162	22	C	3	2 ob, 2 hn, 2 tpt, str	Salzburg, 19 [?29] April 1773 (D)	VIII/ii, 1	IV:11/iv, 1		40
181	162b	23	D	3	2 ob, 2 hn, 2 tpt, str	Salzburg, 19 May 1773 (D)	VIII/ii, 13	IV:11/iv, 57		40
182	173dA	24	Bb	3	2 ob/fl, 2 hn, str	Salzburg, 3 Oct 1773 (D)	VIII/ii, 39	IV:11/iv, 75		40
183	173dB	25	g	4	2 ob, 2 bn, 4 hn, str	Salzburg, 5 Oct 1773 (D)	VIII/ii, 39	IV:11/iv, 87		40
201	186a	29	A	4	2 ob, 2 hn, str	Salzburg, 6 April 1774 (D)	VIII/ii, 117	IV:11/v, 1		41
202	186b	30	D	4	2 ob, 2 hn, 2 tpt, str	Salzburg, 5 May 1774 (D)	VIII/ii, 141	IV:11/v, 26		41
200	189k	28	C	4	2 ob, 2 hn, 2 tpt, timp, str	Salzburg, 17 [?12] Nov 1774 [?1773] (D)	VIII/ii, 95	IV:11/iv, 107		41
121	207a		D	1	2 ob, 2 hn, str	Salzburg, end 1774–early 1775	X, 42	IV:11/v, 44	finale, to form sym. with ov. La finta giardiniera K196	
			D	4	2 ob, 2 bn, 2 hn, 2 tpt, str		—	IV:11/vii, 1	movts from Serenade K204/213a	

K	K	BH	Key	Movts	Scoring	Composition	MW	NMA	Remarks	
102	213c		C	1	2 ob/fl, 2 hn, 2 tpt, str	Salzburg, April and Aug 1775	XXIV, no.8	IV:11/v, 139	finale, to form sym. with versions of ov. and 1st aria of Il rè pastore K208	
			D	4	2 ob, 2 bn, 2 hn, 2 tpt, timp, str		—	IV:11/vii, 31	movts from Serenade K250/248b with new timp pt.	107
297	300a	31	D	3	2 fl, 2 ob, 2 cl, 2 bn, 2 hn, 2 tpt, timp, str	Paris, June 1778	VIII/ii, 157	IV:11/v, 57	'Paris'; 2 slow movts, original in 1st edn. (Paris, 1788)	
A8	311A						—	—	never written; see Zaslaw, MT, cxix (1978), 753	
318	318	32	G	1	2 fl, 2 ob, 2 bn, 4 hn, 2 tpt, timp, str	Salzburg, 26 April 1779 (D)	VIII/ii, 197	IV:11/vi, 3	ov., ? for Zaide K344/336b	66, 67
319	319	33	Bb	4	2 ob, 2 bn, 2 hn, str	Salzburg, 9 July 1779 (D)	VIII/ii, 213	IV:11/vi, 23	3rd movt (minuet) later addn: (Vienna, 1785) as op.7 no.2	66, 67
			D	3	2 ob, 2 bn, 2 hn, 2 tpt, timp, str		—	IV:11/viii, 89	movts from Serenade K320 with added timp	
338	338	34	C	3	2 ob, 2 bn, 2 hn, 2 tpt, timp, str	Salzburg, 29 Aug 1780 (D)	VIII/ii, 239	IV:11/vi, 59	minuet (after 1st movt) cancelled in autograph; see K409/383f	67, 132
409	383f		C	1	2 fl, 2 ob, 2 bn, 2 hn, 2 tpt, timp, str	?Vienna, May 1782	X, 48	IV:11/x, 3	minuet, ? for K338	67
385	385	35	D	4	2 fl, 2 ob, 2 cl, 2 bn, 2 hn, 2 tpt, timp, str	Vienna, July 1782 (D)	VIII/iii, 1	IV:11/vi, 113	'Haffner'; orig. intended as serenade, with March K408.2/385a and another minuet (lost); fls and cls later addns; (Vienna, 1785) as op.7 no.1	82, 107, 126
425	425	36	C	4	2 ob, 2 bn, 2 hn, 2 tpt, timp, str	Linz, Oct–Nov 1783	VIII/iii, 37	IV:11/viii, 3	'Linz'	84, 107
444	425a	37	G	2	2 ob, 2 hn, str	?Linz, Nov 1783, or later	VIII/iii, 81		introduction for M. Haydn: Sym. P16	
504	504	38	D	3	2 fl, 2 ob, 2 bn, 2 hn, 2 tpt, timp, str	Vienna, 6 Dec. 1786 (C)	VIII/iii, 97	IV:11/viii, 63	'Prague'	112, 126, 128, 151

543	39	Eb	4 fl, 2 cl, 2 bn, 2 hn, 2 tpt, timp, str	Vienna, 26 June 1788 (C)	VIII/iii, 137	IV:11/ix, 1		128, 130, 132
550	40	g	4 fl, 2 ob, (2 cl,) 2 bn, 2 hn, str	Vienna, 25 July 1788 (C)	VIII/iii, 181	IV:11/ix, 63, 125	2 versions, 1st without cls	128, 130, 133
551	41	C	4 fl, 2 ob, 2 bn, 2 hn, 2 tpt, timp, str	Vienna, 10 Aug 1788 (C)	VIII/iii, 230	IV:11/ix, 187	'Jupiter'	128, 130, 132

Frags., sketches: K.A100/383g, Eb, lost, pt. of 1st movt formerly extant: K383i, C, ? for sym. or ov.
Doubtful or spurious: K17/C11.02, Bb [BH no.2] MW, VIII/i, 13: K.A216/C11.03, Bb, MW, XXIV, no.63; K18/A51, Eb [BH no.3], MW, VIII/i, 23 (by C. F. Abel); 'New Lambach', A-LA, G (see Abert, 1964 and Zaslaw, 1983); K98/C11.04, F, MW, XXIV, no.56; K291/A52, Fugue, D, by M. Haydn, MW, XXIV, no.11; K311a/C11.05, Bb, ?spurious, '2nd Paris symphony'

CASSATIONS, SERENADES, DIVERTIMENTOS, MISCELLANEOUS WORKS

K	Kᵃ	Title	Key, movts	Scoring	Composition	MW	NMA	Remarks	
32	32	Gallimathias musicum		hpd, 2 ob, 2 hn, 2 bn, str	The Hague, March 1766	XXIV, no.12	IV:12/i, 3		
41a	41a	6 divertimentos			Salzburg, 1767	—	—	lost; in LC	
100	62a	Cassation	D, 8	fl, hn, tpt, trbn. vn, va, vc	Salzburg, 1769	IX/i, 33	IV:12/i, 67	with march K62	23, 24
63	63	Cassation	G, 7	2 ob/fl, 2 hn, 2 tpt, str	Salzburg, 1769	IX/i, 1	IV:12/i, 25		23
—	—	Cassation	C	2 ob, 2 hn, str	?Salzburg, 1769	—	—	lost; see letter, 18 Aug 1771	
99	63a	Cassation	Bb, 7	2 ob, 2 hn, str	Salzburg, 1769	IX/i, 19	IV:12/i, 45		23
113	113	Divertimento	Eb, 4	2 cl, 2 hn (or 2 ob, ?2 cl, 2 eng hn, ?2 bn, 2 hn), str	Milan, Nov 1771	IX/ii, 1	IV:12/ii, 3	'Concerto o sia Divertimento'; rev. orch. early 1773	?28
136-8	125a-c	3 Divertimentos			Salzburg, 1772			see 'Chamber Music: String Quartets'	28, 29
131	131	Divertimento	D, 7	fl, ob, bn, 4 hn, str	Salzburg, June 1772	IX/ii, 15	IV:12/ii, 29		28
205	167A	Divertimento	D, 5	2 bn, bn, str (solo)	Salzburg, ?1773	IX/ii, 73	VII:18, 7	with march K290/167AB	39
185	167a	Serenade	D, 7	2 ob/fl, 2 hn, 2 tpt, vn solo, str	Vienna, July–Aug 1773	IX/i, 61	IV:12/ii, 76	with march K189/167b	39
203	189b	Serenade	D, 8	2 ob/fl, bn, 2 hn, 2 tpt, vn solo, str	Salzburg, Aug 1774 (D)	IX/i, 97	IV:12/iii, 7	with march K237/189c	42

K	K*	Title	Key, movts	Scoring	Composition	MW	NMA	Remarks	
204	213a	Serenade	D, 7	2 ob/fl, bn, 2 hn, 2 tpt, vn solo, str	Salzburg, 5 Aug 1775 (D)	IX/i, 133	IV:12/iii, 60	with march K215/213b; see also 'Symphonies'	48
239	239	Serenata notturna	D, 3	2 vn, va, db (solo); str, timp	Salzburg, Jan 1776 (D)	IX/i, 177	IV:12/iii, 114		51
247	247	Divertimento	F, 6	2 hn, str (solo)	Salzburg, June 1776 (D)	IX/ii, 98	VII:18, 28	with march K248; sk, K288/246c	51
250	248b	Serenade	D, 9	2 ob/fl, 2 bn, 2 hn, 2 tpt, vn solo, str	Salzburg, June 1776 (D)	IX/i, 193	IV:12/iv, 8	'Haffner'; with march K249; see also 'Symphonies'	51, 250
251	251	Divertimento	D, 6	ob, 2 hn, str (solo)	Salzburg, July 1776 (D)	IX/ii, 121	VII:18, 67		51
286	269a	Notturno	D, 3	4 groups, each 2 hn, str (solo)	Salzburg, Dec 1776–Jan 1777	IX/i, 293	IV:12/v		51
287	271H	Divertimento	B♭, 6	2 hn, str (solo)	Salzburg, June 1777	IX/ii, 168	VII:18, 103		51
320	320	Serenade	D, 7	2 fl/pic, 2 ob, 2 bn, 2 hn, posthorn, 2 tpt, timp, str	Salzburg, 3 Aug 1779 (D)	IX/i, 325	IV:12/v	'Posthorn'; with 2 marches, K335/320c; see also 'Symphonies', 'Concertos (wind insts)'	67, 69
334	320b	Divertimento	D, 6	2 hn, str (solo)	Salzburg, 1779–80	IX/ii, 208	VI:18. 158	with march K445/320c	68
477	479a	Maurerische Trauermusik	c	2 ob, cl, 3 basset hn, dbn, 2 hn, str	Vienna, Nov 1785	X, 53	IV:11/x,11	July 1785 (C)	
522	522	Ein musikalischer Spass	F, 4	2 hn, str (solo)	Vienna, 14 June 1787 (C)	X, 58	VII:18, 223	sk, KA108/522a	118
525	525	Eine kleine Nachtmusik	G, 4	2 vn, va, vc, b (solo)	Vienna, 10 Aug 1787 (C)	XIII, 181	IV:12/vi, 43	orig. 5 movts, 2nd lost; sk KA69/525a	118

Frag.: K246b/320B, 2 hn, str, end 1772–early 1773

WIND ENSEMBLE

K	K⁶	Title	Key	Scoring	Composition	MW	NMA	Remarks	
33a	33a	Solos		fl, [?bc]	Lausanne, Sept 1766	—	—	lost; in LC	
33h	33h	Piece		hn [+?]	?Salzburg, 1766	—	—	lost; mentioned in Leopold's letter, 16 Feb 1778	
41b	41b	Pieces		2 tpt/2 hn/2 basset hn	Salzburg, 1767	—	—	lost; in LC	
186	159b	Divertimento	B♭	2 ob, 2 cl, 2 eng hn, 2 hn, 2 bn	Milan, March 1773	IX/ii, 57	VII:17/i		
166	159d	Divertimento	E♭	2 ob, 2 cl, 2 eng hn, 2 hn, 2 bn	Salzburg, 24 March 1773 (D)	IX/ii, 47	VII:17/i		
213	213	Divertimento	F	2 ob, 2 bn, 2 hn	Salzburg, July 1775 (D)	IX/ii, 83	VII:17/i		
240	240	Divertimento	B♭	2 ob, 2 bn, 2 hn	Salzburg, Jan 1776 (D)	IX/ii, 89	VII:17/i		
252	240a	Divertimento	E♭	2 ob, 2 bn, 2 hn	Salzburg, early 1776	IX/ii, 147	VII:17/i		
188	240b	Divertimento	C	2 fl, 5 tpt, timp	Salzburg, mid-1773	IX/ii, 69	VII:17/i		
253	253	Divertimento	F	2 ob, 2 bn, 2 hn	Salzburg, Aug 1776 (D)	IX/ii, 152	VII:17/i		
270	270	Divertimento	B♭	2 ob, 2 bn, 2 hn	Salzburg, Jan 1777 (D)	IX/ii, 159	VII:17/i		
289	271g	Divertimento	E♭	2 ob, 2 bn, 2 hn	?Salzburg, 1777	IX ii, 198	VII:17/i	?doubtful	51
361	370a	Serenade	B♭	2 ob, 2 cl, 2 basset hn, 2 bn, 4 hn, db	Vienna, 1781 or 1781-4	IX/i, 399	VII:17/ii, 141		76, 86, 99
375	375	Serenade	E♭	(2 ob,) 2 cl, 2 bn, 2 hn	Vienna, Oct 1781	IX/i, 455	VII:17/ii, 3, 41	obs added in 2nd version, July 1782 arr. as str qnt, K406/516b	25, 98
388	384a	Serenade	c	2 ob, 2 cl, 2 bn, 2 hn	Vienna, ?July 1782 or late 1783	IX/i, 481	VII:17/ii, 97		98, 133
A229	439b	5 divertimentos	B♭	2 basset hn/cl, bn; 3 basset hn	Vienna, ?1783 or later	XXIV, no.62	VIII:21, 67, 78, 89, 105, 114 (also 167)	see Whewell, MT, ciii (1962), 19; Flothuis, MJb 1973-4, 202	98
411	484a	Adagio	B♭	2 cl, 3 basset hn	?Vienna, end 1785	X, 80	VII:17/ii, 223		
410	440d	Adagio	F	2 basset hn, bn	?Vienna, end 1785	X, 79	VIII:21, 120		
487	496a	12 Duos		2 hn [?basset hn]	Vienna, 27 July 1785 (D)	XXIV, no.58	VIII:21, 49		

Frags., sketches: Andante K384B, 2 ob, 2 cl, 2 bn, 2 hn; March K384b, 2 ob, 2 cl, 2 bn, 2 hn; Allegro K384c, 2 ob, 2 cl, 2 bn, 2 hn; Allegro assai, Bb, KA95/484b, 2 cl, 3 basset hn; Adagio, F, KA93/484c, cl, 3 basset hn; Allegro, F, K484e, basset hn, str inst; Adagio, C, KA94/580a, ? cl, 3 basset hn (or eng hn, 2 hn/basset hn, bn)

Doubtful: 4 partitas, 2 ob, 2 cl, 2 bn, 2 hn, F, Bb, Eb, Bb, incl. movts from KA17.04–5, arrs. of movts from K361/370a, movts in CS-Pu; 5 Pièces d'harmonie, 2 ob, 2 cl, 2 bn, 2 hn (Leipzig, 1802); Bb, after K361/370a; Eb, KA226/C17.01; Bb, after K361/370a; Bb, KA227/C17.02; Eb, KA228/C17.03; Partita, Eb, 2 ob, 2 cl, 2 bn, 2 hn, KAC13.07, inc., CS-Pu; see Leeson and Whitwell, ML, liii (1972), 377

Spurious: Divertimento, C, K187/C17.12, 2 fl, 5 tpt, timp, MW, IX/ii, 63, arr. by Leopold of dances by Starzer and Gluck; see also 'Arrangements', K626b, 28

MARCHES

K	K⁶	Key	Scoring	Composition	MW	NMA	Remarks
41c	41c		2 ob, bn, 2 hn, 2 vn, b	Salzburg, 1767	—	—	lost; in LC
62	62	D	2 ob, 2 hn, 2 tpt, str	Salzburg, 1769	—	IV:12/i, 63	quoted in letter, 4 Aug 1770; used in Mitridate, K87/74a ? for Cassation, K100/62a
290	167AB	D	2 hn, str	Salzburg, sum. 1772	X, 19	VII:18, 3	with Divertimento, K205/167A
189	167b	D	2 fl, 2 hn, 2 tpt, 2 vn, b	Vienna, July–Aug 1773	X, 1	IV:12/ii, 70	with Serenade, K185/167a
237	189c	D	2 ob, 2 bn, 2 hn, 2 tpt, 2 vn, b	Salzburg, Aug 1774	X, 10	IV:12/iii, 3	with Serenade, K203/189b
215	213b	D	2 ob, 2 hn, 2 tpt, str	Salzburg, Aug 1775	X, 7	IV:12/iii, 55	with Serenade, K204/213a
214	214	C	2 ob, 2 hn, 2 tpt, str	Salzburg, 20 Aug 1775 (D)	X, 4	IV:13/1/ii	
248	248	F	2 hn, str	Salzburg, June 1776 (D)	X, 13	VII:18, 23	with Divertimento, K247
249	249	D	2 ob, 2 bn, 2 hn, 2 tpt, str	Salzburg, 20 July 1776 (D)	X, 16	IV:12/iv, 3	with Serenade, K250/248b
335	320a	D	2 ob/fl, 2 hn, 2 tpt, str	Salzburg, Aug 1779	X, 22	IV:13/1/ii	2; with Serenade, K320
445	320c	D	2 hn, str	Salzburg, sum. 1780	X, 114	VII:18, 155	with Divertimento, K334/320b
408/1	383e	C	2 ob, 2 hn, 2 tpt, timp, str	Vienna, 1782	X, 28	IV:13/1/ii	
408/3	383F	C	2 fl, 2 bn, 2 hn, 2 tpt, timp, str	Vienna, 1782	X, 36	IV:13/1/ii	
408/2	385a	D	2 ob, 2 bn, 2 hn, 2 tpt, timp, str	Vienna, 1782	X, 32	IV:13/1/ii	
544	544	D	fl, hn, str	Vienna, June 1788 (C)	—		lost

All surviving marches listed above in NMA IV:13/1/ii

DANCE MUSIC

K	K°	No.	Keys	Scoring	Composition	MW	NMA	Remarks
					Minuets (* – without trio)			
41d 65a	41d 61b	7	G, D, A, F, C, G, D	various 2 vn, b	Salzburg, 1767 Salzburg, 26 Jan 1769	XXIV, no.13	IV:13/1/i, 1	lost; in LC
103	61d	19	C, G, D, F, C, A*, D, F, C, G, F, C, G, Bb, Eb, E*, A*, D, G*	2 ob/fl, 2 hn/tpt, 2 vn, b	Salzburg, spr.–sum. 1772		IV:13/1/i, 11, 78, 80	orig. 20; rearranged by Mozart as 19
104	61e	6	C, F, C, A*, G, G	pic, 2 ob, 2 hn/tpt, 2 vn, b	Salzburg, late 1770–early 1771		IV:13/1/i, 28	nos.1, 2 arr. from M. Haydn P79, nos.1, 3; see Senn, MJb 1964, 71
61g	61g	2	A*, C	2 fl, str	Salzburg, early 1770		IV:13/1/i, 40, 92	no.1 doubtful; no.2 known only in kbd transcr., trio also in K104/61e, 3
122	73t	1	Eb*	2 ob, 2 hn, 2 vn, b	?Bologna, Aug 1770	XXIV, no.13a	IV:13/1/i, 10	
164	130a	6	D, D, D, G, G, G, G	fl, ob, 2 hn/tpt, 2 vn, b	Salzburg, June 1772 (D)	XXIV, no.57	IV:13/1/i, 45	
176	176	16	C, G, Eb*, Bb*, F, D, A, C, G, Bb*, F, D, G, C, F, D	2 ob/fl, bn, 2 hn/tpt, 2 vn, b	Salzburg, Dec 1773 (D)		IV:13/1/i, 51	
363	363	3	D*, Bb*, D*	2 ob, 2 bn, 2 hn, 2 tpt, timp, 2 vn, b	?Vienna, c1782–3	XXIV, no.14	IV:13/1/ii	
409	383f	1	C					see 'Symphonies', K409/383f no.6 inc.
461	448a	6	C, Eb, G, Bb, F, D*	2 ob/fl, 2 bn, 2 hn, 2 vn, b	Vienna, early 1784	XI, 158	IV:13/1/ii	
463	448c	2	F*, Bb*	2 ob, bn, 2 hn, 2 vn, b	Vienna, early 1784	XI, 169	IV:13/1/ii	short minuets with contredanses (Vienna, 1789)
568	568	12	C, F, Bb, Eb, G, D, A, F, Bb, D, G, C	2 fl/pic, 2 ob/cl, 2 bn, 2 hn, 2 tpt, timp, 2 vn, b	Vienna, 24 Dec 1788 (C)	XI, 1	IV:13/1/ii	
585	585	12	D, F, Bb, Eb, G, C, A, F, Bb, Eb, G, D	2 fl/pic, 2 ob/cl, 2 bn, 2 hn, 2 tpt, timp, 2 vn, b	Vienna, Dec 1789 (C)	XI, 19	IV:13/1/ii	

K	K°	No.	Keys	Scoring	Composition	MW	NMA	Remarks
599	599	6	C, G, Eb, Bb, F, D	2 fl/pic, 2 ob/cl, 2 bn, 2 hn, 2 tpt, timp, 2 vn, b	Vienna, 23 Jan 1791 (C)	XI, 37	IV:13/1/ii	
601	601	4	A, C, G, D	2 fl/pic, hurdy-gurdy, 2 ob/cl, 2 bn, 2 hn, 2 tpt, timp, 2 vn, b	Vienna, 5 Feb 1791 (C)	XI, 46	IV:13/1/ii	with German Dances κ602
604	604	2	Bb, Eb	2 fl, 2 cl, 2 bn, 2 tpt, timp, 2 vn, b	Vienna, 12 Feb 1791 (C)	XI, 53	IV:13/1/ii	with German Dances κ605

Doubtful or spurious (see Plath, *MJb* 1971–2, 33); 6 Minuets, D, D, G, G, G, κ105/61f, NMA IV:13/1/i, 34; 6 Minuets, C, A*, D*, Bb, G, C, κ61h, NMA, IV:13/1/i, 40; Minuet, D, κ64 (? by Leopold)

German dances, ländler

K	K°	No.	Keys	Scoring	Composition	MW	NMA	Remarks
509	509	6	D, G, Eb, F, A, C	2 fl/pic, 2 fl, 2 ob, 2 cl, 2 bn, 2 hn, 2 tpt, timp, 2 vn, b	Prague, 6 Feb 1787 (C)	XI, 56	IV:13/1/ii	
536	536	6	C, G, Bb, D, F, F	pic, 2 fl, 2 ob/cl, 2 bn, 2 hn/tpt, timp, 2 vn, b	Vienna, 27 Jan 1788 (C)	XI, 72	IV:13/1/ii	(Vienna, 1789)
567	567	6	Bb, Eb, G, D, A, C	pic, 2 fl, 2 ob/cl, 2 bn, 2 hn, 2 tpt, timp, 2 vn, b	Vienna, 6 Dec 1788 (C)	XI, 80	IV:13/1/ii	(Vienna, 1789)
571	571	6	D, A, C, G, Bb, D	2 fl/pic, 2 ob/cl, 2 bn, 2 hn/tpt, timp, perc, 2 vn, b	Vienna, 21 Feb 1789 (C)	XI, 92	IV:13/1/ii	
586	586	12	C, G, Bb, F, A, D, G, Eb, Bb, F, A, C	2 fl/pic, 2 ob/cl, 2 bn, 2 hn, 2 tpt, timp, perc, 2 vn, b	Vienna, Dec 1789 (C)	XI, 106	IV:13/1/ii	
600	600	6	C, F, Bb, Eb, G, D	pic, 2 fl, 2 ob/cl, 2 bn, 2 hn, 2 tpt, timp, 2 vn, b	Vienna, 29 Jan 1791 (C)	XI, 127	IV:13/1/ii	
602	602	4	Bb, F, C, A	2 fl/pic, 2 ob/cl, 2 bn, 2 hn/tpt, timp, hurdy-gurdy, 2 vn, b	Vienna, 5 Feb 1791 (C)	XI, 139	IV:13/1/ii	with Minuets κ601
605	605	3	D, G, C	2 fl/pic, 2 ob, 2 bn, 2 hn/tpt, 2 post-horns, timp, 5 sleighbells, 2 vn, b	Vienna, 12 Feb 1791 (C)	XI, 145	IV:13/1/ii	with Minuets κ604; no.3, Die Schlittenfahrt, ? composed separately

	K.	No.	Keys	Scoring	Place, date			Remarks
606	606	6	B♭	2 vn, b [wind pts. lost]	Vienna, 28 Feb 1791 (C)	XXIV, no.16	IV:13/1/ii	'Ländlerische'; with Contredanse K607/605a
611	611	1	C	2 fl, 2 ob, 2 bn, 2 tpt, timp, hurdy-gurdy, 2 vn, b	Vienna, 6 March 1791 (C)	XI, 144	IV:13/1/ii	'Die Leyerer' = K602, no.3
					Contredanses			
123	73g	1	B♭	2 ob, 2 hn, 2 vn, b	Rome, 13–14 April 1770	XI, 152	IV:13/1/i, 7	
101	250a	4	F, G, D, F	2 ob/fl, bn, 2 hn, 2 vn, b	Salzburg, ?early 1776	IX/1, 57	IV:13/1/i, 67	'Serenade'
—	269b	12	G, G, C, D	vn, b	Salzburg, ?early 1776			nos.1, 2, 3, 12 extant in kbd red. only; others lost; nos.2, 12 = K101/250a nos.2, 3
267	271c	4	G, E♭, A, D	2 ob/fl, bn, 2 hn, 2 vn, b	Salzburg, early 1777	XI, 154	IV:13/1/i, 71	
462	448b	6	C, E♭, B♭, D, B♭, F	2 ob, 2 hn, 2 vn, b	Vienna, Jan 1784	XI, 165	IV:13/1/ii	wind insts added later
463	448c	2	F, B♭	2 ob, bn, 2 hn, 2 vn, b	Vienna, Jan 1784	XI, 169	IV:13/1/ii	each preceded by a minuet
510	C13.02	9	D, D, D, B♭, D, D, F, B♭, C	2 pic, 2 ob/fl, 2 cl, 2 hn, 2 tpt, timp, 2 vn, b	?Prague, early 1787	XI, 173	IV:13/1/ii	probably not authentic
534	534	1	D	pic, 2 ob, 2 hn, side drum, 2 vn, b	Vienna, 14 Jan 1788 (C)	XXIV, no.27	IV:13/1/ii	Das Donnerwetter; extant only in pf red.
535	535	1	C	pic, 2 cl, bn, tpt, side drum, 2 vn, b	Vienna, 23 Jan 1788 (C)	XI, 184	IV:13/1/ii	La bataille [The Siege of Belgrade]
535a	535a	3	C, G, G		Vienna, ?early 1788			only pf version extant
565	565	2	B♭, D	2 ob, 2 hn, 2 vn, b	Vienna, 30 Oct 1788 (C)	—	—	lost
587	587	1	C	fl, ob, bn, tpt, 2 vn, b	Vienna, Dec 1789 (C)	XI, 188	IV:13/1/ii	Der Sieg vom Helden Coburg
106	588a	3	D, A, B♭	2 ob, 2 bn, 2 hn, 2 vn, b	Vienna, Jan 1790	XXIV, no.15	IV:13/1/ii	with ov.
603	603	2	D, B♭	pic, 2 ob, 2 bn, 2 hn, 2 tpt, timp, 2 vn, b	Vienna, 5 Feb 1791 (C)	XI, 191	IV:13/1/ii	?sk K.A107/535b
607	605a	1	E♭	fl, ob, bn, 2 hn, 2 vn, b	Vienna, 28 Feb 1791 (C)	XXIV, no.17	IV:13/1/ii	Il trionfo delle dame; with German Dances K606

K	K⁶	No.	Keys	Scoring	Composition		MW	NMA	Remarks
609	609	5	C, Eb, D, C, G	fl, side drum, 2 vn, b	Vienna, 1791		XI, 194	IV:13/1/ii	Les filles malicieuses
610	610	1	G	2 fl, 2 hn, 2 vn, b	Vienna, 6 March 1791 (C)		XI, 200	IV:13/1/ii	

CONCERTOS, CONCERTO MOVEMENTS
piano

K	K⁶	Title	BH	Key	Scoring	Composition	Cadenzas K624/626a	MW	NMA	Remarks
37,39, 41, 107, 1-3	37,39, 41, 107, 1-3		1-4							see 'Arrangements' see 'Arrangements'
175	175	Concerto	5	D	pf, 2 ob, 2 hn, 2 tpt, timp, str	Salzburg, Dec 1773 (D)	1-4	XVI/i, 131	V:15/i, 3	(Vienna, 1785), op.7; see K382 below	39
238	238	Concerto	6	Bb	pf, 2 ob/fl, 2 hn, str	Salzburg, Jan 1776 (D)	5-7	XVI/i, 165	V:15/i, 89	49
242	242	Concerto	7	F	3 pf, 2 ob, 2 hn, str	Salzburg, Feb 1776 (D)	—	XVI/i, 197	V:15/i, 155	also version for 2 pf	49
246	246	Concerto	8	C	pf, 2 ob, 2 hn, str	Salzburg, April 1776 (D)	8-14	XVI/i, 289	V:15/ii, 3	49
271	271	Concerto	9	Eb	pf, 2 ob, 2 hn, str	Salzburg, Jan 1777 (D)	15-22	XVI/ii, 1	V:15/ii, 65	49, 68, 124,
365	316a	Concerto	10	Eb	2 pf, 2 ob, 2 bn, 2 hn, str	Salzburg, 1779	23-4	XVI/ii, 53	V:15/ii, 145	68
382	382	Rondo		D	pf, fl, 2 ob, 2 hn, 2 tpt, timp, str	Vienna, March 1782	25-6	XVI/iv, 359	V:15/i, 67	new finale for K175 (Vienna, 1785)	50, 103
414	385p	Concerto	12	A	pf, 2 ob, 2 hn, str	Vienna, 1782	27-36	XVI/ii, 133	V:15/iii, 3	(Vienna, 1785) as op.4 no.1: sk K385o	86, 103, 104
386	386	Rondo		A	pf, 2 ob, 2 hn, str	Vienna, 19 Oct 1782 (D)	—		V:15/viii, 173 (inc.)	? intended as finale for K414/385p	
413	387a	Concerto	11	F	pf, 2 ob, 2 bn, 2 hn, str	Vienna, 1782-3	37-8	XVI/ii, 101	V:15/iii, 67	(Vienna, 1785) as op.4 no.2	86, 103, 104
415	387b	Concerto	13	C	pf, 2 ob, 2 bn, 2 hn, 2 tpt, timp, str	Vienna, 1782-3	39-41	XVI/ii, 163	V:15/iii, 127	(Vienna, 1785) as op.4 no.3	86, 103, 125, 132
449	449	Concerto	14	Eb	pf, 2 ob, 2 hn, str	Vienna, 9 Feb 1784 (DC)	42	XVI/ii, 205	V:15/iv, 3	25, 86, 104

				Instrumentation	Date				Notes	References
450	Concerto	15	B♭	pf, fl, 2 ob, 2 bn, 2 hn, str	Vienna, 15 March 1784 (C)	43–5	XVI/ii, 241	V:15/iv, 67		104, 105, 106, 124, 126
451	Concerto	16	D	pf, fl, 2 ob, 2 bn, 2 hn, 2 tpt, timp, 2 vn	Vienna, 22 March 1784 (C)	46–7	XVI/ii, 285	V:15/iv, 137	(Paris, c1785); ornamentation of ii, k624/626αII, M	104, 105, 106, 125, 126, 132
453	Concerto	17	G	pf, fl, 2 ob, 2 bn, str	Vienna, 12 April 1784 (C)	48–51	XVI/iii, 22	V:15/v, 3	(Speyer, 1789) as op.9; sk κA65/452c, κA59/459a [466a in κ3]	105, 106
456	Concerto	18	B♭	pf, fl, 2 ob, 2 bn, 2 hn, str	Vienna, 30 Sept 1784 (C)	52–7	XVI/iii, 55	V:15/v, 71		105, 106, 126, 134
459	Concerto	19	F	pf, fl, 2 ob, 2 bn, 2 hn, str	Vienna, 11 Dec 1784 (C)	58–60	XVI/iii, 119	V:15/v, 151		106, 137, 138
466	Concerto	20	d	pf, fl, 2 ob, 2 bn, 2 tpt, timp, str	Vienna, 10 Feb 1785 (C)	—	XVI/iii, 181	V:15/vi, 3		123, 124, 125, 130
467	Concerto	21	C	pf, fl, 2 ob, 2 bn, 2 tpt, timp, str	Vienna, 9 March 1785 (C)	—	XVI/iii, 237	V:15/vi, 93	sk κA60/502a	123, 124, 125, 132
482	Concerto	22	E♭	pf, fl, 2 cl, 2 bn, 2 hn, 2 tpt, timp, str	Vienna, 16 Dec 1785 (C)	—	XVI/iv, 1	V:15/vi, 177		25, 124, 125, 126
488	Concerto	23	A	pf, fl, 2 cl, 2 bn, 2 hn, str	Vienna, 2 March 1786 (C)	61	XVI/iv, 67	V:15/vii, 3	sk κA58/488a, A63/488b, A64/488c, 488d	124, 125, 126, 133
491	Concerto	24	c	pf, fl, 2 ob, 2 cl, 2 bn, 2 hn, 2 tpt, timp, str	Vienna, 24 March 1786 (C)	—	XVI/iv, 121	V:15/vii, 85	sk κA62/491a	124, 126, 133
503	Concerto	25	C	pf, fl, 2 ob, 2 bn, 2 hn, 2 tpt, timp, str	Vienna, 4 Dec 1786 (C)	—	XVI/iv, 185	V:15/vii, 256		113, 125, 126, 132, 151
537	Concerto	26	D	pf, fl, 2 ob, 2 bn, 2 hn, 2 tpt, timp, str	Vienna, 24 Feb 1788 (C)	—	XVI/iv, 253	V:15/viii, 3	'Coronation'	126, 132, 134, 137, 138
595	Concerto	27	B♭	pf, fl, 2 ob, 2 bn, 2 hn, str	Vienna, ?1788–91, 5 Jan 1791 (C)	62–4	XVI/iv, 309	V:15/viii, 93	(Vienna, 1791) as op.17	156

Frag.: for vn, pf, in D, κA56/315f, MW, XXIV, no.21a; for pf, sk, D, κA57/537a, ?1786; for pf, slow movt sk, d, κA61/537b, ?end 1786; sk material noted above is in NMA, V:15/viii, 188ff *strings*

K	K°	Title	Key	Solo	Accompaniment	Composition	MW	NMA	Remarks	
190	186E	Concertone	C	2 vn	solo ob, vc; 2 ob, 2 hn, 2 tpt, str	Salzburg, 31 May 1774 (D)	XII/i, 167	V:14/ii, 3		42
207	207	Concerto	B♭	vn	2 ob, 2 hn, str	Salzburg, 14 April 1775 (D)	XII/i, 1	V:14/i		48, 49
211	211	Concerto	D	vn	2 ob, 2 hn, str	Salzburg, 14 June 1775 (D)	XII/i, 27	V:14/i		48
216	216	Concerto	G	vn	2 ob, 2 hn, str	Salzburg, 12 Sept 1775 (D)	XII/i, 49	V:14/i		48
218	218	Concerto	D	vn	2 ob, 2 hn, str	Salzburg, Oct 1775 (D)	XII/i, 83	V:14/i		48
219	219	Concerto	A	vn	2 ob, 2 hn, str	Salzburg, 20 Dec 1775 (D)	XII/i, 113	V:14/i		49
261	261	Adagio	E	vn	2 fl, 2 hn, str	Salzburg, 1776	XII/i, 145	V:14/i	for K219	49
269	261a	Rondo	B♭	vn	2 ob, 2 hn, str	Salzburg, 1776	XII/i, 150	V:14/i	? for K207	49
364	320d	Sinfonia concertante	E♭	vn, va	2 ob, 2 hn, str	Salzburg, 1779	XII/i, 211	V:14/ii, 57		25, 68, 132
373	373	Rondo	C	vn	2 ob, 2 hn, str	Vienna, 2 April 1781 (D)	XII/i, 159	V:14/i	fl arr. in D KA184 not authentic	78
470	470	Andante	A	vn	2 ob, 2 hn, str	Vienna, 1 April 1785 (C)	—		lost; ? for concerto	

Lost and frag.: vc, F, K206a, lost; Sinfonia concertante, vn, va, vc, A, KA104/320e
Doubtful and spurious violin concertos: in D, K271a/271i, NMA, X/29/i, 81 (see King, 1978, pp31f, and Mahling, *MJb 1978* 9, 252); in E♭, K268/C14.04, MW, XXIV, ?incl. authentic material (see Oldman, *ML*, xii, 1931, p.174; King, 1978, pp.31ff); 'Adelaide Concerto', in D, KA294a/C14.05, by its 'editor', H. Casadesus (Mainz, 1930)

wind instruments

K	K°	Title	Key	Solo	Accompaniment	Composition	MW	NMA	Remarks	
47c	47c	Concerto		tpt		Vienna, Nov 1768	—	—	lost; see Leopold's letter, 12 Nov 1768	12
191	186e	Concerto	B♭	bn	2 ob, 2 hn, str	Salzburg, 4 June 1774 (D)	XII/ii, 1	V:14/iii, 133		42
271k	271k	Concerto		ob	2 ob, 2 hn, str	Salzburg, 1777			mentioned in letter, 14 Feb 1778: ?lost, or K314/285d	
313	285c	Concerto	G	fl	2 ob, 2 hn, str	Mannheim, early 1778	XII/ii, 73	V:14/iii, 3		64
314	285d	Concerto	C/D	ob/fl	2 ob, 2 hn, str	Mannheim, early 1778	XII/ii, 104	V:14/iii, 53, 97 ob version, ?k271k		

K	K6	Title	Key	Scoring	Composition	MW	NMA	Remarks	
315	285e	Andante	C	fl; 2 ob, 2 hn, str	?Salzburg, 1779–80	XII/ii, 129	V:14/iii, 89	lost (if written); see A9/C14.01	64
A9	297B	Sinfonia concertante		fl, ob, bn, hn				doubtful; K3 297b; ?later arr. of KA9/297B; see *MJb 1971–2*, 56; and Leeson and Levin, *MJb 1976–7*, 70	57
A9	C14.01	Sinfonia concertante	E♭	ob, cl, bn, hn; 2 ob, 2 hn, str	? Paris, April 1778	XXIV, no.7a	X:29/i, 3		57
299	297c	Concerto	C	fl, harp; 2 ob, 2 hn, str	Paris, April 1778	XII/ii, 21	V:14/iii		64
320	320	Sinfonia concertante	G	2 fl, 2 ob, 2 bn				iii and iv of Serenade K320; see letter of 29 March 1783; inc. sk K370b	
371	371	Rondo	E♭	hn; 2 ob, 2 hn, str	Vienna, 21 March 1781 (D)	XXIV, no.21	V:14/v		106
412	386b	Concerto	D	hn; 2 ob, 2 bn, str	Vienna, 1791	XII/ii, 135	V:14/v	ii inc.; version in *USSR-Lit* (K514) is ?1792 completion	106
417	417	Concerto	E♭	hn; 2 ob, 2 hn, str	Vienna, 27 May 1783	XII/ii, 149	V:14/v		106
447	447	Concerto	E♭	hn; 2 cl, 2 bn, str	Vienna, ?1784–7	XII/ii, 167	V:14/v		106
495	495	Concerto	E♭	hn; 2 ob, 2 hn, str	Vienna, 26 June 1786 (C)	XII/ii, 187	V:14/v		106
622	622	Concerto	A	cl; 2 fl, 2 bn, 2 hn, str	Vienna, Oct 1791	XII/ii, 207	V:14/iv	orig. solo part, with range to written c, lost	156

Frag. movts: ob, F, K293/416f; MW, XXIV, no.20; hn, E, K494a; basset hn, G, K584b/621b (= i of K622)

Doubtful: bn, F, KA230/196d; bn, B♭, AC14.03, spurious; ?others for bn, lost

CHAMBER
Strings and wind

K	K6	Title	Key	Scoring	Composition	MW	NMA	Remarks	
292	196c	Duo	B♭	bn, vc	Munich, early 1775	X, 75	VIII:21, 7		45
285	285	Quartet	D	fl, vn, va, vc	Mannheim, 25 Dec 1777 (D)	XIV, 307	VIII:20/2, 3		64
285a	285a	Quartet	G	fl, vn, va, vc	Mannheim, Jan–Feb 1778		VIII:20/2, 25		64

K	K⁶	Title	Key	Scoring	Composition	MW	NMA	Remarks	
A171	285b	Quartet	C	fl, vn, va, vc	?Vienna, 1781–2		VIII:20/2, 33	ii, arr., ?not by Mozart, from Serenade K361/370a; see Leavis, ML, xliii (1962), 48; (Speyer, 1788) as op.14	119
298	298	Quartet	A	fl. vn. va. vc	Vienna, 1786–7	XIV, 310	VIII:20/2, 51		76
370	368b	Quartet	F	ob. vn. va. vc	Munich, early 1781	XIV, 327	VIII:20/2, 65		
407	386c	Quintet	E♭	hn. vn. 2 va. vc	Vienna, end 1782	XIII, 41	VIII:19/2, 1		
581	581	Quintet	A	cl. 2 vn, va, vc	Vienna, 29 Sept 1789 (C)	XIII, 112	VIII:19/2, 15		155, 157

Frags.: B♭, K.A91/516c and E.♭, K516d, cl, 2 vn, va, vc; F, K.A90/580b, cl, basset hn, vn, va, vc; A, K.A88/581a

String quintets: 2 vn, 2 va, vc

K	K⁶	Key	Composition	MW	NMA	Remarks	
174	174	B♭	Salzburg, Dec 1773	XIII, 1	VIII:19/1, 3		39
515	515	C	Vienna, 19 April 1787 (C)	XIII, 54	VIII:19/1, 27	(Vienna, 1789); sk K.A80/514a	116, 154
516	516	g	Vienna, 16 May 1787 (C)	XIII, 85	VIII:19/1, 63	(Vienna, 1790); sk K.A86/516a	116
406	516b	c	Vienna, 1788	XIII, 23	VIII:19/1, 91	arr. from Serenade K388/384a	116, 133, 154
593	593	D	Vienna, Dec 1790 (C)	XIII, 132	VIII:19/1, 113		98
614	614	E♭	Vienna, 12 April 1791 (C)	XIII, 156	VIII:19/1, 143	sk K.A81/613a, A82/613b	154, 155

Frags.: K.A83/592b, D, ?1788; K87/515a, F, a,?1791
Doubtful: 3 preludes, see 'Arrangements'; spurious: K46, MW, XXIV, no.22: arr. of movts from Serenade K361/370a

String quartets

K	K⁶	Title	Key	Composition	MW	NMA	Remarks	
80	73f	Quartet	G	Lodi, 15 March 1770 (D)	XIV, 1; XXIV, no.55	VIII:20/1/i, 3	iv added Vienna, late 1773, or Salzburg, early 1774	15, 29
136	125a	Divertimento	D	Salzburg, early 1772	XIV, 278	IV:12/vi, 3		
137	125b	Divertimento	B♭	Salzburg, early 1772	XIV, 287	IV:12/vi, 19		
138	125c	Divertimento	F	Salzburg, early 1772	XIV, 294	IV:12/vi, 30		
155	134a	[Quartet]	D	Bolzano, Verona, Oct–Nov 1772	XIV, 8	VIII:20/1/i, 17		29
156	134b	Quartet	G	Milan, end 1772	XIV, 15	VIII:20/1/i, 31		29
157	157	Quartet	C	Milan, end 1772–early 1773	XIV, 21	VIII:20/1/i, 41		

K	K⁶	Title	Key	Composition	XIV	VIII:20/1	Remarks	pp.
158	158	Quartet	F	Milan, end 1772–early 1773	XIV, 29	VIII:20/1/i, 57		29
159	159	Quartet	Bb	Milan, early 1773	XIV, 36	VIII:20/1/i, 69		29
160	159a	Quartet	Eb	Milan, early 1773	XIV, 45	VIII:20/1/i, 85		
168	168	Quartet	F	Vienna, Aug 1773	XIV, 52	VIII:20/1/i, 99		38
169	169	Quartet	A	Vienna, Aug 1773 (D)	XIV, 60	VIII:20/1/i, 113		38
170	170	Quartet	C	Vienna, Aug 1773 (D)	XIV, 69	VIII:20/1/i, 129		38
171	171	Quartet	Eb	Vienna, Aug 1773 (D)	XIV, 77	VIII:20/1/i, 145		38
172	172	Quartet	Bb	Vienna, ?Sept 1773	XIV, 86	VIII:20/1/i, 159		38
173	173	Quartet	d	Vienna, [Sept] 1773 (D)	XIV, 96	VIII:20/1/i, 175		38, 97
387	387	Quartet	G	Vienna, 31 Dec 1782 (D)	XIV, 106	VIII:20/1/ii, 3	(Vienna, 1785) as op.10 no.1	90, 97, 122, 131
421	417b	Quartet	d	Vienna, June 1783	XIV, 124	VIII:20/1/ii, 33	(Vienna, 1785) as op.10 no.2	84, 96, 97, 133
428	421b	Quartet	Eb	Vienna, June–July 1783	XIV, 137	VIII:20/1/ii, 85	(Vienna, 1785) as op.10 no.4	96
458	458	Quartet	Bb	Vienna, 9 Nov 1784 (C)	XIV, 152	VIII:20/1/ii, 57	'Hunt' (Vienna, 1785) as op.10 no.3; sk KA68/589a	96
464	464	Quartet	A	Vienna, 10 Jan 1785 (C)	XIV, 168	VIII:20/1/ii, 111	(Vienna, 1785) as op.10 no.5; sk KA72/464a	96, 97
465	465	Quartet	C	Vienna, 14 Jan 1785 (C)	XIV, 186	VIII:20/1/ii, 145	'Dissonance' (Vienna, 1785) as op.10 no.6	96
499	499	Quartet	D	Vienna, 19 Aug 1786 (C)	XIV, 206	VIII:20/1/iii, 3	'Hoffmeister' (Vienna, 1786)	116
546	546	Adagio and Fugue	c	Vienna, 26 June 1788 (C)	XIV, 301	IV:11/x, 47	?for str orch; fugue arr. from K426	100, 118
575	575	Quartet	D	Vienna, June 1789	XIV, 226	VIII:20/1/iii, 37	'Prussian'	135, 152, 153, 154
589	589	Quartet	Bb	Vienna, May 1790 (C)	XIV, 242	VIII:20/1/iii, 65	'Prussian': sk KA75/458a, 71/458h	135, 152, 154
590	590	Quartet	F	Vienna, June 1790 (C)	XIV, 258	VIII:20/1/iii, 93	'Prussian': sk KA73/589b	136, 152, 154

Frags.: F, K168a, early 1775; C, K77/405a, c1790; K76/417c, after 1786; c, K417d, c1789; with K453b, ?1783; g, KA47/587a, c1789; for sk dating see Tyson: *Mozart's Workshop*

Doubtful: 6 preludes, see 'Arrangements'; spurious: Bb, C, A, Eb, KA210–13/C20.01–04 (Mainz, 1932) by J. Schuster; see Finscher, *Mf*, xix (1966), 270

String sonatas, duos, trios

K	K⁶	Title	Key	Scoring	Composition	MW	NMA	Remarks
33b	33b	Solos		vc, b	Donaueschingen, Oct 1766	—	—	lost; in LC (incipit ? = 2nd pt of that in K⁶ for 196d)
—	—			viola da gamba, b		—	—	lost; in LC (incipit ?as 33b)
41g	41g	Nachtmusik		2 vn, b	?Salzburg, 1767			
—	46d	6 trios		2 vn, vc	before 1768	—	VIII:21, 3	lost; see Nannerl's letter, 8 Feb 1800
46d	46d	Sonata	C	vn, b	Vienna, 1 Sept 1768 (D)	—		lost; in LC
46e	46e	Sonata	F	vn, b	Vienna, 1 Sept 1768 (D)	—	VIII:21, 5	

210

K	K*	Title	Key	Scoring	Composition	MW	NMA	Remarks	
266	271f	Trio	B♭	2 vn, b	Salzburg, early 1777	XXIV, no.23	VIII:21, 61		
404a	404a	4 preludes		vn, va, vc	Vienna, 1782			doubtful; for fugues by J. S. and W. F. Bach; see 'Arrangements'	
423	423	Duo	G	vn, va	?Salzburg, sum. 1783	XV, 1	VIII:21, 15		
424	424	Duo	B♭	vn, va	?Salzburg, sum. 1783	XV, 9	VIII:21, 33		
563	563	Trio	E♭	vn, va, vc	Vienna, 27 Sept 1788 (C)	XV, 19	VIII:21, 121	'Ein Divertimento . . . di sei pezzi'; sk κA66/562e	118, 134

Frags.: G, κA66/562c, vn, va, vc; Fugue, G, κ443/404b, completed by M. Stadler

Keyboard and two or more instruments

K	K*	Title	Key	Scoring	Composition	MW	NMA	Remarks	
10–15	10–15	6 sonatas		hpd, vn [vc]				see 'Keyboard and violin' below	
254	254	Divertimento	B♭	pf, vn, vc	Salzburg, Aug 1776 (D)	XVII/2, 2	VIII:22/2, 56	(Paris, c1782) as op.3	
442	442	Trio	d	pf, vn, vc	Vienna, ?1783–90	XVII/2, 20	—	inc.; finished by M. Stadler; ? three separate movts, in d, G, D, associated fortuitously sk κA54/452a	98, 155
452	452	Quintet	E♭	pf, ob, cl, bn, hn	Vienna, 30 March 1784 (C)	XVII/1, 2; XXIV, no.59	VIII:22/1, 107		
478	478	Quartet	g	pf, vn, va, vc	Vienna, 16 Oct 1785 (D)	XVII/1, 32	VIII:22/1, 1	(Vienna, 1785-6)	119, 128
493	493	Quartet	E♭	pf, vn, va, vc	Vienna, 3 June 1786 (C)	XVII/1, 62	VIII:22/1, 53	(Vienna, 1787) as op.13; sk κA53/493a	119, 133
496	496	Trio	G	pf, vn, vc	Vienna, 8 July 1786 (C)	XVII/2, 46	VIII:22/2, 78	(Vienna, 1786); sk κA52/495a	119
498	498	Trio	E♭	pf, cl, va	Vienna, 5 Aug 1786 (C)	XVII/2, 68	VIII:22/2, 104	(Vienna, 1788) as op.14	120
502	502	Trio	B♭	pf, vn, vc	Vienna, 18 Nov 1786 (C)	XVII/2, 86	VIII:22/2, 129	(Vienna, 1788) as op.15 no.1	119
542	542	Trio	E	pf, vn, vc	Vienna, 22 June 1788 (C)	XVII/2, 110	VIII:22/2, 160	(Vienna, 1788) as op.15 no.2	120, 133
548	548	Trio	C	pf, vn, vc	Vienna, 14 July 1788 (C)	XVII/2, 132	VIII:22/2, 188	(Vienna, 1788) as op.15 no.3	120

K	K⁶	Title	Key	Scoring	Composition				Remarks	
564	564	Trio	G	pf, vn, vc	Vienna, 27 Oct 1788 (C)	XVII/2, 150			(London, 1789)	119
617	617	Adagio and Rondo	c	armonica, fl, ob, va, vc	Vienna, 23 May 1791 (C)	VIII/22/2, 212	X, 85	VIII/22/1, 146	sk KA92/616a	

Frag.: KA51/501a, pf, vn, vc, B♭, 1784-5

Keyboard and violin

K	K⁶	Title	Key	Composition	MW	NMA	Remarks	
6-7	6-7	2 sonatas	C, D	Salzburg, Paris, 1762-4	XVIII/i, 2, 12	VIII/23/i, 2, 12	(Paris, 1764) as op.1	21
8-9	8-9	2 sonatas	B♭, G	Paris, 1763-4	XVIII/i, 20, 26	VIII:23/i, 20, 26	(Paris, 1764) as op.2	21
10-15	10-15	6 sonatas	B♭, G, A, F, C, B♭	London, 1764	XVIII/i, 34, 42, 47, 54, 62, 72	VIII:22/? 2, 12, 18, 25, 36, 48	(London, 1765) as op.3; vc ad lib	22
26-31	26-31	6 sonatas	E♭, G, C, D, F, B♭	The Hague, Feb 1766	XVIII/i. 78, 84, 90, 96, 100, 106	VII:23/i. 34, 40, 45, 50, 54, 59	(The Hague and Amsterdam, 1766) as op.4	22
301	293a	Sonata	G	Mannheim, early 1778	XVIII/ii, 18	VIII:23/i, 66	(Paris, 1778) as op.1 no.1	63
302	293b	Sonata	E♭	Mannheim, early 1778	XVIII/ii, 32	VIII:23/i, 78	(Paris, 1778) as op.1 no.2	63
303	293c	Sonata	C	Mannheim, early 1778	XVIII/ii, 44	VIII:23/i, 88	(Paris, 1778) as op.1 no.3	
305	293d	Sonata	A	Mannheim, early 1778	XVIII/ii, 64	VIII:23/i, 107	(Paris, 1778) as op.1 no.5	
296	296	Sonata	C	Mannheim, 11 March 1778 (D)	XVIII/ii, 2	VIII:23/i, 139	(Vienna, 1781) as op.2 no.2	63, 92
304	300c	Sonata	e	Paris, early sum. 1778	XVIII/ii, 54	VIII:23/i, 98	(Paris, 1778) as op.1 no.4	133
306	300l	Sonata	D	Paris, sum. 1778	XVIII/ii, 76	VIII:23/i, 118	(Paris, 1778) as op.1 no.6	63, 66
378	317d	Sonata	B♭	Salzburg, early 1779 or Vienna, 1781	XVIII/ii, 140	VIII:23/i, 154	(Vienna, 1781) as op.2 no.4	68, 92
372	372	Sonata	B♭	Vienna, 24 March 1781	XVIII/ii, 98	VIII:23/ii, 154	Allegro only, inc.; completed by M. Stadler	
379	373a	Sonata	G	Vienna, April 1781	XVIII/ii, 160	VIII:23/ii, 3	(Vienna, 1781) as op.2 no.5	78, 92
359	374a	Variations	G	Vienna, June 1781	XVIII/ii, 290	VIII:23/ii, 136	on La bergère Célimène, Fr. song, anon. (Vienna, 1786)	
360	374b	Variations	g	Vienna, June 1781	XVIII/ii, 300	VIII:23/ii, 144	on Hélas, j'ai perdu mon amant, Fr. song, anon. (Vienna, 1786)	
376	374d	Sonata	F	Vienna, sum. 1781	XVIII/ii, 108	VIII:23/ii, 16	(Vienna, 1781) as op.2 no.1	92
377	374e	Sonata	F	Vienna, sum. 1781	XVIII/ii, 124	VIII:23/ii, 32	(Vienna, 1781) as op.2 no.3	92, 97
380	374f	Sonata	E♭	Vienna, sum. 1781	XVIII/ii, 172	VIII:23/ii, 48	(Vienna, 1781) as op.2 no.6	92
403	385c	Sonata	C	Vienna, Aug–Sept 1782	XVIII/ii, 198	VIII:23/ii, 152	inc.; completed by M. Stadler	
404	385d	Sonata	C	Vienna, ?1782 (? or c1788)	XVIII/ii, 208	VIII:23/ii, 164	Andante and Allegretto, inc.	

K	K°	Title	Key	Composition	MW	NMA	Remarks	
402	385e	Sonata	A	Vienna, Aug–Sept 1782	XVIII/ii, 190	VIII:23/ii, 173	inc.; completed by M. Stadler	86, 93
396	385f	Sonata movt	c	Vienna, Aug–Sept 1782	—	VIII:23/ii, 181	inc.; completed by M. Stadler; see Eppstein, *Mf*, xxi (1968), 205	93
454	454	Sonata	B♭	Vienna, 21 April 1784 (C)	XVIII/ii, 210	VIII:23/ii, 64	(Vienna, 1784) as op.7 no.3	
481	481	Sonata	E♭	Vienna, 12 Dec 1785 (C)	XVIII/ii, 232	VIII:23/ii, 82	(Vienna, 1786)	
526	526	Sonata	A	Vienna, 24 Aug 1787 (C)	XVIII/ii, 252	VIII:23/ii, 100	(Vienna, 1787); sk KA50/526a	120
547	547	Sonata	F	Vienna, 10 July 1788 (C)	XVIII/ii, 276	VIII:23/ii, 122	'für Anfänger'	

Frags.: G, KA47/546a; A, KA48/385E; B ♭, KA46/374g [pf, vc]
Spurious: K55–60/C23.01–6, MW, XVIII, 114ff; see Neumann, *MJb* 1965–6, 152; Plath, *MJb* 1968–70, 368ff; K61, MW, XVIII, 172, by H. F. Raupach

KEYBOARD
Sonatas

K	K°	Key	Composition	MW	NMA	Remarks	
			(solo keyboard)				
A199–202	33d–g	G, B♭, C, F	1766	—	—	lost; known from Breitkopf catalogue	
279–83	189d–h	C, F, B♭, E♭, G	Munich, early 1775	XX, 1	IX:25		45
284	205b	D	Munich, Feb–March 1775	XX, 46	IX:25	(Vienna, 1784) as op.7 no.2	45, 86
309	284b	C	Mannheim, Oct–Nov 1777	XX, 64	IX:25	(Paris, 1782) as op.4 no.1	62
311	284c	D	Mannheim, Nov 1777	XX, 92	IX:25	(Paris, 1782) as op.4 no.2	62, 66
310	300d	a	Paris, sum. 1778	XX, 78	IX:25	(Paris, 1782) as op.4 no.3	62, 133
330	300h	C	Munich or Vienna, 1781–3	XX, 106	IX:25	(Vienna, 1784) as op.6 no.1	76, 86
331	300i	A	Munich or Vienna, 1781–3	XX, 118	IX:25	(Vienna, 1784) as op.6 no.2	76, 86
332	300k	F	Munich or Vienna, 1781–3	XX, 130	IX:25	(Vienna, 1784) as op.6 no.3	76, 86
333	315c	B♭	Linz and Vienna, 1783–4	XX, 146	IX:25	(Vienna, 1784) as op.7 no.1	84, 86
457	457	c	Vienna, 14 Oct 1784 (C)	XX, 160	IX:25	pubd with Fantasia K475 (Vienna, 1785) as op.11	100, 133
533	533	F	Vienna, 3 Jan 1788 (C)	XXII, 44	IX:25	incl. rev. of Rondo K494; (Vienna, 1788)	121
545	545	C	Vienna, 26 June 1788 (C)	XX, 174	IX:25	'für Anfänger'	122
A135	547a	F	?Vienna, summer 1788	—	IX:25	doubtful; finale = transposed version of K545, iii	
570	570	B♭	Vienna, Feb 1789 (C)	XX, 182	IX:25	first edn. (1796) with vn acc., probably spurious; sk KA31/569a	155
576	576	D	Vienna, July 1789 (C)	XX, 194	IX:25		155

Frags., sketches: F, KA29, 30, 37/590a–c, 1789–90

(keyboard duet)

K	K⁶	Key	Composition	MW		NMA	Remarks	
19d	19d	C	London, May 1765	—			(Paris, 1788); see Tyson, *MR*, xxx (1969), 98	
381	123a	D	Salzburg, mid-1772	XIX, 32		IX:24/2, 20	(Vienna, 1783) as op.3 no.1	
358	186c	Bb	Salzburg, late 1773–early 1774	XIX, 18		IX:24/2, 36	(Vienna, 1783) as op.3 no.2	
497	497	F	Vienna, 1 Aug 1786 (C)	XIX, 46		IX:24/2, 54	(Vienna, 1787) as op.12	120
521	521	C	Vienna, 29 May 1787 (C)	XIX, 80		IX:24/2, 106	(Vienna, 1787)	120

(for 2 keyboards)

K	K⁶	Key	Composition	MW		NMA	Remarks	
448	375a	D	Vienna, Nov 1781	XIX, 126		IX:24/1, 2		100

Frags.: ? Sonata, G (Allegro, k357/497a (98 bars) and Andante, k357/500a (158 bars)], MW, XIX, 2, 10 and NMA, IX:24/2, 142

Variations

(solo keyboard)

K	K⁶	Theme	Key	Composition	MW	NMA	Remarks
A206	21a	?orig.	C	?London, 1765	—	—	lost; in Breitkopf catalogue
24	24	Dutch song (Laat ons juichen) by C. E. Graaf	G	The Hague, Jan 1766	XXI, 1	IX:26, 3	(The Hague, 1766)
25	25	Willem van Nassau (Dutch national song)	D	Amsterdam, Feb 1766	XXI, 6	IX:26, 9	(The Hague, 1766)
180	173c	Mio caro Adone from Salieri: La fiera di Venezia (Vienna, 1772)	G	Vienna, aut. 1773	XXI, 22	IX:26, 15	(Paris, 1778)
179	189a	Minuet (finale of Ob Conc. no.1, 1768) by J. C. Fischer	C	Salzburg, sum. 1774	XXI, 12	IX:26, 20	(Paris, 1778)
354	299a	Je suis Lindor (song in Beaumarchais: Le barbier de Séville, by A. L. Baudron)	Eb	Paris, early 1778	XXI, 58	IX:26, 34	(Paris, 1778)
265	300e	Ah vous dirai-je, maman (Fr. song)	C	Vienna, 1781–2	XXI, 36	IX:26, 49	(Vienna, 1785)
353	300f	La belle françoise (Adieu donc, dame françoise, Fr. song)	Eb	Vienna, 1781–2	XXI, 50	IX:26, 58	(Vienna, 1786)
264	315d	Lison dormait from N. Dezède: Julie (Paris, 1772)	C	Paris, late sum. 1778	XXI, 26	IX:26, 67	shortened (Paris, 1786); (Vienna, 1786)
352	374c	Dieu d'amour (March), chorus from Grétry: Les mariages samnites (Paris, 1776)	F	Vienna, June 1781	XXI, 44	IX:26, 82	(Vienna, 1786)
398	416e	Salve tu, Domine, chorus from Paisiello: I filosofi immaginarii (Vienna, 1781)	F	Vienna, March 1783	XXI, 68	IX:26, 90	(Vienna, 1786)

214

K	K⁶	Theme	Key	Composition	MW	NMA	Remarks	
460	454a	Come un agnello from Sarti: Fra i due litiganti (Milan, 1782)	A	Vienna, ?June 1784	XXI, 84	IX:26, 154	autograph has 2 variations; version with 8 variations doubtful: see MJb 1958, 18: MJb 1959, 127, 140; MJb 1971–2, 55; MJb 1978–9, 112; (Vienna, 1784)	100
455	455	Les hommes pieusement (Unser dummer Pöbel meint) from Gluck: La rencontre imprévue	G	Vienna, 25 Aug 1784 (C)	XXI, 74	IX:26, 98	(Vienna, 1785); earlier version 1783	100
500	500	probably orig.	B♭	Vienna, 12 Sept 1786 (C)	XXI, 94	IX:26, 112		
54	547b	probably orig.	F	Vienna, July 1788		IX:26, 157	1st edn. (1795) has spurious 4th variation; re-used by Mozart, with vn, K547	
573	573	Minuet [from Vc Sonata op.4 no.6] by J. P. Duport	D	Potsdam, 29 April 1789 (C)	XXI, 100	IX:26, 120	(Berlin, 1791); see Hortschansky, Mf, xvi (1963), 265	
613	613	Ein Weib ist das herrlichste Ding, by B. Schack or F. Gerl	F	Vienna, March 1791	XXI, 108	IX:26, 132	theme from music to Schikaneder play Der dumme Gärtner, 1789 (Vienna, 1791)	

Frag.: E♭, K236/588b, theme by Gluck, ?intended for variations; K438/383c, ?org

(piano duet)

K	K⁶	Theme	Key	Composition	MW	NMA	Remarks	
501	501	probably orig.	G	Vienna, 4 Nov 1786 (C)	XIX, 108	IX:24/ii, 96		

Miscellaneous

(solo keyboard)

K	K⁶	Title	Key	Composition	MW	NMA	Remarks	
—	1a	Andante	C	Salzburg, early 1761	—			2
—	1b	Allegro	C	Salzburg, early 1761	—			2
—	1c	Allegro	F	Salzburg, 11 Dec 1761	—			
—	1d	Minuet	F	Salzburg, 16 Dec 1761	—			
1	1e	Minuet	G	Salzburg, Dec–Jan 1761–2	XII, 2			
—	1f	Minuet	C	Salzburg, Dec–Jan 1761–2	—			

2	2	Minuet	F	Salzburg, Jan 1762	XXII, 3			
3	3	Allegro	Bb	Salzburg, 4 March 1762	XXII, 38			
4	4	Minuet	F	Salzburg, 11 May 1762	XXII, 3			
5	5	Minuet	F	Salzburg, 5 July 1762	XXII, 4			
9a	5a	Allegro	C	sum. 1763	—			
9b	5b	Andante	Bb	sum. 1763	—			
—	33B	[without title]	F	Zurich, Oct 1766	—			
41e	41e	Fugue		Salzburg, 1767	—			
72a	72a	Allegro	G	?Verona, Jan 1770	—	—	lost; only source is S. dalla Rosa portrait	13, 14
94	73h	Minuet	D	Salzburg, 1769	XXII, 5			
284a	284a	4 preludes		Mannheim, Nov 1777	—	—	identical with K395/300g	
284f	284f	Rondo					lost; mentioned in letter, 29 Nov 1777	
395	300g	Capriccio	C	Munich, Oct 1777	XXIV, no.24			
315a	315g	8 minuets		Salzburg, late 1773	—			
400	372a	Allegro	Bb	Vienna, 1781	XXIV, no.26		inc.; completed by M. Stadler	
401	375e	Fugue	g	Vienna, early 1782	XXII, 34		inc.; completed by M. Stadler; also duet version	
153	375f	Fugue	Eb	?Salzburg, 1783	XXIV, no.25		inc.; completed by S. Sechter	
394	383a	Prelude and fugue	C	Vienna, early 1782	XX, 20	IX:25		99
396	385f	Fantasia	c	Vienna, early 1782	XX, 214	IX:25	inc.; orig. with vn, see 'Chamber music'	
397	385g	Fantasia	d	Vienna, early 1782 or 1786–7	XX, 220	IX:25	last 10 bars (not in 1st edn.) probably spurious; see Plath, MJb 1971–2, 31	99
399	385i	Suite	C	Vienna, early 1782	XXII, 28		sarabande inc.	
154	385k	Fugue	g	Vienna, early 1782	XXIV		inc.	99
453a	453a	Funeral march	c	Vienna, 1784	—			
475	475	Fantasia	c	Vienna, 20 May 1785 (C)	XX, 224	IX:25	pubd with Sonata K457 (Vienna, 1785) as op.11	133
485	485	Rondo	D	Vienna, 10 Jan 1786 (D)	XXII, 8	IX:25	(Vienna, c1786)	121
494	494	Rondo	F	Vienna, 10 June 1786 (D)	XXII, 14	IX:25	(London, 1788), (Speyer, 1788); rev. version in Sonata K533	121
511	511	Rondo	a	Vienna, 11 March 1787 (CD)	XXII, 20	IX:25	(Vienna, 1787)	121

K	K°	Title	Key	Composition	MW	NMA	Remarks	
540	540	Adagio	b	Vienna, 19 March 1788 (C)	XXII, 56		?(Vienna, 1788)	121, 133
574	574	Gigue	G	Leipzig, 16 May 1789 (D)	XXII, 60			155
355	576b	Minuet	D	Vienna, ?1786–7	XXII, 6		trio by M. Stadler; see King (1955, 3/1970), 222f; Badura-Skoda, NZM, Jg. 127 (1966), 468	
236	588b	Andantino	E♭		XXII, 55		see 'Arrangements'	
312	590d	Allegro	g	Vienna, 1789–90	XXII, 39		inc.; ? for a sonata; see Plath, MJb 1971–2, 30f; Tyson, Mozart's Workshop	156

Frags.: Fugue, D, K73w, early 1773; Fugue, G, KA41/375g, 1777; Fugue, F, K375h; Fugue, F, KA33 and 40/383b, ?1788–9; Fugue, c, KA39/383d; Adagio, d, KA34/385h, 1786–7; Fantasia, f, KA32/383C; Minuet, D, KA34/576a, 1786–7

(2 keyboards)

K	K°	Title	Key	Composition	MW	NMA	Remarks	
426	426	Fugue	c	Vienna, 29 Dec 1783 (D)	XIX, 118	IX:24/1, 39	(Vienna, 1788); arr., with new introduction, for str, K546	100, 118, 166
—	—	Larghetto and Allegro	E♭	?Vienna, 1782–3	—	IX:24/1, suppl.	inc.; completed by M. Stadler; see Croll, MJb 1962–3, 708; MJb 1964, 28	100

Frags.: Grave-Presto, B♭, KA42/375b (52 bars), MW, XXIV, 60 and NMA, IX:24/1, 46; movt, B♭, KA43/375c (15 bars), NMA, IX:24/1, 49; Fugue, G, KA45/375d (23 bars), NMA, IX:24/1, 50; Allegro, c, KA44/426a (22 bars), NMA, IX:24/1, 51

(for mechanical organ or armonica)

K	K°	Title	Instrument	Key	Composition	MW	NMA	Remarks	
594	594	Adagio and Allegro	mechanical org	f	Vienna and elsewhere, Oct–Dec 1790	XXIV, no.27a	IX:27		155, 156
608	608	[Fantasia]	mechanical org	f	Vienna, 3 March 1791 (C)	X/100	IX:27		156
616	616	Andante	mechanical org	F	Vienna, 4 May 1791	X/109	IX:27		
356	617a	Adagio	armonica	C	Vienna, 1791	X/84	IX:27	arr. pf (Venice, 1791)	

Frags. for mechanical org.: Adagio, d, KA35/593a; Andante, F, K615a

MISCELLANEOUS

K	K*	Title	Key	Composition	MW	NMA	Remarks
A109b, 15a-ss	15a-ss	London Sketchbook		London, 1765	—	—	short pieces on 2 staves for kbd or sketches for orch
—	32a	Capricci		?1764–6	—	—	lost; see Constanze's letter to André, 2 March 1799; ?in LC
41f	41f	Fugue a 4		Salzburg, 1767	—	—	lost; in LC
393	385b	Solfeggios for voice		Vienna, ?Aug 1782	XXIV, no.49		
—	385n	Fugue a 4	A	Vienna, ?1782	—		frag.
443	404b	Fugue a 3	G	Vienna, ?1782	—		inc.; completed by M. Stadler facs. in Lach, Mozart als Theoretiker (Vienna, 1918)
—	453b	Exercise book for Barbara Ployer			—		
485a	506a	Attwood Studies		Vienna, 1785–6	—	X:30, 1	
A294d	516f	Musikalisches Würfelspiel	C	Vienna, 1787	—		
A78	620b	[contrapuntal study]	b	Vienna, ?Sept 1791	—		chorale setting; ?sketch for Die Zauberflöte K620

ARRANGEMENTS ETC

K	K*	Orig. composer, work	Orig. scoring	Key	Mozart's scoring	Date of arr.	MW	NMA	Remarks
37	37	i H. F. Raupach, op.1 no.5 ii ? iii L. Honauer, op.2 no.3	kbd	F	kbd, 2 ob, 2 hn, str	Salzburg, April 1767	XVI/i, 1	X:28/ii, 3	
39	39	i Raupach, op.1 no.1 ii J. Schobert, op.17 no.2 iii Raupach, op.1 no.1	kbd	B♭	kbd, 2 ob, 2 hn, str	Salzburg, June 1767	XVI/i, 35	X:28/ii, 45	
40	40	i Honauer, op.2 no.1 ii J. G. Eckard, op.1 no.4 iii C. P. E. Bach, w117	kbd	D	kbd, 2 ob, 2 hn, str	Salzburg, July 1767	XVI/i, 67	X:28/ii, 84	cadenza K624/626aII, C

K	K⁶	Orig. composer, work	Orig. scoring	Key	Mozart's scoring	Date of arr.	MW	NMA	Remarks	
41	41	i Honauer, op.1 no.1 ii Raupach, op.1 no.1 iii Honauer, op.1 no.1	kbd	G	kbd, 2 ob, 2 hn, str	Salzburg, July 1767	XVI/i, 99	X:28/ii, 125		
107, 1	107, 1	J. C. Bach, op.5 no.2	kbd	D	kbd, 2 vn, b	1772	—	X:28/ii, 165	cadenzas k624/626aII. A–B	26, 27
107, 2	107, 2	J. C. Bach, op.5 no.3	kbd	G	kbd, 2 vn, b	1772	—	X:28/ii, 187		26
107, 3	107, 3	J. C. Bach, op.5 no.4	kbd	E♭	kbd, 2 vn, b	1772	—	X:28/ii, 203		26
284e	284e	J. B. Wendling, conc.	fl, str		?addl. wind	Mannheim, Nov 1777	—	—	lost; see letter, 21 Nov 1777	
404a	404a	6 preludes and fugues 1 p ?orig., f J. S. Bach BWV853 2 p ?orig., f BWV883 3 p ?orig., f BWV882 4 p BWV527/ii, f BWV1080 no.8 5 p, f BWV526/ii, iii 6 p, f W. F. Bach Fugue no.8	kbd	d g F F E♭ f	vn, va, vc	Vienna, 1782	—	—	doubtful; see Kirkendale, JAMS, xvii (1964), 43 and MJf, xviii (1965), 195; Holschneider, MJf, xvii (1964), 51	
405	405	J. S. Bach 5 fugues BWV871, 876, 878, 877, 874	kbd	c, E♭, E, d, D	2 vn, va, vc	Vienna, 1782	—	—	see Kirkendale, MJb 1962–3, 140	
—	—	J. S. Bach BWV891	kbd	c	2 vn, va, vc	?Vienna, 1782	—	—	see Croll, ÖMz, xxi (1966), 508	
—	—	6 preludes and fugues 1 p ?orig., f J. S. Bach BWV548 2 p ?orig., f BWV877 3 p ?orig., f BWV876 4 p ?orig., f BWV891 5 p ?orig., f BWV874 6 p ?orig., f BWV878	kbd	e d E♭ b D E	2 vn, va, vc	?Vienna, 1782	—	—	very doubtful; see Kirkendale, JAMS, xvii (1964), 43	

			kbd					
—	—	3 preludes and fugues 1 p ?orig., f J. S. Bach BWV849 d 2 p ?orig., f BWV867 a 3 p ?orig., f BWV546 c		2 vn, 2 va, vc	?Vienna, 1782	—		very doubtful; see Kirkendale, *JAMS*, xvii (1964), 43
470a	470a	G. B. Viotti, Vn Conc. no.16		addl tpt, timp	Vienna, April 1785	—		lost Andante K470 ? intended for this
A109g no.19	537d	C. P. E. Bach, Ich folge dir, from Auferstehung und Himmelfahrt Jesu (1787)	T, tpt, str	addl fl, ob, tpt	Vienna, Feb 1788	—		
566	566	G. F. Handel, Acis and Galatea (1718)	S, T, T, T, B, rec, 2 ob, bn, 2 vn, va, bc	addl 2 fl, 2 cl, bn, 2 hn	Vienna, Nov 1788	—	X:28/1/i	115
572	572	Handel, Messiah (1742)	S, A, T, B, SATB, 2 ob, 2 tpt, timp, str	addl 2 fl, 2 cl, 2 bn, 2 hn, 3 trbn, rev. tpt parts	Vienna, March 1789	—	X:28/1/ii	
591	591	Handel, Alexander's Feast (1736)	S, T, B, SATB, 2 rec, 2 ob, 3 bn, 2 hn, 2 tpt, timp, str	addl 2 fl, 2 cl, rev. tpt parts	Vienna, July 1790	—	X:28/1/iii	
592	592	Handel, Ode for St Cecilia's Day (1739)	S, T, SATB, fl, 2 ob, 2 tpt, timp, lute, str	addl fl, 2 cl, 2 bn, 2 hn, rev. tpt parts	Vienna, July 1790	—	X:28/1/iv	
625	592a	? B. Schack, Nun liebes Weibchen, duet, in Schikaneder's play Der Stein der Weisen	S, B, ?pf	S, B, fl, 2 ob, 2 bn, 2 hn, str	Vienna, Aug 1790	—	VI/2, 235	?orig.

K	K⁶	Orig. composer, work	Orig. scoring	Key	Mozart's scoring	Date of arr.	MW	NMA	Remarks
624	626aII, D–O	Cadenzas	kbd			various			D(A61a), F–G, H for J. S. Schroeter op.3 nos.1, 4, 6; K for I. von Beecke Conc. in D: N, O for unknown conc; L lost; E, I unauthentic
	626b, 28	C. W. Gluck, gavotte from Paride ed Elena (1769)	orch		2 fl, 5 tpt, timp				? Mozart's contribution to Divertimento K187
—	—	L. Mozart: Litaniae de venerabili altaris sacramento (1762)	S, A, T, B, SATB, 2 hn, str		various changes		—	X:28/3–5/i	

19 cadenzas K293e for J. C. Bach arias, 1772–3, some not authentic: see Plath, *MJb 1960–61*, 106, and *MJb 1971–2*, 20

Bibliography

CATALOGUES, BIBLIOGRAPHIES, LETTERS, DOCUMENTS

L. von Köchel: *Chronologisch-thematisches Verzeichnis sämtlicher Tonwerke Wolfgang Amade Mozarts* (Leipzig, 1862; 2/1905 ed. P. Graf von Waldersee; 3/1937 ed. A. Einstein, repr. 4/1958, 5/1963, with suppl. 3/1947; 6/1964 ed. F. Giegling, A. Weinmann and G. Sievers, repr. 7/1965) [reviews by A. H. King, *Mf*, xviii (1965), 307 and B. E. Wilson, *Notes*, xxi (1963–4), 531; corrections and suppls. by P. W. van Reijen, *MJb 1971–2*, 342–401]

C. von Wurzbach: *Mozart-Buch* (Vienna, 1869)

H. de Curzon: *Essai de bibliographie mozartienne: revue critique des ouvrages relatifs à W. A. Mozart et ses oeuvres* (Paris, 1906)

L. Schiedermair, ed.: *Die Briefe W. A. Mozarts und seiner Familie: erste kritische Gesamtausgabe* (Munich and Leipzig, 1914)

O. Keller: *W. A. Mozart: Bibliographie und Ikonographie* (Berlin, 1927)

E. Anderson, ed.: *Letters of Mozart and his Family* (London, 1938; rev. 2/1966 ed. A. H. King and M. Carolan)

O. E. Deutsch, ed.: *Wolfgang Amadeus Mozart: Verzeichnis aller meiner Werke: Faksimile der Handschrift mit dem Beiheft 'Mozarts Werkverzeichnis 1784–1791'* (Vienna, 1938; Eng. edn., 1956)

E. Müller von Asow, ed.: *Gesamtausgabe der Briefe und Aufzeichnungen der Familie Mozart* (Berlin, 1942)

——: *Wolfgang Amadeus Mozart: Verzeichnis aller meiner Werke und Leopold Mozart: Verzeichnis der Jugendwerke W. A. Mozarts* (Vienna, 1943, 2/1956)

O. E. Deutsch: *Mozart: die Dokumente seines Lebens, gesammelt und erläutert* (Kassel, 1961; Eng. trans., 1965, 2/1966; suppl. 1978)

W. A. Bauer, O. E. Deutsch and J. H. Eibl, eds.: *Mozart: Briefe und Aufzeichnungen* (Kassel, 1962–75) [complete edn.; for later discoveries see G. Croll, *MJb 1967*, 12, and R. Angermüller and S. Dahms-Schneider, *MJb 1968–70*, 211–41]

O. Schneider and A. Algatzy: *Mozart-Handbuch: Chronik, Werk, Bibliographie* (Vienna, 1962)

R. Angermüller and O. Schneider: 'Mozart-Bibliographie (bis 1970)', *MJb 1975*

——: *Mozart-Bibliographie 1971–1975 mit Nachträgen bis 1970* (Kassel, 1978)

O. Wessely: 'Ergänzerungen zur Mozart-Bibliographie', *SMw*, xxix (1978), 37–68

ICONOGRAPHY

O. Keller: *W. A. Mozart: Bibliographie und Ikonographie* (Berlin, 1927)

R. Tenschert: *Wolfgang Amadeus Mozart 1756–1791: sein Leben in Bildern* (Leipzig, 1935)

R. Bory: *La vie et l'oeuvre de Wolfgang-Amadeus Mozart par l'image* (Geneva, 1948) [also Eng. edn.]

G. Rech: *Wolfgang Amadeus Mozart: ein Lebensweg in Bildern* (Munich and Berlin, 1955)

O. E. Deutsch: 'Mozart's Portraits', *The Mozart Companion*, ed. H. C. R. Landon and D. Mitchell (London, 1956, 2/1965), 1

R. Petzoldt: *Wolfgang Amadeus Mozart: sein Leben in Bildern* (Leipzig, 1956, 2/1956)

E. Valentin: *Mozart: eine Bildbiographie* (Munich, 1959; Eng. trans., 1959)

O. E. Deutsch: *Mozart und seine Welt in zeitgenössischen Bildern* (Kassel, 1961) [in Ger. and Eng.]

A. Hutchings: *Mozart: the Man, the Musician* (London, 1976)

SPECIALIST PUBLICATIONS

Mitteilungen für die Mozartgemeinde in Berlin (1895–1925)

Mozarteums-Mitteilungen (1918–21)

Mozart-Jb, i–iii (1923–9)

Bulletin de la Société d'Etudes Mozartiennes, i (Paris, 1930–32)

Tagung der Internationalen Stiftung Mozarteum: Salzburg 1931

Wiener Figaro, Mitteilungen der Mozartgemeinde Wien (1931–)

Neues Mozart-Jb, i–iii (1941–3)

MJb 1950– [with annual bibliography up to 1975]

Mitteilungen der Internationalen Stiftung Mozarteum (1952–)

Acta Mozartiana, Mitteilungen der Deutschen Mozart-Gesellschaft (1954–)

Prefaces and Critical Commentaries to all vols. of *W. A. Mozart: Neue Ausgabe sämtlicher Werke* (Kassel, 1955–)

Internazionale Mozartkonferenz: Praha 1956

Kongressbericht: Wien Mozartjahr 1956

Les influences étrangères dans l'oeuvre de Mozart: CNRS Paris 1956

'W. A. Mozart emlékére', *Zenetudományi tanulmányok*, v (1957)

'Mozart und Italien: Rom 1974', *AnMc*, no.18 (1978)

MT, cxxii/7 (1981)

SKETCHES, FRAGMENTS, RESEARCH, AUTHENTICITY, MANUSCRIPTS, SOURCES, PUBLICATION

L. Schiedermair: *W. A. Mozarts Handschrift in zeitlich geordneten Nachbildungen* (Bückeburg and Leipzig, 1919)

M. Blaschitz: *Die Salzburger Mozart-Fragmente* (diss., U. of Bonn, 1924; part pubd in *Jb der philosophischen Fakultät, Bonn 1924–5*)

O. E. Deutsch and C. B. Oldman: 'Mozart-Drucke: eine bibliographische Ergänzung zu Köchels Werkverzeichnis', *ZMw*, xiv (1931–2), 135, 337

C. B. Oldman: 'Mozart and Modern Research', *PRMA*, lviii (1931–2), 43

G. de Saint-Foix: *Les éditions françaises de Mozart (1765–1801)* (Paris, 1933)

H. G. Farmer and H. Smith: *New Mozartiana: the Mozart Relics in the Zavertal Collection at the University of Glasgow* (Glasgow, 1935/R1976)

A. H. King: 'A Census of Mozart Musical Autographs in England', *MQ*, xxxviii (1952), 566; repr. in King (1955)

O. E. Deutsch: 'Mozarts Nachlass: aus den Briefen Constanzes an den Verlag André', *MJb 1953*, 32

——: 'Mozarts Verleger', *MJb 1955*, 49

R. Engländer: 'Die Mozart-Skizzen der Universitätsbibliothek Uppsala: eine entstehungsgeschichtliche Studie', *STMf*, xxxvii (1955), 96; suppl. in *Mf*, ix (1956), 307

A. H. King: *Mozart in the British Museum* (London, 1956/R1975)

H. Moldenhauer: 'Übersicht der Musikmanuskripte W. A. Mozarts in den Vereinigten Staaten von Amerika (1956)', *MJb 1956*, 88

Mozart en France (Paris, 1956) [*F-Pn* exhibition catalogue]

L. Nowak: 'Die Wiener Mozart-Autographen', *ÖMz*, xi (1956), 180

A. Weinmann: *Wiener Musikverleger und Musikalienhändler von Mozarts Zeit bis gegen 1860* (Vienna, 1956)

E. Hertzmann: 'Mozart's Creative Process', *MQ*, xliii (1957), 187 [repr. in Lang, 1963]

W. Plath: 'Das Skizzenblatt KV.467a', *MJb 1959*, 114

M. and C. Raeburn: 'Mozart's Manuscripts in Florence', *ML*, xl (1959), 334

L. Finscher: 'Maximilian Stadler und Mozarts Nachlass', *MJb 1960–61*, 168

W. Plath: 'Beiträge zur Mozart-Autographie I: die Handschrift Leopold Mozarts', *MJb 1960–61*, 82–118

W. Senn: 'Mozarts Skizze der Ballettmusik zu Le gelosie del serraglio', *AcM*, xxxiii (1961), 169

A. Holschneider: 'Neue Mozartiana in Italien', *Mf*, xv (1962), 227

W. Senn: 'Die Mozart-Überlieferung im Stift Heilig Kreuz zu Augsburg', *Neues Augsburger Mozartbuch* (Augsburg, 1962), 333–68

K.-H. Köhler: 'Die Erwerbung der Mozart-Autographe der Berliner Staatsbibliothek: ein Beitrag zur Geschichte des Nachlasses', *MJb 1962–3*, 55

'Mozart-Autographe: Verzeichnis der verschollenen Mozart-Autographe der ehemaligen Preussischen Staatsbibliothek Berlin', *MJb 1962–3*, 306 [see also *Acta Mozartiana*, xii (1965), 66]

W. Plath: 'Miscellanea Mozartiana I', *Festschrift Otto Erich Deutsch* (Kassel, 1963), 135

W. Rehm: 'Miscellanea Mozartiana II', *Festschrift Otto Erich Deutsch* (Kassel, 1963), 141

224   *Mozart*

A. A. Abert: ' Methoden der Mozartforschung', *MJb 1964*, 22 [on Lambach symphonies]

H. Engel: 'Probleme der Mozartforschung', *MJb 1964*, 38

E. Hess: 'Ein neu entdecktes Skizzenblatt Mozarts', *MJb 1964*, 185

W. Plath: 'Bemerkungen zu einem missdeuteten Skizzenblatt Mozarts', *Festschrift Walter Gerstenberg* (Wolfenbüttel, 1964)

——: 'Der Ballo des "Ascanio" und die Klavierstücke KV Anh. 207', *MJb 1964*, 111

——: 'Der gegenwärtige Stand der Mozart-Forschung', *IMSCR, ix Salzburg 1964*, 47, 88

G. Rech: 'Mozart: Results of Present-day Research on his Works', *Universitas*, vii (1965), 355

H. Federhofer: 'Mozartiana im Musikaliennachlass von Ferdinand Bischoff', *MJb 1965–6*, 15

W. Plath: 'Überliefert die dubiose Klavierromanze in As, KV-Anh.205, das verschollene Quintett-Fragment KV-Anh.54 (452a)?', *MJb 1965–6*, 71

G. Croll: 'Zu den Verzeichnissen von Mozarts nachgelassenen Fragmenten und Entwürfen', *ÖMz*, xxi (1966), 250

D. Kolbin: 'Autographe Mozarts und seiner Familie in der UdSSR', *MJb 1968–70*, 281

R. D. Levin: 'Das Konzert für Klavier und Violine D-Dur KV Anh. 56/315f und das Klarinettenquintett B-Dur, KV Anh. 91/516c: ein Ergänzungsversuch', *MJb 1968–70*, 304 [in Eng.]

W. Plath: 'Mozartiana in Fulda und Frankfurt', *MJb 1968–70*, 333

M. H. Schmid: *Die Musiksammlung der Erzabtei, St. Peter in Salzburg: Katalog I. Teil: Leopold und Wolfgang Mozart, Joseph und Michael Haydn*, Schriftenreihe der Internationalen Stiftung Mozarteum, iii–iv (Salzburg, 1970)

K. Pfannhauser: 'Epilegomena Mozartiana', *MJb 1971–2*, 268–312

W. Plath: 'Leopold Mozarts Notenbuch für Wolfgang (1762): eine Fälschung?', *MJb 1971–2*, 337

W. Plath and others: 'Zur Echtheitsfrage bei Mozart', *MJb 1971–2*, 19–67 [incl. discussions]

N. Zaslaw: 'A Rediscovered Mozart Autograph at Cornell University', *MJb 1971–2*, 419

D. N. Leeson and D. Whitwell: 'Mozart's Thematic Catalogue', *MT*, cxiv (1973), 781

A. H. King: 'Some Aspects of Recent Mozart Research', *PRMA*, c (1973–4), 1

W. Senn: 'Beiträge zur Mozartforschung', *AcM*, xlviii (1976), 205

W. Plath: 'Beiträge zur Mozart-Autographie II: Schriftchronologie 1770–1780', *MJb 1976–7*, 131–73

A. Tyson: 'A Reconstruction of Nannerl Mozart's Music Book (Notenbuch)', *ML*, lx (1979), 389

C. Wolff, ed.: *The String Quartets of Haydn, Mozart, and Beethoven:*

Studies of the Autograph Manuscripts: Isham Memorial Library 1979 [articles on Mozart by L. Finscher, M. Flothuis, A. Tyson and C. Wolff]

A. Tyson: 'The Origin of Mozart's "Hunt" Quartet, K.458', *Music and Bibliography: Essays in Honour of Alec Hyatt King* (London, 1980), 132

——: 'The Date of Mozart's Piano Sonata in B flat, KV 333/315c: The 'Linz' Sonata?', *Musik – Edition – Interpretation: Gedenkschrift Günter Henle* (Munich, 1980)

——: 'The Mozart Fragments', *JAMS*, xxxiv (1981), 471–510

——: 'The Two Slow Movements of Mozart's Paris Symphony K297', *MT*, cxxii (1981), 17

N. Zaslaw: 'Leopold Mozart's List of his Son's Works', *Essays on Music of the Classic Era in Honor of Barry S. Brook* (New York, 1982)

A. Tyson: *Mozart's Workshop* (Berkeley and Los Angeles, in preparation)

BIOGRAPHIES, STUDIES OF LIFE AND WORKS

F. Schlichtegroll: 'Johannes Chrysostomus Wolfgang Gottlieb Mozart', *Nekrolog auf das Jahr 1791* (Gotha, 1793), ed. L. Landshoff (Munich, 1924); as *Mozarts Leben* (Graz, 1794/R1974) [see also Favier, 1976]

F. X. Niemetschek: *Leben des k.k. Kapellmeisters Wolfgang Gottlieb Mozart nach Originalquellen beschrieben* (Prague, 1798, enlarged 2/1808; Eng. trans., 1956) [see also Favier, 1976]

[I. F. Arnold]: *Mozarts Geist: seine kurze Biographie und ästhetische Darstellung* (Erfurt, 1803)

I. F. Arnold: *Galerie der berühmtesten Tonkünstler des 18. und 19. Jahrhunderts . . . W. A. Mozart und Joseph Haydn: Versuch einer Parallele* (Erfurt, 1810, 2/1816)

Stendhal [M.-H. Beyle]: *Lettres . . . sur le célèbre compositeur Haydn: suivies d'une vie de Mozart et considérations sur Métastase* (Paris, 1814, rev. 2/1817 as *Vies de Haydn, de Mozart et de Métastase*; Eng. trans., 1972)

P. Lichtenthal: *Cenni biografici intorno al celebre maestro Wolfgang Amadeo Mozart* (Milan, 1816)

G. N. Nissen: *Biographie W. A. Mozarts nach Originalbriefen* (Leipzig, 1828/R1964 and 1972)

A. D. Oulibicheff: *Nouvelle biographie de Mozart* (Moscow, 1843, 2/1890–92)

E. Holmes: *The Life of Mozart* (London, 1845, 2/1878, repr. 1932)

O. Jahn: *W. A. Mozart* (Leipzig, 1856, 2/1867; ed. H. Deiters, 3/1889–91, 4/1905–7; Eng. trans., 1882) [for later edns. see H. Abert, 1919–21]

L. Nohl: *Mozart* (Leipzig, 1863, enlarged 2/1877 as *Mozarts Leben*, rev. 3/1906)

G. Nottebohm: *Mozartiana* (Leipzig, 1880/*R*1972)

W. W. F[owler]: *Stray Notes on Mozart and his Music* (Edinburgh, 1910)

T. de Wyzewa and G. de Saint-Foix: *Wolfgang Amédée Mozart: sa vie musicale et son oeuvre* (Paris, 1912–46/*R*1979) [iii–v by Saint-Foix alone]

A. Schurig: *Wolfgang Amadeus Mozart: sein Leben und sein Werk* (Leipzig, 1913, 2/1923)

H. de Curzon: *Mozart* (Paris, 1914, 2/1927)

E. W. Engel: *Wolfgang Amade Mozart* (Vienna, 1914)

H. Abert: *W. A. Mozart: neu bearbeitete und erweiterte Ausgabe von Otto Jahns 'Mozart'* (Leipzig, 1919–21, 3/1955–66)

J. S. J. Kreitmeier: *W. A. Mozart: eine Charakterzeichnung des grossen Meisters nach literarischen Quellen* (Düsseldorf, 1919)

L. Schiedermair: *Mozart: sein Leben und seine Werke* (Munich, 1922, rev., enlarged 2/1948)

B. Paumgartner: *Mozart* (Berlin, 1927, enlarged 6/1967)

D. Hussey: *Wolfgang Amade Mozart* (London, 1928)

M. Davenport: *Mozart* (New York, 1932)

H. Ghéon: *Promenades avec Mozart* (Paris, 1932, 7/1948; Eng. trans., 1932 as *In Search of Mozart*)

R. Haas: *Wolfgang Amadeus Mozart* (Potsdam, 1933, 2/1950)

E. F. Schmid: *W. A. Mozart* (Lübeck, 1934, enlarged 3/1955)

E. Blom: *Mozart* (London, 1935, 3/1975)

A. Boschot: *Mozart* (Paris, 1935, 2/1949)

W. J. Turner: *Mozart: the Man and his Works* (London, 1938, 3/1966)

A. Einstein: *Mozart: his Character, his Work* (Eng. trans., New York, 1945; Ger. orig., 1947, 4/1960)

R. Tenschert: *Wolfgang Amadeus Mozart* (Salzburg, 1951; Eng. trans., 1952)

E. Schenk: *Wolfgang Amadeus Mozart: eine Biographie* (Vienna and Zurich, 1955, rev. 2/1975; Eng. trans., abridged, 1960 as *Mozart and his Times*)

F. Hadamowsky and L. Nowak: *Mozart: Werk und Zeit* (Vienna, 1956)

J. N. Burk: *Mozart and his Music* (New York, 1959)

J. and B. Massin: *Wolfgang Amadeus Mozart: biographie, histoire de l'oeuvre* (Paris, 1959, 2/1971)

C. Haldane: *Mozart* (London, 1960)

F. Blume: 'Mozart, Wolfgang Amadeus', *MGG* [iconography by W. Rehm, bibliography and work-list by F. Lippmann, list of edns. by R. Schaal]

S. Sadie: *Mozart* (London, 1966)

A. H. King: *Mozart: a Biography with a Survey of Books, Editions and Recordings* (London, 1970)

M. Levey: *The Life and Death of Mozart* (London, 1971)

G. Favier, ed.: *Vie de W. A. Mozart par Franz Xaver Niemetschek précedée du nécrologe de Schlichtegroll* (St Etienne, 1976) [in Ger. and Fr., with introduction and notes]

A. Hutchings: *Mozart: the Man, the Musician* (London, 1976)

W. Hildesheimer: *Mozart* (Frankfurt am Main, 1977; Eng. trans., 1979)

I. Keys: *Mozart: his Life in his Music* (London, 1980)

LIFE: PARTICULAR ASPECTS AND EPISODES

F. Rochlitz: 'Verbürgte Anekdoten aus Wolfgang Gottlieb Mozarts Leben: ein Beitrag zur richtigeren Kenntnis dieses Mannes, als Mensch und Künstler', *AMZ*, i (1798–9), 17, 49, 81, 113, 145, 177, 289, 480, 854; iii (1800–01), 450, 493, 590

L. da Ponte: *Memorie di Lorenzo da Ponte, da Ceneda: scritte da esso* (New York, 1823–7; Eng. trans., 1929/*R*1967)

E. Mörike: *Mozart auf der Reise nach Prag* (Stuttgart and Augsburg, 1856; Eng. trans., 1934, 1946) [novel]

C. F. Pohl: *Mozart and Haydn in London* (Vienna, 1867/*R*1970)

A. J. Hammerle: *Mozart und einige Zeitgenossen: neue Beiträge für Salzburgische Geschichte, Literatur und Musik* (Salzburg, 1877)

K. Prieger: *Urtheile bedeutender Dichter, Philosopher und Musiker über Mozart* (Wiesbaden, 1885–6)

R. Procházka: *Mozart in Prag* (Prague, 1899; rev. and enlarged by P. Nettl as *Mozart in Böhmen*, 1938)

E. K. Blümml: *Aus Mozarts Freundes- und Familienkreis* (Leipzig, 1923)

O. E. Deutsch: *Mozart und die Wiener Logen: zur Geschichte seiner Freimaurer-Kompositionen* (Vienna, 1932)

P. Nettl: *Mozart und die königliche Kunst: die freimaurerische Grundlage der Zauberflöte* (Berlin, 1932, enlarged 2/1956)

W. Kipp: *Mozart und das Elsass* (Colmar, 1941)

H. A. Thies: *Mozart und München: ein Gedenkbuch* (Munich, 1941)

E. F. Schmid: 'Mozart und das geistliche Augsburg, insonderheit das Chorherrenstift Heiligkreuz', *Augsburger Mozartbuch* (Augsburg, 1942–3), 40

E. J. Luin: 'Mozarts Aufenthalt in Rom', *Neues Mozart-Jb*, iii (1943), 45

E. Schenk: 'Neues zu Mozarts erster Italienreise: Mozart in Verona', *Neues Mozart-Jb*, iii (1943), 22

I. Hoesli: *W. A. Mozart: Briefstil eines Musikgenies* (Zurich, 1948)

A. B. Gottron: *Mozart und Mainz* (Baden-Baden and Mainz, 1951)

M. Fehr and L. Caflisch: *Der junge Mozart in Zürich: ein Beitrag zur Mozart-Biographie auf Grund bisher unbekannter Dokumente* (Zurich, 1952)

M. Kenyon: *Mozart in Salzburg* (London, 1952)

E. J. Luin: 'Mozart: Ritter vom Goldenen Sporn', *SMw*, xxii (1955), 30

N. Medici di Marignano and R. Hughes: *A Mozart Pilgrimage: Being the Travel Diaries of Vincent and Mary Novello in the Year 1829* (London, 1955/*R*1975)

A. Ostoja: *Mozart e l'Italia* (Bologna, 1955)

E. Schenk: 'Mozart in Mantua', *SMw*, xx (1955), 1

G. Barblan and A. della Corte: *Mozart in Italia* (Milan, 1956)

O. E. Deutsch: 'Phantasiestücke aus der Mozart-Biographie', *MJb 1956*, 46

L. E. Staehelin: 'Neues zu Mozarts Aufenthalten in Lyon, Genf und Bern', *SMz*, xcvi (1956), 46

O. E. Deutsch: 'Aus Schiedenhofens Tagebuch', *MJb 1957*, 15

P. Nettl: *Mozart and Masonry* (New York, 1957/*R*1970)

A. Greither: *Wolfgang Amadé Mozart: seine Leidensgeschichte aus Briefen und Dokumenten zusammengestellt* (Heidelberg, 1958)

W. Hummel: *Nannerl Mozarts Tagebuchblätter, mit Eintragungen ihres Bruders Wolfgang Amadeus* (Salzburg, 1958)

E. F. Schmid: 'Zur Entstehungszeit von Mozarts italienischen Sinfonien', *MJb 1958*, 71

E. Winternitz: 'Gangflow Trazom: an Essay on Mozart's Script, Pastimes, and Nonsense Letters', *JAMS*, xi (1958), 200

H. F. Deininger and J. Herz: 'Beiträge zur Genealogie der ältesten schwäbischen Vorfahren W. A. Mozarts', *Neues Augsburger Mozartbuch* (Augsburg, 1962), 1–76

O. E. Deutsch: 'Mozart in Zinzendorfs Tagebüchern', *SMz*, cii (1962), 211

H. W. Hamann: 'Mozarts Schülerkreis', *MJb 1962–3*, 115; suppl. by C. Bär, *Acta Mozartiana*, xi (1964), 58

O. E. Deutsch: 'Die Legende von Mozarts Vergiftung', *MJb 1964*, 7 [with discussion by C. Bär]

L. Wegele: 'Die Mozart: neue Forschungen zur Ahnengeschichte Wolfgang Amadeus Mozarts', *Acta Mozartiana*, xi (1964), 18; also in *Mitteilungen der Internationalen Stiftung Mozarteum*, xii/3–4 (1964), 1

W. Lievense: *De familie Mozart in Nederland: een reisverslag* (Hilversum, 1965)

C. Bär: *Mozart: Krankheit, Tod, Begräbnis*, Schriftenreihe der Internationalen Stiftung Mozarteum, i (Kassel, 1966, rev. 2/1972)

A. R. Mohr: *Das Frankfurter Mozart-Buch* (Frankfurt, 1968)

L. E. Staehelin: *Die Reise der Familie Mozart durch die Schweiz* (Berne, 1968)

A. Greither: *Die sieben grossen Opern Mozarts: mit ein Pathographie Mozarts* (Heidelberg, 2/1970) ['Pathographie' not in 1956 edn.]

H. Schuler: *Die Gesamtverwandschaft Wolfgang Amadeus Mozarts* (Essen, c1972)

——: *Die Vorfahren Wolfgang Mozarts* (Essen, 1972)

J. H. Eibl: 'Die Mozarts und der Erzbischof', *ÖMz*, xxx (1975), 329

M. H. Schmid: *Mozart und die Salzburger Tradition* (Tutzing, 1976)

K. Thomson: 'Mozart and Freemasonry', *ML*, lvii (1976), 25

———: *The Masonic Thread in Mozart* (London, 1977)

C. Bär: 'Er war ... kein guter Wirth: eine Studie über Mozarts Verhältnis zum Geld', *Acta Mozartiana*, xxv (1978), 30

ESSAYS, COLLECTIVE WORKS

D. F. Tovey: *Essays in Musical Analysis* (London, 1935–44) [on к297/300*a*, 338, 425, 543, 550, 551; 250/248*b*; 414/385*p*, 450, 453, 488, 491; 218, 219, 261, 313/285*c*, 314/285*d*, 315/285*e*, 299/297*c*, 622; 452; 497]

H. F. Deininger, ed.: *Augsburger Mozartbuch: Zeitschrift des historischen Vereins für Schwaben*, lv–lvi (Augsburg, 1942–3)

E. F. Schmid: *Ein schwäbisches Mozartbuch* (Stuttgart, 1948)

A. H. King: *Mozart in Retrospect: Studies in Criticism and Bibliography* (London, 1955, 3/1970/*R*1976)

A. Einstein: *Essays on Music* (New York, 1956) [incl. 8 on Mozart]

H. C. R. Landon and D. Mitchell, eds.: *The Mozart Companion* (London, 1956, 2/1965)

P. Schaller and H. Kühner, eds.: *Mozart-Aspekte* (Olten and Freiburg, 1956) [symposium]

Neues Augsburger Mozartbuch: Zeitschrift des historischen Vereins für Schwaben, lxii–lxiii (Augsburg, 1962)

F. Blume: *Syntagma musicologicum: gesammelte Reden und Schriften* (Kassel, 1963) ['Haydn und Mozart', 571; 'Wolfgang Amadeus Mozart', 583; 'Wolfgang Amadeus Mozart: Geltung und Wirkung', 670; 'Mozarts Konzerte und ihre Überlieferung', 686; 'Requiem und kein Ende', 714]

P. H. Lang, ed.: *The Creative World of Mozart* (New York, 1963)

Mozartgemeinde Wien 1913 bis 1963: Forschung und Interpretation (Vienna, 1964)

E. Wellesz and F. Sternfeld, eds.: *The Age of Enlightenment 1745–1790*, NOHM, vii (1973)

Festschrift Erich Valentin zum 70. Geburtstag (Regensburg, 1976) [incl. 12 essays on Mozart]

WORKS: STYLE, INFLUENCES, PARTICULAR ASPECTS

A. Heuss: 'Das dämonische Element in Mozarts Werken', *ZIMG*, vii (1905–6), 175

G. Schünemann, ed.: *Mozart als achtjähriger Komponist: ein Notenbuch Wolfgangs* (Leipzig, 1909)

R. Lach: *W. A. Mozart als Theoretiker* (Vienna, 1918)

F. Torrefranca: 'Le origini dello stile Mozartiano', *RMI*, xxviii (1921), 263; xxxiii (1926), 321, 505; xxxiv (1927), 1, 169, 493; xxxvi (1929), 373

W. Lüthy: *Mozart und die Tonartencharakteristik* (Strasbourg,

1931/*R*1974)

C. Thieme: *Der Klangstil des Mozartorchesters* (Leipzig, 1936)

A. Einstein: 'Mozart's Choice of Keys', *MQ*, xxvii (1941), 415; repr. in Einstein (1945)

A. H. King: 'Mozart's Counterpoint: its Growth and Significance', *ML*, xxvi (1945), 12; repr. in King (1955)

J. Chantavoine: *Mozart dans Mozart* (Paris, 1948)

E. J. Dent: 'Mozart: Lecture on a Master Mind', *Proceedings of the British Academy*, xxxix (1953), 181

J. A. Westrup: 'Cherubino and the G minor Symphony', *Fanfare for Ernest Newman* (London, 1955), 181

D. Bartha: 'Mozart et le folklore musical de l'Europe centrale', *Les influences étrangères dans l'oeuvre de Mozart: CNRS Paris 1956*, 157

F. Blume: 'Mozart's Style and Influence', *The Mozart Companion*, ed. H. C. R. Landon and D. Mitchell (London, 1956, 2/1965), 10

I. M. Bruce: 'A Note on Mozart's Bar-rhythms', *MR*, xvii (1956), 35

H. T. David: 'Mozartean Modulations', *MQ*, xlii (1956), 193; repr. in Lang (1963)

H. Engel: 'Mozarts Instrumentation', *MJb 1956*, 51

E. E. Lowinsky: 'On Mozart's Rhythm', *MQ*, xlii (1956), 162; repr. in Lang (1963)

E. F. Schmid: 'Mozart and Haydn', *MQ*, xlii (1956), 145

B. Szabolcsi: 'Die "Exotismen" Mozarts', *Internazionale Mozartkonferenz: Praha 1956*, 181; Eng. trans., *ML*, xxxvii (1956), 323

E. Valentin: *Der früheste Mozart* (Munich, 1956) [in Ger. and Eng.]
——: *Leopold Mozart: Nannerls Notenbuch 1759* (Munich, 1956)

E. Hertzmann: 'Mozart's Creative Process', *MQ*, xliii (1957), 187; repr. in Lang (1963)

W. Siegmund-Schultze: *Mozarts Melodik und Stil* (Leipzig, 1957)

K. F. Müller: *Leopold Mozart: Werkverzeichnis für W. A. Mozart (1768): ein Beitrag zur Mozartforschung* (Salzburg, 1958)

H. Engel: 'Haydn, Mozart und die Klassik', *MJb 1959*, 46–79

G. Massenkeil: *Untersuchungen zum Problem der Symmetrie in der Instrumentalmusik W. A. Mozarts* (Wiesbaden, 1962)

H. Engel: 'Nochmals: thematische Satzverbindungen und Mozart', *MJb 1962–3*, 14

I. R. Eisley: 'Mozart and Counterpoint: Development and Synthesis', *MR*, xxiv (1963), 23

M. Chusid: 'The Significance of D minor in Mozart's Dramatic Music', *MJb 1965–6*, 87

S. Davis: 'Harmonic Rhythm in Mozart's Sonata Form', *MR*, xxvii (1966), 25

W. Kirkendale: *Fuge und Fugato in der Kammermusik des Rokoko und der Klassik* (Tutzing, 1966), 184–215; Eng. trans., enlarged (1979), 152–81

H. Beck: 'Harmonisch-melodische Modelle bei Mozart', *MJb 1967*, 90

I. Kecskeméti: 'Barockelemente in den langsamen Instrumentalsätzen Mozarts', *MJb 1967*, 182

M. S. Cole: 'The Rondo Finale: Evidence for the Mozart–HaydnExchange?', *MJb 1968–70*, 242

M. Flothuis: *Mozarts Bearbeitungen eigener und fremder Werke*, Schriftenreihe der Internationalen Stiftung Mozarteum, ii (Salzburg, 1969)

H. Federhofer: 'Mozart als Schüler und Lehrer in der Musiktheorie', *MJb 1971–2*, 89

K. J. Marx: *Zur Einheit der zyklischen Form bei Mozart* (Stuttgart, 1971)

C. Rosen: *The Classical Style: Haydn, Mozart, Beethoven* (London, 1971, 2/1973), 183–325

D. Heartz: 'Thomas Attwood's Lessons in Composition with Mozart', *PRMA*, c (1973–4), 175

'Tonartenplan und Motivstruktur (Leitmotivtechnik?) in Mozarts Musik', *MJb 1973–4*, 82–144 [discussions]

'Typus und Modell in Mozarts Kompositionsweise', *MJb 1973–4*, 145–78 [discussions]

U. Toeplitz: *Die Holzbläser in der Musik und ihr Verhältnis zur Tonartwahl* (Baden-Baden, 1978)

A. Forte: 'Generative Chromaticism in Mozart's Music: The Rondo in A minor, K.511', *MQ*, lxvi (1980), 459

SACRED WORKS

W. Pole: *The Story of Mozart's Requiem* (London, 1879)

E. Lewicki: 'Über Mozarts grosse c-Moll-Messe und die Endgestaltung ihrer Ergänzung', *Mozart-Jb*, i (1923), 69

K. A. Rosenthal: 'The Salzburg Church Music of Mozart and his Predecessors', *MQ*, xviii (1932), 559

——: 'Mozart's Sacramental Litanies and their Forerunners', *MQ*, xxvii (1941), 433

K. G. Fellerer: *Mozarts Kirchenmusik* (Salzburg, 1955)

G. Reichert: 'Mozarts "Credo-Messen" und ihre Vorläufer', *MJb 1955*, 117

K. Geiringer: 'The Church Music', *The Mozart Companion*, ed. H. C. R. Landon and D. Mitchell (London, 1956, 2/1965), 361

H. Federhofer: 'Probleme der Echtheitsbestimmung der kleineren kirchenmusikalischen Werke W. A. Mozarts', *MJb 1958*, 97; suppl., *MJb 1960–61*, 43

E. Hess: 'Zur Ergänzung des Requiems von Mozart durch F. X. Süssmayr', *MJb 1959*, 99

K. Pfannhauser: 'Mozarts kirchenmusikalische Studien im Spiegel seiner Zeit und Nachwelt', *KJb*, xliii (1959), 155

F. Blume: 'Requiem but no Peace', *MQ*, xlvii (1961), 147; repr. in Lang (1963) and [Ger.] in Blume (1963)

I. Kecskeméti: 'Beiträge zur Geschichte von Mozarts Requiem', *SM*, i (1961), 147

K. Marguerre: 'Mozart und Süssmayer', *MJb 1962–3*, 172

O. E. Deutsch: 'Zur Geschichte von Mozarts Requiem', *ÖMz*, xix (1964), 49

L. Nowak: 'Das Requiem von W. A. Mozart', *ÖMz*, xx (1965), 395

R. Federhofer-Königs: 'Mozarts "Lauretanische Litaneien" KV 109 (74e) und 195 (186d)', *MJb 1967*, 111

A. Holschneider: 'C. Ph. E. Bachs Kantate "Auferstehung und Himmelfahrt Jesu" und Mozarts Aufführung des Jahres 1788', *MJb 1968–70*, 264

F. Beyer: 'Mozarts Komposition zum Requiem: zur Frage der Ergänzung', *Acta Mozartiana*, xviii (1971), 27

G. Duda: 'Neues aus der Mozartforschung', *Acta Mozartiana*, xviii (1971), 32 [on Requiem]

C. Rosenthal: 'Der Einfluss der Salzburger Kirchenmusik auf Mozarts kirchenmusikalische Kompositionen', *MJb 1971–2*, 173

L. Nowak: 'Wer hat die Instrumentalstimmen in der Kyrie-Fuge des Requiems von W. A. Mozart geschrieben? Ein vorläufiger Bericht', *MJb 1973–4*, 191

K. G. Fellerer: 'Liturgische Grundlagen der Kirchenmusik Mozarts', *Festschrift Walter Senn* (Munich and Salzburg, 1975), 64

'Sektion Kirchenmusik', *MJb 1978–9*, 14 [4 articles]

OPERA

A. D. Oulibicheff: *Mozarts Opern: kritische Erläuterungen* (Leipzig, 1848)

C. Gounod: *Le Don Juan de Mozart* (Paris, 1890; Eng. trans., 1895/*R*1970)

E. Komorzynski: *Emanuel Schikaneder: ein Beitrag zur Geschichte des deutschen Theaters* (Vienna, 1901, rev. 2/1951, 3/1955)

E. J. Dent: *Mozart's Operas: a Critical Study* (London, 1913, 2/1947)

E. Lert: *Mozart auf dem Theater* (Berlin, 1918)

A. Lorenz: 'Das Finale in Mozarts Meisteropern', *Musik*, xix (1926–7), 621

E. Blom: 'The Literary Ancestry of Figaro', *MQ*, xiii (1927), 528

R. Dumesnil: *Le 'Don Juan' de Mozart* (Paris, 1927)

F. Brukner: *Die Zauberflöte: unbekannte Handschriften und seltene Drucke aus der Frühzeit der Oper* (Vienna, 1934)

P. Stefan: *Die Zauberflöte: Herkunft, Bedeutung, Geheimnis* (Vienna, 1937)

E. Komorzynski: 'Die Zauberflöte: Entstehung und Bedeutung des Kunstwerks', *Neues Mozart-Jb*, i (1941), 147

H. F. Redlich: 'L'oca del Cairo', *MR*, ii (1941), 122

P. J. Jouve: *Le Don Juan de Mozart* (Fribourg, 1942; Eng. trans., 1957)

L. Conrad: *Mozarts Dramaturgie der Oper* (Würzburg, 1943)

E. Wellesz: 'Don Giovanni and the dramma giocoso', *MR*, iv (1943), 121

C. Benn: *Mozart on the Stage* (London, 1946, 2/1947)

A. H. King: 'The Melodic Sources and Affinities of Die Zauberflöte', *MQ*, xxxvi (1950), 241; repr. in King (1955)

S. Levarie: *Mozart's 'Le nozze di Figaro': a Critical Analysis* (Chicago, 1952/R1977)

H. Engel: 'Die Finali der Mozartschen Opern', *MJb 1954*, 113

C. Raeburn: 'An Evening at Schönbrunn', *MR*, xvi (1955), 96

A. Greither: *Die sieben grossen Opern Mozarts: Versuche über das Verhältnis der Texte zur Musik* (Heidelberg, 1956, enlarged 2/1970)

L. F. Tagliavini: 'L'opéra italien du jeune Mozart', *Les influences étrangères dans l'oeuvre de Mozart: CNRS Paris 1956*, 125

C. Raeburn: 'Die textlichen Quellen des "Schauspieldirektor" ', *ÖMz*, xiii (1958), 4

J. A. Westrup: 'Two First Performances: Monteverdi's "Orfeo" and Mozart's "La clemenza di Tito" ', *ML*, xxxix (1958), 327

T. Volek: 'Über den Ursprung von Mozarts Oper "La clemenza di Tito" ', *MJb 1959*, 274

C. Bitter: *Wandlungen in den Inszenierungsformen des 'Don Giovanni' von 1787 bis 1928* (Regensburg, 1961)

B. Szabolcsi: 'Mozart et la comédie populaire', *SM*, i (1961), 65

S. Kunze: 'Mozarts Schauspieldirektor', *MJb 1962–3*, 156

F.-H. Neumann: 'Zur Vorgeschichte der Zaide', *MJb 1962–3*, 216–47

A. Livermore: 'The Origins of Don Juan', *ML*, xliv (1963), 257

B. Brophy: *Mozart the Dramatist: a New View of Mozart, his Operas and his Age* (London, 1964)

C. Floros: 'Das "Programm" in Mozarts Meisterouvertüren', *SMw*, xxvi (1964), 140–86

C. Raeburn: 'Die Entführungsszene aus "Die Entführung aus dem Serail', *MJb 1964*, 130

A. Rosenberg: *Die Zauberflöte: Geschichte und Deutung* (Munich, 1964)

R. Moberly and C. Raeburn: 'Mozart's "Figaro": the Plan of Act III', *ML*, xlvi (1965), 134; repr. in *MJb 1965–6*, 161

R. Münster: 'Die verstellte Gärtnerin: neue Quellen zur authentischen Singspielfassung von W. A. Mozarts La finta giardiniera', *Mf*, xviii (1965), 138

P. Branscombe: ' "Die Zauberflöte": some Textual and Interpretative Problems', *PRMA*, xcii (1965–6), 45

M. Chusid: 'The Significance of D minor in Mozart's Dramatic Music', *MJb 1965–6*, 87

D. J. Keahey: 'Così fan tutte: Parody or Irony', *Paul A. Pisk: Essays in his Honor* (Austin, 1966), 116

A. A. Abert: 'Beiträge zur Motivik von Mozarts Spätopern', *MJb 1967*, 7

B. Brophy: 'The Young Mozart', *Opera 66*, ed. C. Osborne (London, 1967)

F. Giegling: 'Zu den Rezitativen von Mozarts Oper "Titus" ', *MJb 1967*, 121

G. Gruber: 'Das Autograph der "Zauberflöte" ', *MJb 1967*, 127–49; *MJb 1968–70*, 99–110

D. Heartz: 'The Genesis of Mozart's Idomeneo', *MJb 1967*, 150; repr. in *MQ*, lv (1969), 1

K.-H. Köhler: 'Mozarts Kompositionsweise: Beobachtungen am Figaro-Autograph', *MJb 1967*, 31

R. B. Moberly: *Three Mozart Operas: Figaro, Don Giovanni, The Magic Flute* (London, 1967)

A. A. Abert: ' "La finta giardiniera" und "Zaide" als Quellen für spätere Opern Mozarts', *Musik und Verlag: Karl Vötterle zum 65. Geburtstag* (Kassel, 1968), 113

J. Chailley: *'La flûte enchantée', opéra maçonnique: essai d'explication du livret et de la musique* (Paris, 1968; Eng. trans., 1972)

F. R. Noske: 'Musical Quotation as a Dramatic Device: the Fourth Act of Le nozze di Figaro', *MQ*, liv (1968), 185; repr. in Noske (1977)

L. F. Tagliavini: 'Quirino Gasparini and Mozart', *New Looks at Italian Opera: Essays in Honor of Donald J. Grout* (Ithaca, 1968), 151 [on *Mitridate*]

S. Döhring: 'Die Arienformen in Mozarts Opern', *MJb 1968–70*, 66

H. Federhofer: 'Die Harmonik als dramatischer Ausdrucksfaktor in Mozarts Meisteropern', *MJb 1968–70*, 77

F. Giegling: 'Metastasios Oper "La clemenza di Tito" in der Bearbeitung durch Mazzola', *MJb 1968–70*, 88

K.-H. Köhler: 'Figaro-Miscellen: einige dramaturgische Mitteilungen zur Quellensituation', *MJb 1968–70*, 119

C.-H. Mahling: 'Typus und Modell in Opern Mozarts', *MJb 1968–70*, 145

G. Rech: 'Bretzner contra Mozart', *MJb 1968–70*, 186

E. M. Batley: *A Preface to The Magic Flute* (London, 1969)

C. Henning: 'Thematic Metamorphoses in Don Giovanni', *MR*, xxx (1969), 22

F. Noske: 'Social Tensions in "Le nozze di Figaro" ', *ML*, l (1969), 45; repr. in Noske (1977)

A. A. Abert: *Die Opern Mozarts* (Wolfenbüttel, 1970); Eng. version in *NOHM*, vii (1973)

B. Brophy: ' "Figaro" and the Limitations of Music', *ML*, li (1970), 26

F. R. Noske: 'Don Giovanni: Musical Affinities and Dramatic Structure', *SM*, xii (1970), 167–203; repr. in *Theatre Research/Recherches téâtrales*, xiii (1973), 60 and in Noske (1977)

A. Williamson: 'Who was Sarastro?', *Opera*, xxi (1970), 297; see also 695f

H. H. Eggebrecht: *Versuch über die Wiener Klassik: die Tanzszene in*

Mozarts 'Don Giovanni' (Wiesbaden, 1972)

H. Keller: 'Mozart's Wrong Key Signature', *Tempo* (1972), no.98, p.21 [*Così fan tutte*]

S. Kunze: *Don Giovanni vor Mozart: die Tradition der Don Giovanni-Opern im italienischen Buffo-Theater des 18. Jahrhunderts* (Munich, 1972)

H. Goldschmidt: 'Die Cavatina des Figaro', *BMw*, xv (1973), 185

R. B. Moberly: 'Mozart and his Librettists', *ML*, liv (1973), 161

B. Williams: 'Passion and Cynicism: Remarks on "Così fan tutte" ', *MT*, cxiv (1973), 361

D. Heartz: 'Raaff's last Aria: a Mozartian Idyll in the Spirit of Hasse', *MQ*, lx (1974), 517 [from *Idomeneo*]

——: 'Tonality and Motif in Idomeneo', *MT*, cxv (1974), 2

H. Lühning: 'Zur Entstehungsgeschichte von Mozarts "Titus" ', *Mf*, xxvii (1974), 300; see also xxviii (1975), 77, 312; xxix (1976), 127

R. B. Moberly: 'The Influence of French Classical Drama on Mozart's "La clemenza di Tito" ', *ML*, lv (1974), 286

G. Gruber: 'Bedeutung und Spontaneität in Mozarts "Zauberflöte" ', *Festschrift Walter Senn* (Munich and Salzburg, 1975), 118

D. Koenigsberger: 'A New Metaphor for Mozart's *Magic Flute*', *European Studies Review*, v (1975), 229–75

H. L. Scheel: ' "Le mariage de Figaro" von Beaumarchais und das Libretto der "Nozze di Figaro" von Lorenzo da Ponte', *Mf*, xxviii (1975), 156

A. Tyson: ' "La clemenza di Tito" and its Chronology', *MT*, cxvi (1975), 221

H. Abert: *Mozart's 'Don Giovanni'* (London, 1976) [Eng. trans. from Abert, 1919–21]

C. Gianturco: *Le opere del giovane Mozart* (Pisa, 1976, enlarged 2/1978, Eng. trans., enlarged, 1981)

R. Angermüller: 'Wer war der Librettist von "La finta giardiniera"?', *MJb 1976–7*, 1

W. Mann: *The Operas of Mozart* (London, 1977)

F. Noske: *The Signifier and the Signified: Studies in the Operas of Mozart and Verdi* (The Hague, 1977)

R. Angermüller: 'Mozart and Metastasio', *Mitteilungen der Internationalen Stiftung Mozarteum*, xxvi/1–2 (1978), 12

D. Heartz: 'Mozart's Overture to Titus as Dramatic Argument', *MQ*, lxiv (1978), 29

——: 'Mozart, his Father and "Idomeneo" ', *MT*, cxix (1978), 228

C. Osborne: *The Complete Operas of Mozart* (London, 1978)

S. Vill, ed.: *Così fan tutte: Beiträge zur Wirkungsgeschichte von Mozarts Oper* (Bayreuth, 1978)

D. Heartz: 'Mozart and his Italian Contemporaries: La clemenza di Tito', *MJb 1978–9*, 275

J. Godwin: 'Layers of Meaning in *The Magic Flute*', *MQ*, lxv (1979), 471

D. Heartz: 'Goldoni, Don Giovanni and the dramma giocoso', *MT*, cxx (1979), 993

J. Rushton: *W. A. Mozart: Don Giovanni* (Cambridge, 1981)

A. Tyson: 'Le nozze di figaro: Lessons from the Autograph Score', *MT*, cxxii (1981), 456

A. Steptoe: 'The Sources of "Così fan tutte": a Reappraisal', *ML*, lxii (1981)

A. Tyson: 'The Great Quartet in Mozart's *Idomeneo*', *Music Forum*, v (in preparation)

MISCELLANEOUS VOCAL

M. J. E. Brown: 'Mozart's Songs for Voice and Piano', *MR*, xvii (1956), 19

A. Orel: 'Mozarts Beitrag zum deutschen Sprechtheater: die Musik zu Geblers "Thamos" ', *Acta Mozartiana*, iv (1957), 43, 74

H. Engel: 'Hasses Ruggiero und Mozarts Festspiel Ascanio', *MJb 1960–61*, 46

C. B. Oldman: 'Mozart's Scena for Tenducci', *ML*, xlii (1961), 44

S. Kunze: 'Die Vertonungen der Arie "Non sò d'onde viene" von J. Chr. Bach und von W. A. Mozart', *AnMc*, no.2 (1965), 85

A. Dunning: 'Mozarts Kanons', *MJb 1971–2*, 227

S. Dahms: 'Mozarts festa teatrale "Ascanio in Alba" ', *ÖMz*, xxxi (1976), 15

ORCHESTRAL

D. Schultz: *Mozarts Jugendsinfonien* (Leipzig, 1900)

S. Sechter: *Das Finale von W. A. Mozarts Jupiter-Symphonie*, ed. F. Eckstein (Vienna, 1923)

H. Schenker: 'Mozart: Sinfonie g-Moll', *Das Meisterwerk in der Musik*, ii (1926), 105

A. E. F. Dickinson: *A Study of Mozart's Last Three Symphonies* (London, 1927, 2/1940)

G. de Saint-Foix: *Les symphonies de Mozart* (Paris, 1932; Eng. trans., 1947)

N. Broder: 'The Wind-instruments in Mozart's Symphonies', *MQ*, xix (1933), 238

C. M. Girdlestone: *W. A. Mozart et ses concertos pour piano* (Paris, 1939, rev. 2/1953, 3/1978; Eng. trans., enlarged, 1948)

G. Dazeley: 'The Original Text of Mozart's Clarinet Concerto', *MR*, ix (1948), 166; see also J. Kratchovíl, *Internazionale Mozartkonferenz: Praha 1956*, 262, and E. Hess, *MJb 1967*, 18

A. Hutchings: *A Companion to Mozart's Piano Concertos* (London, 1948, 2/1950)

G. de Saint-Foix: 'La jeunesse de Mozart: 1771: les diverses orientations de la symphonie', *MJb 1950*, 14, 116

(handwritten annotation in left margin:) D. Heartz

(handwritten annotation:) 1980. P. 233 - 256.

H. Engel: 'Über Mozarts Jugendsinfonien', *MJb 1951*, 22

G. Hausswald: *Mozarts Serenaden: ein Beitrag zur Stilkritik des 18. Jahrhunderts* (Leipzig, 1951, rev. 2/1975)

H. Engel: 'Der Tanz in Mozarts Kompositionen', *MJb 1952*, 29

J. N. David: *Die Jupiter-Sinfonie: eine Studie über die thematisch-melodischen Zusammenhänge* (Göttingen, 1953)

H. Beck: 'Zur Entstehungsgeschichte von Mozarts D-Dur Sinfonie, KV.297: Probleme der Kompositionstechnik und Formentwicklung in Mozarts Instrumentalmusik', *MJb 1955*, 95

F. Blume: 'The Concertos, I: their Sources', *The Mozart Companion*, ed. H. C. R. Landon and D. Mitchell (London, 1956, 2/1965), 200

H. Keller: 'K503: the Unity of Contrasting Themes and Movements', *MR*, xvii (1956), 48, 120

H. C. R. Landon: 'The Concertos, II: their Musical Origin and Development', *The Mozart Companion*, ed. H. C. R. Landon and D. Mitchell (London, 1956, 2/1965), 234

J. P. Larsen: 'The Symphonies', *The Mozart Companion*, ed. H. C. R. Landon and D. Mitchell (London, 1956, 2/1965), 156

E. J. Simon: 'Sonata into Concerto: a Study of Mozart's First Seven Concertos', *AcM*, xxxi (1959), 170

C. Bär: 'Die "Musique vom Robinig" ', *Mitteilungen der Internationalen Stiftung Mozarteum*, ix/3–4 (1960), 6

——: 'Die Lodronschen Nachtmusiken', *Mitteilungen der Internationalen Stiftung Mozarteum*, x/1–2 (1961), 19

——: 'Zum "Nannerl-Septett" KV 251', *Acta Mozartiana*, ix (1962), 24

——: 'Die "Andretterin-Musik": Betrachtungen zu KV 205', *Acta Mozartiana*, x (1963), 30

A. A. Abert: 'Stilistischer Befund und Quellenlage: zu Mozarts Lambacher Sinfonie KV Anh. 221 = 45a', *Festschrift Hans Engel* (Kassel, 1964), 43

H. Tischler: *A Structural Analysis of Mozart's Piano Concertos* (New York, 1966)

I. Kecskeméti: 'Opernelemente in den Klavierkonzerten Mozarts', *MJb 1968–70*, 111

M. W. Cobin: 'Aspects of Stylistic Evolution in two Mozart Concertos: K.271 and K.482', *MR*, xxxi (1970), 1

J. Kerman, ed.: *Mozart: Piano Concerto in C Major, K.503* (New York, 1970) [score and essays]

D. Forman: *Mozart's Concerto Form: the First Movements of the Piano Concertos* (London, 1971)

W. Plath and others: 'Zur Echtheitsfrage bei Mozart', *MJb 1971–2*, 19–67 [with discussions of ᴋAnh.9/Anh.C14.01 and ᴋ84/73*q*]

P. Benary: 'Metrum bei Mozart: zur metrischen Analyse seiner letzten drei Sinfonien', *SMz*, cxiv (1974), 201

S. Wollenberg: 'The Jupiter Theme: New Light on its Creation', *MT*, cxvi (1975), 781

L. Meyer: 'Grammatical Simplicity and Relational Richness: the Trio of Mozart's G minor Symphony', *Critical Inquiry*, ii (1976), 693–761

A. H. King: *Mozart String and Wind Concertos* (London, 1978)

C. Wolff: 'Zur Chronologie der Klavierkonzert-Kadenzen Mozarts', *MJb 1978–9*, 235

R. Strohm: 'Merkmale italienischer Versvertonung in Mozarts Klavierkonzerten', *AnMc*, no.18 (1978), 219

A. Tyson: 'The Two Slow Movements of Mozart's Paris Symphony K297', *MT*, cxxii (1981), 17

N. Zaslaw: 'The "Lambach" Symphonies of Wolfgang and Leopold Mozart', *Music and Civilization: Essays Presented to Paul Henry Lang* (New York, 1983)

CHAMBER AND ENSEMBLE MUSIC

T. F. Dunhill: *Mozart's String Quartets* (London, 1927, 2/1948)

A. Einstein: 'Mozart's Ten Celebrated String Quartets', *MR*, iii (1942), 159

R. S. Tangemann: 'Mozart's Seventeen Epistle Sonatas', *MQ*, xxxii (1946), 588

W. Fischer: 'Mozarts Weg von der begleiteten Klaviersonate zur Kammermusik mit Klavier', *MJb 1956*, 16

J. Kratochvíl: 'Betrachtungen über die Urfassung des Konzerts für Klarinette und des Quintetts für Klarinette und Streicher von W. A. Mozart', *Internazionale Mozartkonferenz: Praha 1956*, 262

S. T. M. Newman: 'Mozart's G minor Quintet (KV.516) and its Relationship to the G minor Symphony (KV.550)', *MR*, xvii (1956), 287

A.-E. Cherbuliez: 'Bemerkungen zu den "Haydn"-Streichquartetten Mozarts und Haydns "Russischen" Streichquartetten', *MJb 1959*, 28

E. Hess: 'Die "Varianten" im Finale des Streichquintettes KV.593', *MJb 1960–61*, 68

K. Marguerre: 'Mozarts Klaviertrios', *MJb 1960–61*, 282

M. Whewell: 'Mozart's Bassethorn Trios', *MT*, ciii (1962), 19

A. Palm: 'Mozarts Streichquartett d-Moll, KV 421, in der Interpretation Momignys', *MJb 1962–3*, 256

W. Kirkendale: 'More Slow Introductions by Mozart to Fugues of J. S. Bach?', *JAMS*, xvii (1964), 43

L. Finscher: 'Mozarts Mailänder Streichquartette', *Mf*, xix (1966), 270

A. H. King: *Mozart Chamber Music* (London, 1968)

K. Marguerre: 'Die beiden Sonaten-Reihen für Klavier und Geige', *MJb 1968–70*, 327

G. Croll and K. Birsak: 'Anton Stadlers "Bassettklarinette" und das "Stadler-Quintett" KV581: Versuch einer Anwendung', *ÖMz*, xxiv (1969), 3

W. J. Mitchell: 'Giuseppe Sarti and Mozart's Quartet K.421', *CMc*, no.9 (1969), 147

W. S. Newman: 'The Duo Texture of Mozart's K.526: an Essay in Classic Instrumental Style', *Essays in Musicology in Honor of Dragan Plamenac* (Pittsburgh, 1969), 191

W. Hümmeke: *Versuch einer strukturwissenschaftlichen Darstellung der ersten und vierten Sätze der zehn letzten Streichquartette von W. A. Mozart* (Münster, 1970)

I. Hunkemöller: *W. A. Mozarts frühe Sonaten für Violine und Klavier* (Berne and Munich, 1970)

F. László: 'Untersuchungen zum Mozarts "zweiten" Opus 1, Nr. 1', *MJb 1971–2*, 149

D. N. Leeson and D. Whitwell: 'Mozart's "Spurious" Wind Octets', *ML*, liii (1972), 377

R. Hellyer: 'Mozart's Harmoniemusik', *MR*, xxxiv (1973), 146

M. Flothuis: 'Die Bläserstücke KV 439b', *MJb 1973–4*, 202

J. A. Vertrees: 'Mozart's String Quartet K465: the History of a Controversy', *CMc*, no.17 (1974), 96

A. Tyson: 'New Light on Mozart's "Prussian" Quartets', *MT*, cxvi (1975), 126

D. N. Leeson and D. Whitwell: 'Concerning Mozart's Serenade in B♭ for Thirteen Instruments, K.361 (370a)', *MJb 1976–7*, 97–130

C. Wolff, ed.: *The String Quartets of Haydn, Mozart, and Beethoven: Studies of the Autograph Manuscripts: Isham Memorial Library 1979* [articles on Mozart by L. Finscher, M. Flothuis, A. Tyson and C. Wolff]

R. Hellyer: 'Mozart's Harmoniemusik and its Publishers', *MT*, cxxii (1981), 468

KEYBOARD

F. Lorenz: *W. A. Mozart als Klavierkomponist* (Breslau, 1866)

H. Schenker: 'Mozart: Sonate a-Moll', *Der Tonwille*, ii (1922), 7

———: 'Mozart: Sonate C-Dur', *Der Tonwille*, iv (1923), 19

N. Broder: 'Mozart and the "Clavier" ', *MQ*, xxvii (1941), 422; repr. in Lang (1963)

H. Ferguson: 'Mozart's Duets for One Pianoforte', *PRMA*, lxxiii (1946–7), 35

W. Mason: 'Melodic Unity in Mozart's Piano Sonata K332', *MR*, xxii (1961), 28

K. von Fischer: 'Mozarts Klaviervariationen: zur Editions- und Aufführungspraxis des späten 18. und frühen 19. Jahrhunderts', *Hans Albrecht in memoriam* (Kassel, 1962), 168

G. Croll: 'Zu Mozarts Larghetto und Allegro Es-Dur für 2 Klaviere', *MJb 1964*, 28

H. Neumann and C. Schachter: 'The Two Versions of Mozart's Rondo K494', *Music Forum*, i (1967), 1–34

R. Rosenberg: *Die Klaviersonaten Mozarts: Gestalt- und Stilanalyse* (Hofheim, Hesse, 1972)

W. Plath: 'Zur Datierung der Klaviersonaten KV 279–284', *Acta*

Mozartiana, xxi (1974), 26
Piano Quarterly, no.95 (1976) [Mozart issue]

PERFORMING PRACTICE

R. Elvers: *Untersuchungen zu den Tempi in Mozarts Instrumentalmusik* (diss., U. of Berlin, 1952)

W. Fischer: 'Selbstzeugnisse Mozarts für die Aufführungsweise seiner Werke', *MJb 1955*, 7

H. Albrecht, ed.: *Die Bedeutung der Zeichen Keil, Strich und Punkt bei Mozart* (Kassel, 1957)

E. and P. Badura-Skoda: *Mozart-Interpretation* (Vienna and Stuttgart, 1957; Eng. trans., 1962 as *Interpreting Mozart on the Keyboard*)

P. Mies: 'Die Artikulationszeichen Strich und Punkt bei Wolfgang Amadeus Mozart', *Mf*, xi (1958), 428

A. B. Gottron: 'Wie spielte Mozart die Adagios seiner Klavierkonzerte', *Mf*, xiii (1960), 334

C. Bär: 'Zum Begriff des "Basso" in Mozarts Serenaden', *MJb 1960–61*, 133

W. Gerstenberg: 'Authentische Tempi für Mozarts "Don Giovanni" ', *MJb 1960–61*, 58

R. Münster: 'Authentische Tempi zu den sechs letzten Sinfonien W. A. Mozarts?', *MJb 1962–3*, 185

C. Bär: 'Zu einem Mozart'schen Andante-Tempo', *Acta Mozartiana*, x (1963), 78

Z. Śliwiński: 'Ein Beitrag zum Thema: Ausführung der Vorschläge in W. A. Mozarts Klavierwerken', *MJb 1965–6*, 179

C.-H. Mahling: 'Mozart und Orchesterpraxis seiner Zeit', *MJb 1967*, 229

S. Babitz: 'Some Errors in Mozart Performance', *MJb 1968–70*, 62

H. Engel: 'Interpretation und Aufführungspraxis', *MJb 1968–70*, 7 [with proceedings of colloquium of Zentralinstitut für Mozartforschung, 1968]

E. Melkus: 'Über die Ausführung der Stricharten in Mozarts Werken', *MJb 1968–70*, 244

——: 'Zur Auszierung der Da-capo-Arien in Mozarts Werken', *MJb 1968–70*, 159

T. Harmon: 'The Performance of Mozart's Church Sonatas', *ML*, xxxiv (1970), 51

N. Zaslaw: 'Mozart's Tempo Conventions', *IMSCR*, xi *Copenhagen 1972*, 720

M. Bilson: 'Some General Thoughts on Ornamentation in Mozart's Keyboard Works', *Piano Quarterly*, no.95 (1976), 26

J. Webster: 'The Scoring of Mozart's Chamber Music for Strings', *Essays on Music of the Classic Era in Honor of Barry S. Brook* (New York, 1982)

Index

242

Mozart